Every Secret Thing

Also by Gillian Slovo

TIES OF BLOOD

Every Secret Thing

My Family,
My Country

GILLIAN
SLOVO

LITTLE, BROWN AND COMPANY
Boston   New York   Toronto   London

FIRST U.S. EDITION

Library of Congress Cataloging-in-Publication Data

Slovo, Gillian
    Every secret thing : my family, my country / Gillian Slovo. — 1st U.S. ed.
        p. cm.
    ISBN 0-316-79923-8
    1. Slovo, Gillian. — Homes and haunts — South Africa. 2. Women novel-
ists, English — 20th century — Family relationships. 3. Anti-apartheid move-
ments — South Africa — Biography. 4. Slovo, Gillian. — Childhood and
youth. 5. Civil rights workers — South Africa — Biography. 6. Political activists
— South Africa — Biography. 7. Women journalists — South Africa —
Biography. 8. Communists — South Africa — Biography. 9. Slovo, Gillian. —
Family. 10. Parent and child — South Africa. 11. Family — South Africa. 12.
First, Ruth. 13. Slovo, Joe. I. Title
PR6069.L56Z465 1997
823'.914 —dc21
[B]   96-53149

10   9   8   7   6   5   4   3   2   1

MV—NY

Printed in the United States of America

Acknowledgements

Although my parents' history was enacted not written down and the raw materials of their past were often destroyed the truth of what happened was lodged in the memories of their friends and comrades. My narrative is constructed from many such sources. Thanks to all those who were unstintingly generous in reliving their pasts for me, and in particular: Ray Alexander, Muff Anderson, Beryl Baker, George Bizos, Clarice Braun, Jeremy Cronin, John Carlin, Betty du Toit, Barry Dwalatsky, Rene and Sammy Ephron, Ronny First, Jack Flior, Moira Forjaz, Steven Goldblatt, Hillary Hamburger, Miriam Hepner, Rica Hodgson, Barbara Hogan, Aboobaker Ismael, Pallo Jordan, Ronnie Kasrils, Ahmed Kathrada, Wolfie Kodesh, Mandla Langa, Steven Laufer, Janet Love, Philip Mabena, Mac Maharaj, Alexei Makarov, Nelson Mandela, David Moise, George Mokoena, Ismael Momonia, Thami Mtenteni, Joe Nhlanhla, Ivan Pillay, Sue Rabkin, Johannes Rasegatla, Reg September, Mo Shaik, Vladimir Shubin, Barney Simon, Walter Sisulu, Molly Sklaar, Mohammed Timol, Donald Turgel and Arnold Urisohn.

Luli Callinicos and Apollum Davidson shared their research with me, and Don Pinnock generously made available the documentation on Ruth that he'd collected over many years.

It couldn't have been easy for Joe's immediate family, his wife, Helena Dolny and my sisters, Robyn and Shawn Slovo, that I was working on this book so soon after Joe's death. I thank them for their patient forbearance. Thanks also to Shawn for reading and commenting on the manuscript and to Robyn for her support and her incisive structural help.

It was my agent Caradoc King who, not for the first time, helped me find the courage to write this book. My thanks to him, to Lennie Goodings and to my editor Richard Beswick for their constant support.

And finally I owe more to my family than I can say. Both Andy Metcalf and our daughter Cassie uprooted themselves so I could do the research for this book, and afterwards, when we returned, Andy lived it with me, using his perceptive eye and astute mind to help me find my way through the morass of my past.

Part One

Chapter One

An hour before she died my mother went shopping. In the company of one of her closest friends, Moira Forjaz, she left the house where they'd given lunch to fifteen. They were due to go their separate ways later that afternoon and so they drove in convoy. It was 17 August 1982 and Maputo's faded elegance glistened in the bright winter sun.

Their lunch had been long and leisurely and they'd drunk more wine than anticipated: now my mother needed to restock for the party to be held that evening in honour of a departing member of staff. But in Mozambique in 1982, where even the most basic of foodstuffs was scarce, the only place to buy alcohol was at the *loja franca* – a shopping oasis for the simple reason that payment had to be in foreign currency. Flushed with the success of the conference she had organised, my mother headed out to spend her carefully amassed cache of dollars.

There is a photograph of her taken on the day before she died. I have it on my London wall – she stares at my back as I sit by my computer. I turn to look at her. I see her carefree, smiling, confident, at home and I conjure her up, as she must have been in those last hours, her feet clicking against the cobbled pavement, her neatly turned ankle lifted up into the ageing Renault 16 that she had shipped from England.

Turning away I close my eyes and am assailed by a different image: my mother as she had once been in England. I see a stylish, handsome woman who had never lost her passion for expensive clothes but who was showing the strain of an enforced exile, a husband who was constantly on the move and three angry daughters.

It is like looking past the fifteen years since her death and finding two completely different women: the one that I had known, the other who had got away. I know what lies between these two images: it is 5,000 miles and the continent she loved, her home – Africa.

I saw her recently, captured on badly preserved, grainy 35 mm celluloid a few weeks before her death. She sits, at a table, facing a row of journalists, talking about the work that was her passion. Her hair is cut short, pulled back from her face to reveal her cheekbones and an ebullient smile she reserved for strangers. She was so engaged then, using her vivaciousness to charm and her hands to emphasise the points she was making in staccato Portuguese. Watching I sat alone in the stalls of a vast movie house in Maputo which had once been all plush reds and velvets but which had since grown tawdry from misuse, and I wondered whether I had ever really known her look so free.

In Mozambique, she had become a different person. She laughed more often. She sat in restaurants sipping at the bottle of weak beer which was each person's meal-time ration, spinning stories. I remember sitting opposite her, the year before she died, as she basked in the admiration of a young economist whose shining eyes showed how stunned he was by her combination of vivaciousness and intellectual rigour. She flirted and was flattered: a butterfly dancing around a flame which I feared might burn her but which never did.

In most families it is the children who leave home. In mine it was the parents. And especially her: we stood on the sidelines, watching as she, who had fought her own inhibitions to make a mark in the world, reached out, openly, for what she wanted.

A new vigour crept into everything she did. I remember her in her Maputo kitchen after nightfall, using one of her beautiful Italian shoes to beat back the encroaching tide of small brown cockroaches. She, whose idea of bliss had once been to come out of a fancy grocer's with a huge array of delicacies to add to a salad lunch, now made jokes about a hundred ways to cook Russian tinned beef. She was happy – able to push off the tide of guilt that had once bound her tightly to her three daughters. Her sharp tongue, which had so often got her into trouble in the movement to which she had dedicated her life, was now an asset. And it was more often stilled – she was no longer on the outside, railing against the enemy within.

Against the grainy background of that last photograph, a band of white light shafts across her head. Her hair fluffs out softly in its own version of an Afro. For over thirty years she had struggled with that unruly, black frizz, making time in her busy schedule to go twice weekly to a hairdresser who washed and rolled and straightened, striving to tame it. But in Maputo, my mother conceded defeat: she didn't have the time, she said, and besides, hairdressers were in short supply. That at least was her excuse. We knew that the truth lay somewhere else. At fifty-seven, Ruth no longer needed a fiercely regimented hairstyle to show control. What she had, she had finally accepted.

A month before she died she had been in London, on her annual visit. I see her as she was then, at the Camden Town house she and my father still owned. I remember standing by the railings, watching as she walked down the steep stairs that lead to her mother's, my grandmother's, basement flat. I had, for many years, been taller than my mother but at that moment I saw clearly for the first time, something that made me shiver. Looking down, I saw a portion of white scalp showing through her thinning hair. From my high vantage the henna that she used to hide the grey couldn't hide her ageing. I had always thought of her as eternally young: now I was no longer so sure. My observation felt like betrayal: I pushed it nervously away.

Soon afterwards we went to a Greek restaurant. Ruth was in high spirits as she described the conversation she'd just had with her mother, Tilly, then aged eighty-four. The interchange between the two women was usually stilted by Ruth's ill-concealed irritation, but this time she had somehow found the courage to speak her mind. She had told Tilly that life was short and that instead of playing the victim, Tilly should grab what was left of it.

In my mind's eye I relive that moment, Ruth sitting opposite me, boasting of the encounter. She was so pleased with herself:

she had managed, finally, to cut the knot of aggravation that her mother's passivity always provoked; she had spoken out for life.

The irony of it – that this was the last contact Ruth was to have with the mother who would outlast her by more than seven years.

We went shopping. Ruth was going to buy me shoes – something that came so easily to her and I in contrast, could rarely ever do. But at the plate glass of a slick Soho shop, the argument we'd started in the restaurant reached a fierce peak. We were on a battle ground that had been ours for years. The terrain was, ostensibly, about what was happening to my younger sister Robyn. Robyn was in crisis and with Ruth so far away I had become my sister's surrogate mother. I felt the unfairness of what Ruth's life had done to me. I protested, knowing that I was only making Ruth feel guilty but when she asked me what she should do to change the situation, I backed down. So we continued arguing, she driven on by guilt and me by righteous indignation, veering away from the catalyst of Robyn's life into a more generalised conflict about Ruth's choices versus mine, about the way she had struggled for recognition in a man's world while my generation was offered, by feminism, a different path. Fine words these – a high-principled dispute about different ways of living. And yet each of us, I think, knew that what we were really fighting about was whether she had been a good enough mother, and whether I, her daughter, would release her from the anchor of her past mistakes.

There had been many times when we had gone over this self-same ground, and on each occasion we had ended by making up, pretending that we'd reached agreement. Not this time. By the shoe shop's plate-glass window, my mother told me she didn't like what I was saying and wasn't going to buy me anything. I nodded acquiescence. I could have found the words to placate her, but I didn't want to. We had moved on and it felt right that a conflict which had been raging for many years should not be resolved by a commercial transaction.

This was a first for us, that neither of us was prepared to make it better. In silence we turned away from the shop and took the tube to Camden Town. There we stood briefly, as people rushed about around us, exchanging a stiff goodbye. I was leaving for holiday the day before she was due to go back to Mozambique. We didn't phone each other before I left – another first.

In Maputo that day, walking into the *loja franca*, Ruth was a long way from her accusing daughter. She was in a euphoric mood. Her conference on southern Africa, funded by the United Nations and bringing together both academics and activists from all over the world, had been hugely successful and she was looking forward to that evening's celebration. Joking with her friend Moira, she walked down the aisles. There wasn't much to choose from: you could buy cheese, or you couldn't; children's clothes from Swaziland and a pair of kid's plimsolls, in the right size if you were extra especially lucky; foodstuffs from South Africa, tins of meat and packets of breakfast cereal that no longer made an appearance in the rest of Mozambique; and wine, of course. My mother grabbed four bottles of red Portuguese *Dao* and paid for them.

At the door of the shop she and Moira parted, each of them going in a different direction. Moira recalls her one last sight of Ruth, a hand, captured in the rear-view mirror, raised in jaunty farewell as Ruth drove towards the university.

In 1975, after Portugal abandoned its colony in Mozambique, there had been a manic renaming of the city which had turned Maputo's street map into something of a who's who of great revolutionaries. In the time that she was there, my mother kept relocating. At first I wrote to her in a flat on *Julius Nyerere*; in 1981, the year before her death, when I visited her, we were ensconced high up in an apartment block on *Mao Tse Tung* which overlooked the sea; and we used to walk in the shade of the jacaranda trees on *Frederick Engels*, trying to connect our two entirely different worlds.

Like the roads around it, the university where Ruth worked had also been rechristened. It was named after a Mozambican, Eduardo Mondlane. Mondlane had never lived to see his party, Frelimo, come to power. One day, in 1969, in exile in Tanzania, he had collected his mail and taken it to a friend's house and opened it. Someone had sent him a book. When he turned its first page a bomb was triggered, killing him instantly.

The university that bore Mondlane's name was a set of sixties characterless, two-storey, buildings off the road that leads to the beach at Machinetta. Ruth worked in the sociology department which had a garden in an internal courtyard that gave the place a modicum of charm. Her office was on the second floor. She climbed the stairs, careful that her high heels did not slip against the over-polished red tiles, and went to her office.

The room was not a fancy one: two windows overlooking a decrepit patch of ground; a couple of steel desks; some second-hand filing cabinets. There were two people waiting for Ruth: Pallo Jordan, a comrade from the ANC; and Bridget O'Laughlin, an American colleague. They were soon joined by a third: Ruth's boss, Aquino da Braganza, who was carrying the post he'd just picked out of his cubby hole. He came in, complaining jovially that, although he was the boss, Ruth always got more mail than him.

'That's because I, unlike you, write letters,' Ruth shot back and added that she'd been in too much of a hurry and hadn't even checked to see if anything was waiting for her. Now, with time to spare before the party was due to begin, she went to fetch her mail.

She returned soon afterwards, carrying her own bundle. She stood by one of the windows, sorting through. Pallo was sitting nearby, at a table, Aquino opposite him, Bridget slightly to one side.

'Look at this,' Aquino said, stretching across the table, holding a letter out to Pallo.

It was at that moment that Ruth must have slit open the buff UN envelope that had been sent to her. In doing so, she broke the circuit that had been carefully laid inside. The bomb went off.

The men who had planned her death had taken no chances: the force of the explosion was powerful enough to blow out the window, sending half of the industrial air-conditioning unit thudding to the ground.

Chapter Two

When the phone rang, my father was at home in Maputo. He was working at his makeshift desk in the house he and Ruth shared inside the Mozambican ministerial compound, opposite the presidential palace. They had recently been moved in: things were hotting up, the Mozambican government had said; it was better that the two have proper security. So, reluctantly, they'd shifted out of the elegance of their Mao Tse Tung high-rise apartment with its sea views, and into this over-large concrete box whose only charm was the spoken rhythm of its street name: Rua Azarua.

My father never told me what he was doing when the phone rang. He did tell me, however, that as soon as he picked it up, one of Ruth's colleagues, a friend to both of them, spoke out. His voice was shaking as he said: 'Joe, come quickly,' and followed that up with a curt, 'Something has happened.'

That was all but it was more than enough. Dropping the receiver Joe ran out to his white Mazda and, without bothering to check it for bombs, he turned the key and drove straight to the university.

There was a commandeered jeep outside the university block, busy ferrying Ruth's three injured companions to hospital. Joe vaulted up the stairs, weaving through a shell-shocked crowd. A finger pointed him in the right direction. He was moving more slowly now. He saw an open door. He went closer.

Her feet, clad in the t-bar, tan high-heel shoes that had been her favourites, poked out from the ruins of the room. My father was no stranger to violent death. The angle and the stillness of her legs told him everything he needed to know. He went no further.

★

Ruth's mother Tilly always went early to bed. Alone in her basement flat, she heard her front door-bell ringing. She lay still, wondering whether she had imagined the sound. When it came again, sharper and more insistent, she knew it was real. She got up, and in that midsummer's half-night gloom, made her way through her living room and into the corridor. Hampered by the arthritis that worsened every year, she walked slowly to the door.

A woman whose beauty and strength still showed in her fierce face, Tilly seemed to have handed the baton of fine clothes to her daughter while she had let her own wardrobe sink into neglect. I imagine her as she was then, her back rigid with the sense of duty that had ruled her life and her body clothed in one of a succession of shapeless house-coats which were never entirely clean. She would have walked past the gallery on her wall – black and white photos of her grandchildren when they were young – past the room which, after the death of her husband, was always kept empty, down the dingy corridor and to the front door.

When she unchained the door and opened up she found a family friend, a woman of Ruth's age, standing on the narrow doorstep. The woman was crying, so hard that although she kept trying to speak, no words emerged. Tilly had no idea what tragedy had propelled her visitor to her doorstep. She stood, waiting to be told. Without success.

'What's wrong?' she asked eventually and it was then that her visitor began to wail.

Who knows what went on in Tilly's head: she was a cynic who expected the worst from others. Perhaps she felt that the display she was witnessing was some act of wanton hysteria in which lesser mortals would sometimes indulge. Or perhaps this account of what happened on the night of 17 August is just Tilly's memory, playing tricks. Perhaps she was told immediately and didn't hear. It's possible. After all, the worst had happened: the daughter whom she had loved so fiercely, the woman who had lived the life that Tilly had always wanted, was dead.

★

We, Ruth's daughters, were all in different locations on that night of Ruth's death. In London, Robyn came back very late to find the house lights blazing. A man with whom she shared the Camden Town house was waiting there for her and he told her what had happened. She didn't believe him. She laughed. And then he told her again.

Shawn was in a different time zone, in New York. She had just come in when the phone rang. She left it alone: whoever it was could leave a message. There was a short pause and then my elder sister heard Ruth's friend Moira's voice, distraught across the satellite, begging Shawn to ring. At that very moment, the door-bell went. Shawn knew already, or she knew enough. Slowly she walked across her apartment and opened the door to the Mozambican ambassador who had come to tell her.

I was also elsewhere. On the night of Ruth's death I was travelling home from holiday. The journey from Santander to Plymouth had taken over twelve hours. I'd spent it either trying to dig my six-year-old step-son, Ben, out of the video-games hall, or lying, miserably, on the outside deck swallowing down nausea. Messages were sent out on the tannoy, calling for me, but my partner, Andy, and I were too far outside and Ben too entranced for us to hear. So it was only after I handed my passport to the bearded man perched behind a high counter, that I knew anything was wrong.

He looked closely at my passport and then across at me. It brought back to me that time in 1965 when I had travelled alone on a cross-channel ferry. With its customary malevolence, the South African government had refused to renew our passports which left us traversing borders with brown-backed identity documents that nobody ever took seriously. Especially when it didn't have the right stamps, as mine didn't in 1965. I was thirteen years old and after berating me for my carelessness, the man at immigration allowed me ten days' grace inside the country during which I had to get the correct permissions.

That was long ago. I was British now. So when this immigration man overlaid my passport with one large hand, I was forewarned.

'Phone your sister, Robyn, or your friend, Susie,' the man said. 'Do you understand?'

Of course I understood. It had come, that moment I'd been expecting throughout my life. One of my parents was dead. Not naturally: one of them had been killed. I knew that. What I didn't know was which one. I got back into the car, told Andy to drive to the nearest telephone box. We didn't speak. We didn't need to.

In a call-box outside Plymouth, I stood with the echo of Susie's voice telling me that it was my mother. I hung up and dialled another number I knew by heart – my mother's London number where Robyn lived. She was about to head out to the airport with my grandmother, to get on a plane I had no time to catch. She handed the receiver to my grandmother. I heard Tilly's crisp, clear, anglicised voice. 'Gilly,' is what she said, 'mother [this the strange way she had of referring to her own daughter] is dead.' One more, brief sentence followed. 'And you weren't there.'

I never asked her what she had meant by that. I never thanked her either for the £50 note she sent along with friends who met us at Heathrow. It was irrelevant; I stuffed it in my pocket. Only when we arrived in the Zimbabwean capital, Harare, and found we had six hours before our onward flight, did I realise that it was the only money that Andy and I had with us.

We'd been told that the Mozambican ambassador to Zimbabwe would look after us during the stopover in Harare, but when we emerged from a claustrophobic customs booth, the airport's small entrance hall was deserted. We waited for a long time and then, realising nobody was coming for us, we took a bus into town.

Weeks later, I saw the ambassador in another airport. He had been away when we'd flown in, he said, taking his children back to the Mozambican village where he'd been born. It was an odd experience, he continued: his six-year-old had never been anywhere without electricity or running water. The child, unable to adjust to these deprivations, spent his two weeks holiday curled up on a grass pallet, whining to go home.

In Harare, I was useless. Andy booked us into the Meikles

Hotel, and while I lay on the bed in the enormous, darkened room, he did desultory laps on the roof-top swimming pool. I roused myself and phoned Maputo. A flustered stranger's voice handed me on to Shawn. I didn't know why I'd rung: there was nothing left to say. I was strangely calm, in a kind of no-man's land which was empty of all feeling. I got up and went through the motions – showering, changing, returning to the airport.

The last leg of our journey: we were on the plane, strapped in, ready for take off, watching as a group of flight attendants huddled in consultation. We found out why when a thick Portuguese accent called out my name, asking that I identify myself. I put up my hand. A collective sigh of relief and a steward came down the aisle to tell me that they'd been instructed by their government that on no account should they take off if Ruth's daughter was not on board.

I was on board. They closed the doors. We were off. I was no longer frightened of flying. Why should I be? What I feared, had already happened. I spent the short trip listening to a Mozambican man raging about the way this new government was destroying his country. Who knows why he latched on to me – perhaps my name sounding out over the plane's intercom had made me seem important. Whatever the reason, he needed me to listen. I had nothing else to do. I listened.

The plane landed in Maputo. Although the doors were open, the passengers were told to keep their seats until Andy and I had left. We walked down the silent aisle and stepped out.

My memory is of darkness much blacker than it could have been, of night, a dense sky, and two men waiting at the bottom of the stairway. One was a Mozambican official who stretched his hand out for our passports. The other was my father.

Chapter Three

We drove through the deserted Maputo streets to my parents' home. My father sat in the front, beside the driver. As we passed a set of street lights he turned. His fair skin was pallid in the neon light, his face strangely bland as if grief had smudged out his familiar features. He muttered something about a concert. I didn't understand what he was talking about and he, gentle but at the same time very distant, didn't explain.

We stopped at his house, dumped our suitcases and were on the move again, passing through a succession of road blocks to the huge Gil Vincente cinema – the same one in which, years later, I was to sit alone, plagued by fleas, and watch Ruth spinning her charm in front of an admiring audience. But in 1982, we were late: a knot of officials hustled us through the rundown lobby, up the wide staircase and in.

A concert was in full swing – South African musician, Abdullah Ibrahim and his band, backed by an immense black and white portrait of Ruth, playing township jazz in an impromptu tribute. A 16 mm camera crew from the Cinema Institute tramped about on stage, turning occasionally to shoot the audience. We were latecomers to a party, shuffling our way into the row where my two sisters and my grandmother were seated.

A man in the row in front of ours in which was seated almost the entire Mozambican cabinet, turned round and pressed his callused brown hand into my damp palm. I didn't know who he was. It didn't seem to matter: I shook his hand and sat down.

We were on display – my sisters and I exchanged quick nods while my grandmother stared straight ahead. A fleeting break in the disjointed piano notes and then Abdullah Ibrahim's fingers skimmed the keys. On any other occasion the elegance of his phrasing would have brought the audience to their feet, but not this time. Perhaps they felt as I did, that in this bizarre setting, the rules of behaviour were up for grabs.

It was all too weird: the calm I'd earlier experienced turned to restlessness. Shawn and I tried to exchange a greeting but were stopped by one of Tilly's reproving glares. We sneaked out. As we closed the auditorium doors, a group of slim, young protocol officials sprang into action, funnelling us out of the way and into a side room. It was a high and narrow enclosure, which no natural light ever touched. It was dusty with misuse, its only furniture a couple of olive green armchairs and a scratched side table planted on a threadbare brown carpet. We were stranded in its middle with our honour guard hovering close by, bound to us in cloying embarrassment. When we asked them to back off, they shuffled a few feet away and then regrouped to stand and watch. But their proximity wasn't what stopped us talking. It was something deeper, the fact that we couldn't find a way to share this loss.

Had it always been like this? Perhaps it had. I stood, remembering us a long, long time before. Shawn was thirteen then and I was eleven, and we were by a window in our airy Johannesburg living room as sheet lightning flashed across a gloomy sky and huge hailstones turned the lawn white. The water that streaked the outside of the plate glass was matched by tears running down Shawn's cheeks.

'She's not coming back,' was what Shawn kept repeating. 'She's gone forever.'

'She' was our grandmother, Tilly, who, a few hours earlier, had set off to deliver supper to our imprisoned mother. Tilly was the only adult member of our close family remaining in South Africa. Joe had left the country and couldn't come back; Ruth was in her third month of solitary detention and recently, and inexplicably, our grandfather, Julius, had taken off – leaving behind, as evidence of his existence, a mug shot accompanied by the words 'most wanted' on the front page of the newspaper.

Which left Tilly. Who should have been back hours ago.

Since she wasn't, logic dictated that she must have disappeared as well. I pretended to defy logic. I stood beside Shawn, calmly telling her that granny was merely late. Inside, of course, I knew Shawn was right, that granny had vanished and that we had been completely abandoned. I just couldn't acknowledge it since that way we would both drown.

There it was: somehow we had absorbed the lesson that if we expressed our fears together, we would be lost. We had grown up, our personal roles defined as either 'panic' or 'reassurance'. In that time, in the early sixties, what was happening in the wider society – a ferocious clampdown by the government – impinged directly on us. We suffered together but at the same time the secrecy that ruled our parents' political activities contaminated our relationship. We had learned not to share experience but to hold it to ourselves.

Back then, as the storm blew leaves off the spreading poplar tree, we saw Tilly's car heading up the driveway. I was proved 'right', Shawn was 'wrong'. Our grandmother was safe. Panic over – for that moment. And yet we learned our lessons then so that now, so many years later when what we had always anticipated had come to pass, when our mother was killed, we couldn't find a way of bridging a relationship forged in competition for such formidable parents. We hugged, briefly, unsubstantially, and went back to being part of the audience.

Before I went to sleep that night, I looked in on my father. I found him on the double bed that he and Ruth had shared. He was lying on top of a mottled brown fur skin that they'd used to keep out the winter's chill. Joe, white South Africa's bogeyman, a 'teddy-bear terrorist' as the South African newspapers later called him, had a joke for every opportunity.

For almost every opportunity. Now he lay alone on their bed, his bulk diminished by her absence. His voice was soft and so was his being. It was as if his outer skin had been removed.

But he had something he wanted to say. 'They targeted her because of who she was,' letting slip the guilt which must have been consuming him, the fear that 'they' had killed *her* because they had not been able to get *him*.

'It was the work she was doing,' he continued. 'It was dangerous to them.'

He could have been right. The research unit that my mother headed was investigating Mozambique's dependence on its powerful neighbour. What she uncovered would have helped the Mozambican government sever its economic ties with South Africa, simultaneously lessening South Africa's power to stop Mozambique from giving ANC guerrillas succour. And more than that: my mother was a symbol of resistance to apartheid – bright, attractive, fiercely independent – she stood as a constant reminder that whites could choose to stand up and be counted.

All this was true. And yet . . . was it reason enough for them to kill her?

I lay down beside my father. He was holding a piece of fur that had become detached, stroking it as if it were a cuddly animal.

'She would play with this,' he said, holding it up for me to see. 'She joked that it was our pet.'

His fingers gripping on to the fur, he lapsed into silence. I wasn't used to seeing my father so quiet, so vulnerable. I lay still, unable to fill the space between us.

Joe spoke again. He told me how, two nights previously, he had woken in the middle of the night and looked over at the sleeping Ruth. Her mouth had been open, he said, and she was very pale. For a moment he had thought she was dead.

I thought I understood what he was saying. He was talking, I thought, about the anticipation of disaster which, as it had been in 1963 with Shawn and I, was still so familiar to me. The risks our parents took had meant that we were always on the look-out for that terrible event which would break through the fragile skin of everyday life. Now, for the first time, I was hearing calm, phlegmatic Joe say that he lived like this as well.

But was that really what he meant? Years later, after Joe had died, a friend recalled a similar conversation she'd had with him. No surprise that he raised the subject with both of us: Joe was a consummate raconteur who saw nothing wrong in repetition. But what was different was the way the friend interpreted what Joe had meant. She had thought he was talking about the fact that days before Ruth had died, Joe had woken up and realised that his wife of thirty-two years was no longer young.

When I think about it now, I remember Joe talking to me, just after her funeral, of Ruth's ageing. She wouldn't have liked getting old, he'd said, she was far too worried about her appearance. I thought he was trying to wipe away some of his own pain and I told him that he was wrong. She was flexible, I said, she could have learned to adjust to the indignities of encroaching age. Joe nodded in apparent agreement but I can still recall the unspoken uncertainty that flickered across his face.

The last time Andy and I had been in Mozambique we had been disturbed each morning by the sound of Ruth's fingers hammering on her Hermes typewriter. Now, on that first morning after her death, I was awakened not by the sound of her typing, but by the lack of it. We were at the top of the house, in a place which Ruth's fine eye for design had not yet reached. I lay, staring at an unpainted wall, until I could lie no more.

I got up and went downstairs. I found my father shifting from one point in the house to the next, unable to settle down. We needed some way of passing the time: we went out for a drive. Under a sky still half-grey with night, we walked along the beach front. As a flat grey sea lapped desultorily against a dirty row of pebbles, a memory – that same beach but many, many years before – came back to me. I couldn't remember how old I was then, eight, or nine or ten. I'd been brought to the city (then called Lourenço Marques) by a friend of my mother's who took me as a companion to her daughter. Although I remember little of what happened that day, I have retained, quite vividly and with the kind of ghoulish horror that comes from childhood, a startling memory of the beach front. It was alive with crabs: small, scuttling creatures that carpeted the sand so densely that each step we took brought us into contact with their soft-shelled bodies.

Over twenty years later, on that same beach in 1982, there were no crabs in sight. I wondered whether my memory was playing tricks. I stood, quite still, watching the first rays of daylight, trying to puzzle out what could have happened to those flitting bodies.

I turned, eventually, and saw my father standing a short distance away staring out to sea. Another memory surfaced – the year before, Andy and I going on a trip with my parents out to the beach at Ponta do Ouro. We'd crossed the bridge at Catembe and driven down the tar road Portugal had built to link its colony to South Africa. We were stopped sporadically by badly dressed Mozambican soldiers who, ostensibly engaged in the official business of checking our passports, were actually cadging cigarettes. As we got closer to the beach, closer to Mozambique's border with South Africa, the road narrowed and became dirt. Through the low scrub that stretched on beyond the track, we caught glimpses of another life: a group of grass huts; a child using a stick to drive on a handful of goats; a woman balancing a jug of water on her head.

One more turn and we were at the resort which had been built for the hordes of South Africans who used to come and feast themselves on Mozambican crabs and prawns and Portuguese beer. This was tourism on a mass scale, designed for people who wanted excess and wanted it cheap. But ever since Mozambique had turned socialist, the South African visitors had stopped coming. Inside the main buildings were tacky lounges and cavernous dining rooms echoing to the sound of waiters far too numerous for the handful of guests who now ate there.

The sky had been overcast then: wild Atlantic Ocean breakers crashed against the white sand. We walked, Andy and I, behind my parents. Their heads were bent together, their lips close enough to nudge each other's ears, not out of affection or against the ferocious wind, but so that no one, not even their daughter, could hear what they were saying about my father's secret work. We walked as far as we could to a sign which told us that a few yards in front Mozambique ended and South Africa began. Just a few yards – that's all my parents had to cross and they would be home.

We didn't cross. We turned instead and walked back to the beach house. My father poured himself a malt whisky while my mother and I began the games of serial patience we used to stop the words we couldn't say to each other from hanging too heavily between us.

Is this what happens, I thought then, that the webs of secrecy enmesh all of life, shrouding not only the details of the military operations that my father had organised, but also the way we feel towards each other? I never found a way of asking her.

Chapter Four

A grimy silver light reflected on the mud flats. Dawn had come, bringing with it the time for official mourning. Joe and I drove to a home which was already teeming with people. A gang of ample, African mamas had taken over, preparing food for the flood of visitors that would follow.

Nobody told us what to do – we were passive in the face of a tradition that we, white children, born into Johannesburg's suburbia and transplanted to England's capital, didn't really understand. Not that anything was required of us, merely that we be there.

People came and went. Some talked of Ruth: others merely sat. There was one amongst them, a thin rake of a man, who outlasted all the rest, sitting quietly by the front door for hours on end. He never spoke to anybody, nor was he acknowledged, but neither did he ever leave. By the second day, I felt sorry for him. He was toying with a chess set – I asked him if he'd like to play.

It took longer to lay the game out than to finish it. I was completely outclassed as his cracked fingers plucked my pieces from the board in quick succession. When it was over, I asked him who he was.

'Oh,' he said, surprised that I didn't know. 'I'm your bodyguard.'

We laughed about it, my sisters and I, that such a frail-looking man was set to be our guard, and that none of us had guessed. But of course, we knew so little. We'd been brought up that way, to tune out whispered conversations. The method that my parents had used on the beach at Ponta do Ouro wasn't new: it had its origins long ago in South Africa when they had stood, with their comrades, on our rolling lawn and talked in code about what their next move should be.

This was the stuff of childhood, a world that I thought I had long left behind. Yet it didn't take long for old habits to slip back into sync. On the third day I overheard someone telling my father about a meeting that had taken place in Cape Town. Just as I had when I was a child, I read between the lines and guessed that the meeting must have been somehow connected to Ruth. I waited for my father to tell me more but all he did was look once at and then beyond me and walk away, silent, shutting me out.

I was just as bad. I didn't ask him. I swallowed down my questions, accepting as I had always done that these secrets were not for me to share. I upheld the taboo.

And yet I wouldn't let myself forget. Fourteen years later, going through South African newspapers, I chanced upon a 1982 report of a memorial meeting for Ruth which, held in Cape Town, had been broken up by the security police. I knew, immediately, that it was this news that had brought the two men's heads so close together. A public meeting, that's all. An act of rebellion by South African students to honour another martyr. A public meeting but we were not told. That was the way the family worked: knowledge, even of the most innocent events, was dangerous and we, the children, had learned to be compliant.

And there we were – Ruth's mother, her three daughters and her husband – closeted together for the first time in many years. A family dominated by women, our mother at the apex, the capable one who held us all together. Old rivalries, old problems jostled but couldn't surface. How could they, without her there to arbitrate? We spent hours in each other's company, saying little.

My grandmother was the only one to find adequate words – regal votes of thanks she produced to satisfy the honour of passing dignitaries. Her face was powder white with strain, her eyes shifting occasionally into confused distress, and yet she stood, ramrod straight, in her old wool skirt and soft wool jumper and thanked the Mozambican vice-president for inviting us to eat. Each word came out, precise and dignified, her hawk-like face still as she spoke, and for the first time I caught a glimpse of the young woman she had once been, that long-haired, fur coated, lively belle who sat on the jump-step of her brother-in-law's gleaming convertible, smiling at the camera – that woman born to rule, before her daughter filled her space.

I don't remember my grandmother beside us on the mortuary steps on the day of Ruth's funeral. Perhaps she was seated in one of the waiting cars. The rest of us, Ruth's family, stood with our backs to the chapel-like mortuary door, looking down on to a large courtyard where a crowd of students and foreign *corporantes*[1] waited. They had started singing when we stepped out of our cars and they continued now – massed ranks of them lilting out the words of South African freedom songs.

I stood there, watching them and I wondered what Ruth would have made of the display. She was a woman whose insecurity made her seem arrogant. Perhaps, somewhere, deep down she knew how much she was worth and this fuelled her anger at the way she had to struggle to be heard. Yet even so, she would have been surprised at the thousands who came to mourn her. And of course, she would not have been able to still her sharp tongue at those whose tears came either from obligation or cheap sentimentality. The daughter of two life-long communists, Ruth hated dogma and empty displays of revolutionary fervour. As I stood watching I thought that she would have distanced herself from the mourners whose songs foretold of the impending victory for which she had given her life.

And yet, maybe I was wrong: maybe Ruth, in her Mozambican incarnation, would have been amongst them. The last photo she sent me had been taken as she marched with members of her university department in a rally. Ruth is in the foreground. On top of her frizzed-out hair perches an incongruous miner's tin hat. She is carrying a flag and smiling proudly – a woman who has finally joined in.

The door behind us opened. We were led into a gloomy high-

---

1. Foreign workers, many of them highly skilled, who had come out on short-term contracts to help Mozambique's transition.

domed room where a stone slab, a coffin and a group of ambassadors were waiting. As we walked closer, Joe whispered that by custom, we should now be viewing the body. But, he added quickly, he'd said no and asked that the coffin be sealed.

For many years afterwards, I wondered about his decision. I listened to bereavement experts talking about the aftermath of sudden death and I believed them when they said that relatives who view their loved ones find it easier to accept what has happened. I used to wonder whether, if Ruth's coffin had been open and we had seen Ruth's corpse, the impact of her murder might have ebbed away in an easier fashion.

Now I know better. I had clung to Joe's account of Ruth's perfectly formed feet lying on her office floor and I had used this image to discount what I was also told: the hole in a brick wall; her four-pronged ring fused into one; the look on the friend's face who talked about identifying the body. I should have known that what lay inside that coffin was not my mother. Not my mother in one piece.

It was years later before I read in a series of descriptions of life in exile, an article by one of Ruth's colleagues where he described the act of scraping what was left of her off the wall.

And there was still more to come. Fourteen years on, I sat in Maputo's dingy Cinema Institute, staring at a screen of an antique Steenbeck editing machine on which was threaded footage on those days. There was a short section that had been excised from the news broadcast that was shown all over Mozambique: a slow pan across the room after the bomb had exploded. I saw the desks, covered in what looked like cinders, the gaping window and then I saw the walls. Was it blood that streaked the corner of two sides of the room? Was it blood, or was it also Ruth's flesh?

I understood then, finally, what Joe had been trying to tell us when he talked of the closed coffin. And I thought: perhaps the mind does everything the experts say it can – including waiting until even the unbearable can be endured.

★

On the day of her funeral, we drove through the streets of Maputo, on the road to the northern industrial suburb of Matola, and through the ornate metal cemetery gates. The walls were mass graves, small drawer-shaped shrines where remains, photographs, inscriptions and plastic flowers had been left as a marker to each separate life. But this was not the place for Ruth. Our cavalcade moved beyond the walls and unloaded us in a special section of the cemetery. In a line were heaps of dry, brown-red earth, the graves of twelve MK soldiers, Joe's boys, who had, the previous year, been killed by South African commandos.

Six people carried Ruth's coffin and laid it carefully down beside the freshly dug grave. I didn't know the pall-bearers, can remember only one in front, a stocky African woman, smart in her women's league uniform of black and green, her lips clenched against an emotion she didn't want to show. She stepped to one side and speeches rained down on us. We stood in front, a mute family line-up, waiting for the words to stop.

My mother had always had an eye for detail: I remember her speaking lyrically at a funeral of her friend's infatuation with garish hats. No one spoke of Ruth like that: no one talked about the silk underwear that she had packed to take to gaol in 1956; about the way she would fall asleep if she was bored; or about her recently developed, and inexplicable passion for overblown jigsaws. They spoke instead of a cardboard heroine, a woman who had given her life to the struggle. I didn't want to hear of that Ruth. I wanted them to talk of the mother I had known.

But if they had been able to, what would they have said? She had lived so many lives, there were so many Ruths. In the weeks that followed, when people spoke of her, they each conjured up a different woman. There seemed no meeting point, no one picture that would join the rest together. And time has changed all that as well. When Shawn's film about the Ruth in 1963, *A World Apart* was in pre-production, we met together with Barbara Hershey who was to play Ruth. While Barbara talked about the kind of woman our mother had been, and about the kind of clothes she would have worn, I sat there thinking: she is nothing like my mother. And yet, years later, on a London tube escalator I caught a glimpse of that same actress's face advertising another film and, before I had time to censor myself, I thought, 'there's my mother'.

A hand touched my elbow: the speeches were over. We moved to the grave and, as the crowd began to sing, we threw roses down. The songs of grief and of revolution swelled: we moved back, supplanted by lines of mourners who queued to heave spadefuls of sand over the coffin until finally it was covered. We turned and left while Ruth stayed there, a lone white woman buried alongside twelve black men.

Three weeks later, Shawn and I were sitting on the plane. Through the small windows we could see Joe on the tarmac, waiting to wave his final goodbye. But the plane didn't move, not for the longest time. As the passengers got increasingly restive, the French pilot appeared. 'Don't complain,' he said. 'We are waiting because I have forced them to repack the luggage hold. The way they had done it before, if we had taken off, our plane would have crashed.'

The baggage was reloaded, the doors closed. My father stepped back, a lonely figure, shrunk by distance on the tarmac. The plane took off. And I sat in it, going back to London, to my home, armed with the jigsaw image of my mother's shoes, and with the first stirrings of a search for the truth that would only really begin more than a decade later.

Part Two

Chapter Five

The bomb that killed Ruth put an end to a marriage which, full of conflict and of passion, lasted more than thirty-two years.

It all began in 1948, the year the South African Nationalist Party won its first election. One ordinary day in '48, Wolfie Kodesh, a Johannesburg-based Communist Party member, got a phone call from a student called Joe Slovo. Joe asked Wolfie to meet him urgently although he wouldn't say why. Wolfie wasn't too surprised. Those were, after all, the beginnings of the conspiratorial years. The Nationalist Party, which was to win every whites-only election for the next forty-six years, had scraped through to its first victory with a vow to stamp out both the 'black peril' and the 'red menace'. Everybody knew that the membership of the Communist Party, which was an explosive combination of both, might soon be made illegal. In anticipation, comrades had begun to be much more circumspect about where they talked, who they talked to, and what they said. Without asking for any further information, Wolfie fixed a meet with Joe.

It was dark by the time Wolfie parked his car in a side street just off Johannesburg's main Harrow Road. He doused his lights and waited. Within minutes, he heard footsteps coming closer. In his rear-view mirror, he could see twenty-two-year-old Joe Slovo heading towards his car. They were part of the same circle, a tight-knit group of right thinkers, and Wolfie knew Joe's history well. He knew how Joe, aged ten, had travelled from Lithuania with his mother and sister to join his father in South Africa. He also knew how Joe's mother had died when he was twelve; how at fourteen, Joe had left school and got a job as a dispatch clerk in a pharmaceutical company; how, at sixteen, he'd led his first successful strike and how, at eighteen, he'd lied about his age and joined the army. It was a move which would stand him in good stead: in 1946 he emerged unscathed from the Italian campaign to find that, as an ex-serviceman, he was not only exempted from university qualification requirements but also eligible for special loans.

And so it was that on that night on a deserted road, Joe was a law student. His was seemingly a typical immigrant's story endlessly narrated. He'd arrived in South Africa a Yiddish speaker, his head shaved against lice, carrying a brown paper bag containing fruit so overripe that its pulp was seeping out. Now, eleven years later, his English was fluent, his skull was blanketed by thick brown hair, and black round-rimmed glasses framed the top half of his genially chubby face. He was a charmer who played the guitar often, if badly, and who always had a steady supply of jokes at hand – a man who liked to party.

On that particular evening Joe was businesslike. He nodded as he opened the passenger door and sat down next to Wolfie. But he was also very nervous. He launched himself into speech.

'Are you in love with Ruth?' is what he said in a question thrown from deep midfield.

It was a well-known fact that Wolfie was a friend of the twenty-four-year-old Ruth First. He had even, since her separation from her boyfriend, escorted her to parties or the movies. But Wolfie felt he had no claim on Ruth. He answered Joe's question with one of his own: 'Why do you ask?'

Joe was insistent: 'I want to know,' he said. 'Are you in love with Ruth?'

Wolfie was, by now, completely flabbergasted. He told Joe that there was nothing like that between Ruth and him, and once again he asked Joe why.

'Because,' was Joe's earnest reply, '*I'm* very much in love with her.'

There are pictures of Joe, pre-Ruth, lounging on a beach towel, surrounded by a bevy of grinning bathing-costumed beauties. But this new crush was different. Joe had fallen hard. He was struck by Ruth's brisk confidence and her stylish presence. The only mystery is why he didn't approach her directly. Perhaps he thought that middle-class Ruth was out of his grasp: perhaps he merely needed someone to give him permission to dare to hope for her. Whatever the reason, it seemed to work. having cleared the air with Wolfie, Joe did eventually summon up the courage to ask Ruth out. She accepted.

She was single at the time, but only just, since she'd recently emerged from four years of passionate entanglement. When she was eighteen she'd fallen in love with Ismael Meer, an Indian militant. Ismael lived in a slovenly flat on Market Street where at any time of day and night there would be crowds of people eating curry, arguing about politics, planning campaigns, and dancing to the gramophone. It was a meeting point for the young lions like Nelson Mandela who were bent on turning the ANC away from its old, unsuccessful conciliatory policies and into direct confrontation with the apartheid government. At the centre of this hotbed of revolt was the charismatic Ismael Meer with Ruth beside him.

Ruth's mother, Tilly, who had long scorned bridge and gossip in favour of left-wing politics, was delighted to see her daughter moving in these radical circles. She wasn't, however, so keen on Ruth's attachment to Ismael Meer. It's not clear why, she never said. Was it something about Ismael's character, or was it merely because he was black? Whatever the reason, Tilly's resistance was an obstacle to be surmounted. Ahmed Kathrada who, along with Nelson Mandela would end up sentenced to life on Robben Island, remembers how in the early days Ruth and Ismael set him up to run interference for their conversations. The routine went like this: Kathrada would phone the First household. When Tilly answered, he would ask for Ruth and then, when Ruth came on the line, he would hand the phone to Meer.

Even today when some people who knew them then talk about Ruth and Ismael Meer, their eyes shimmer with nostalgic regret. It's almost as if this one love affair has been written into the annals of myth. For good reason perhaps: they made a handsome couple and an utterly modern one. He was a rising star of the Transvaal Indian Congress, and she an active member in the young communist league who worked as a journalist for the left-wing newspaper, the *Guardian*. She was white, he was black – a visible defiance against a government bent on securing absolute separation between the races. And they were, so the myth continued, besieged not only by the state but also by their parents. Just as Tilly disliked the arrangement, so must his family have worried about how marrying outside their faith would affect his standing in the community and his prospects.

Yet despite all this, the two stayed together.

For four years, that is. In the end, of course, as must always be the way with myth, their love was doomed. Even before the Nationalist Party grabbed on to power, the sight of a white woman and a black man arm-in-arm was enough to raise eyebrows. After the election, the Immorality Act, one of a gamut of punishing new apartheid laws, would make it illegal. Ruth and Ismael parted: he returning to his home town of Durban and she, so goes the myth, after much soul-searching, staying behind in Johannesburg. Which is why, when Joe asked her out, she was free.

Those same people who hold to the romantic legend of Ruth's ill-fated love affair with Ismael, say that her dating Joe was the act of a woman on the rebound. Whatever the truth of this, by 1949, Ruth and Joe were living together. When they moved into their first flat, some of the rent and all of the furniture was supplied courtesy of her parents. Despite the fact that they were not married, Tilly was thrilled. Joe was every Jewish mother's dream son-in-law: an engaging, clever, witty, white, Jewish, lawyer-to-be.

And there was more as well. Joe and Ruth's parents had a lot in common. Ruth was the odd one out. She was first-generation South African born in a Johannesburg maternity home: the other three – Tilly and Julius and Joe – had all arrived, as children, from the Baltic states. Ruth's life had been one easy progression from school to university: Joe and the Firsts had all, in their early teens, been forced out of school. Ruth's parents were always there to help her financially: Joe, Tilly and Julius had to make their own way. Ruth had continuity: what characterised both her future husband's and her parent's lives, was an abrupt dislocation from the past.

Almost all her life, Tilly kept a picture of her own mother, a gentle fair-haired, blue-eyed beauty above her bed, discarding it only when she was well into her eighties. Despite this, Tilly used to insist she had forgotten what her mother was like. The only details she'd volunteer was that her mother had kept a cow in the yard and that as Tilly grew up, the two could no longer communicate. The problem was literal rather than emotional. Tilly's mother never learned any English while Tilly gradually lost her comprehension of her mother tongue of Yiddish.

I, too, have known disruption in my life, but the cultures between which I was moved were both English-speaking. I found it almost impossible to believe that Tilly, aged twenty-five, didn't share a common language with her mother. When I said as much to Joe, he looked at me, silent for a moment. Then he told me that he believed it, because the same thing had happened to him. By the time he was grown up, Joe and his father quite literally spoke different languages.

The new-in-laws-to-be shared so much history: Ruth, the charismatic, bright, high-achieving focus of her parent's attention had chosen a boyfriend who came from their side of the tracks. No wonder they were delighted. And of course, there was one other overriding quality to recommend Joe to the Firsts: he was a communist with the same grandiose ambition as them; he was determined to change the world.

So it was that Julius and Tilly supplied the furniture and the spare cash, and Ruth the living expenses for the two while Joe continued with his studies. By August of 1949, Ruth was pregnant with the first of their three daughters. They had flouted convention up till then: now they decided to get married.

In the last few months of his life, my father told me about the wedding. He played it down, describing it as a shot-gun event with the bizarre twist that the mother-in-law was ecstatic and the bride cried. In his autobiography, he glosses over the whole event, saying only that he and Ruth took half an hour off from their respective offices to tie the knot.

And yet, was that wedding really so insignificant? I don't think so. When I searched the small blue suitcase which stores blurred snaps of children dancing about the garden decked out in fairy costumes and idyllic picnics on the beach, I found a beige card, stylishly typeset all in lower case: it was an invitation to my parent's wedding party to be held at the bride's parents' home.

By all accounts it turned out to be some celebration. The only no-shows were Joe's father and stepmother. Was Joe so alienated from his father by then that he didn't bother to invite him, or was it his father who administered the snub? It didn't seem to matter then. The cream of radical society, a hundred of them, young and old, black and white, came to parade through Tilly and Julius's double-fronted Kensington home. The alcohol flowed freely at this, the first of the Slovo's many and famous celebrations. By the party's end, the garden was littered with people in varying states of incapacitating inebriation.

Thus did Joe and Ruth mark the beginning of their married life. And they had reason to celebrate. They had everything going for them: they were both well educated with professions tailor made, South Africans in a land where material success was easy to attain so long as you were white. Joe graduated – top of his class – and started practising as an advocate. Ruth continued as a journalist but also did the conventional thing and had a family – three daughters in quick succession: Shawn in 1950; me in 1952 and the youngest, Robyn, in 1953. Their Camelot years had begun.

Chapter Six

The fifties, my parents' Camelot years. How ironic that it was during that time the apartheid laws were being relentlessly solidified. Segregation signposts, the ones that made South Africa infamous – '*net blanke*'/'whites only'; or '*slegs blankes*'/ 'Europeans only' – went up everywhere. In parliament, increasingly divisive laws were laid down on to the statute books. In the newspapers, Nationalist spokesmen used absurd language to justify their deeds.

No matter how preposterous the proposals, nobody laughed. Not, for example, when the Medical Inspector of Schools, Dr J. Coetzee, told a government sponsored commission that school meals were not necessary for Africans, because Africans slept better than their 'European' counterparts. They didn't laugh, but neither did they bother to raise their voices in protest against what was being done in their name. They sequestered themselves in their stiff, well-regulated white lives where the rules of decorum and convention sealed in a society preoccupied by getting rich quick.

Not so my parents. They were the best of their generation and amongst the most outrageous. They existed in the midst of puritanical, apartheid South Africa and they broke all its rules. Africans were not allowed, by law, to buy liquor? Well then, the whites and Indians amongst them would buy it for them, and would hold raucous parties which would be inundated by township dwellers after a good time. Whites were not allowed in 'black' areas without a permit? Well they would use guides to help them sneak in under fences to see what was really happening. Their newspapers were banned? Well they just changed the paper's name and started up again.

And they were so optimistic. It must have seemed to them that they were cresting a wave that would never break. When the Communist Party, the only multiracial body to speak against apartheid, was banned, my parents helped form a new white organisation – the Congress of Democrats – which worked side by side with the young lions of the blacks-only ANC, the Mandelas, Sisulus, and Tambos, who were to become the great heroes of contemporary South Africa. They were fearless, all of them. The more the state cracked down, the more they fought back. Realising that the time for petitions and delegations was gone, they organised the Defiance Campaign where crowds went out, deliberately, to defy the apartheid laws. When the government's response was to vastly increase the penalties for such defiance, my parents and their friends hardly took a breath before they moved on to their next campaign – the drawing up of a new charter, a freedom charter, which would become the ANC's most well-known rallying cry.

Those were exhilarating times and the photos of that period pay tribute to their wonder as black people in their thousands, poor maybe, but incontestably dignified, stand in disciplined formation, determined to resist the horror that was heading closer. Thousands of almost exclusively black people and yet always in each new campaign, there was a small group of whites included, among them my parents. Something – their child-hoods, their parents, some experience at school – had made them different from the rest of their white compatriots. Instead of passively accepting what was happening, they chose resist-ance. They seemed to have no doubts. As each new obstacle reared up, they merely lengthened their stride.

As time went on, as Camelot gave way to a much more dangerous period, they would become pariahs. And Ruth, in particular, as a woman who broke with convention, would be most severely judged.

Yet Ruth did not seem to mind. A woman she might be, but she would never let anyone stand in her way. Not for her the support role that had been her mother's fate. Even though she paid lip service to fashion by producing her three girls within the

then prescribed two-yearly intervals, she refused to let mother-
hood slow her down. Her mother had sacrificed everything for
family: Ruth, well in advance of her time, wouldn't even
surrender her surname. As a friend would later comment, 'The
only two people who ever called her Mrs Slovo were her
hairdresser and the prosecutor in the treason trial.'

By her mid-twenties, Ruth had already begun the long trail
of slotting visits to the hairdresser, the dressmaker and the
headmistress into her political world. If she would not give up
her politics, neither would she forsake her style. Her way was
unique, and she stuck to it – giving, for example, a present not
of some worthy book but of imported Helena Rubenstein
perfume as a thank you to a friend who'd helped with last-
minute preparations for a conference.

Three or four times a year she would visit the shop of
Johannesburg's most exclusive couturier, Eric Pugen and order
outfits. But Ruth's seasons were very different from Pugen's
other clients: while they procured that elegant linen shift for a
pre-dinner cocktail party, she was punctiliously strict about the
hemline of the dress she sported as she climbed up on to some
impromptu township stage. And while Jo'burg's moneyed
madams chose shoes to match their evening's wafting ball wear,
Ruth discarded hers as a raucous party at her house got out of
hand and her guests climbed on top of the piano to continue
dancing.

She was so busy she could not entirely separate her worlds.
She'd drift into Pugen's shop late in the evening, a carefree
stylish woman concerned with her appearance. Then, having
offered her couturier a lift home, would shock him because
when he reached her car, he'd find a black man waiting patiently
for his friend to emerge and finish some inflammatory discussion
they'd been having.

She was always busy: there was so much to be done. In 1950,
as everybody had predicted, the Communist Party was banned.
Both Ruth and Joe were involved in starting it up again, this
time underground, heading deeper into a secret world where

excitement and danger were to run side by side. It was a cosy, in-bred universe they occupied. To make sure their cover wasn't blown, membership was by invitation only. They learned conspiracy in those early years: no meeting was ever pre-advertised, or held in the same place twice running. Phone calls were short and cryptic, conversations often taking place not in the lounge but by a distant garden fence.

Young, talented, passionate, they had broken out of the constraints of the South African colour bar. While the rest of white South Africa looked for its entertainment either to classical European music, or to the naive folk songs of the Afrikaner veld, they danced to township penny whistles and to *kwela* and drew the rest of their music from the wider world: from America and the civil rights movement, as they were swept up in Paul Robson or Harry Belafonte crazes, or from Europe and the latest cult movie – for a while, after *Never on Sunday* came out they could be found in Greek restaurants singing boisterously to the accompaniment of smashing plates.

Perhaps they played harder than others because they knew how close to the edge they were living. But the shadows had not yet closed in: they also felt, black and white together, that they were making history in a world that was going their way. The Russian revolution had framed the lives of their parents' community. To them, the generation that came directly after-wards, to these evangelists against exploitation, China was the next great victory.

They didn't just look to the world; they travelled it as well. Especially Ruth. She had been to Prague, Dubrovnik and Moscow on youth conferences and reporting for her news-papers: now in 1954 she was invited on a study trip to China. No matter that her third daughter, Robyn, was only two months old. As soon as it was offered, Ruth grabbed the invitation and went on a four-month visit.

It was the kind of visit Ruth's mother, Tilly, would have loved to make. But when her daughter went instead, Tilly moved in with us.

★

I was two when Ruth went to China and, while she was away, I learned to walk. It had taken me a long, long time. My parents and my grandparents had watched over me, since I turned one, in anticipation of my first steps. To no avail. I seemed to be developing normally – I learned to talk early in fact – but still I didn't seem able to walk.

My speech was fluent by the time they carted me off to the specialist. Nothing organic wrong, was the doctor's verdict: she'll walk eventually. And so back home I was carried, as always contained by some adult's arms. And then one day, when Ruth was in China, I was sitting in the kitchen and I was hungry.

'I want that,' I said, pointing at a packet of coveted biscuits on the counter, knowing that my black nanny would bring them to me.

'Fetch them yourself,' she said.

Was that all that I'd been waiting for? Someone to tell me to stand up on my own two feet? Perhaps it was: I obeyed. I stood up and I walked.

It was my grandmother who, late in life, told me this story. If I hadn't known her, and known how her life had limited the stretch of her imagination, I would have assumed she'd made it up. It was too apocryphal of white South African life, the white toddler unable to move without the black servant's chiding.

Looking back, I guess the story was invented and that it contained a message. With her reputation of unbearable honesty, my grandmother did sometimes bury her meaning deep. I remember how, on another occasion in 1984, when she had just returned from a visit to South Africa, she chose to describe at length, and with seeming admiration, the beautiful cast-iron fretwork in one of her relatives' Jo'burg home. Only after I had kissed her parchment skin and walked away, did I realise that what she had described were the bars her hosts had erected to keep servants and black intruders out at night.

Perhaps, when she told me the story of how I had learned to walk, what she was really saying was that, once again, it was time for me to get up and stand on my own two feet. Thinking back to the moment she had chosen to tell me the story, and of how angry I had been at the time at something she had chosen to do, I think that this is precisely what she meant. But in those early days, in the fifties, my grandmother was always there and there were no bars separating us from the world. Walk I did, in time for my mother's return. A shadow was lifted. My parents could once again be framed by their own dazzling optimism: with their help, they thought all humanity's problems would soon disappear.

They made choices, brave choices, that others in their country did not make. For this they were heroic. But they were also lucky. There were few commonplace restraints to hem them in. If they had opted for ordinary white lives in South Africa, they could certainly have made much more money yet even though they chose a highly dangerous course, they were still white and well off. Ruth was a working mother and an activist but she had no need to occupy the kitchen: she had domestic workers to do the cooking, the cleaning and the childcare. She also had her parents, ever generous, to supply the extras which included a constant stream of new Citroëns that were my grandfather's obsession. She and Joe worked hard but they played hard too. People fought to get an invitation to their parties: they were, in their circles at least, the king and queen of Jo'burg.

Our family albums are full of those years of gracious living. There's the house that we lived in – a three-bedroomed new-built bungalow in one of Johannesburg's middle-class suburbs, without a swimming pool but with a big garden overlooking an open *veld* and a huge spreading broad-leafed plane tree that we three sisters used to climb.

It was our house, our haven. Even after I was taken away from it, I thought of it as always belonging only to us. And yet when I went back thirty years after we left South Africa, and tried to go inside there was a couple living there who thought of it as theirs. There had been other pilgrims to that place before me: researchers intent on writing of my parents, or activists, trying to relive those days and all of them has been briskly sent away. When I arrived, it was conceded that I did have some claims on the place and I was grudgingly admitted into the living room. No further than that, however: I wasn't allowed to walk down the corridor and visit the bedroom which Robyn and I had once shared, or to open the cupboard where I had once locked and forgotten her.

My second visit, this time with Robyn, was even more curtailed. We got a brief tour of the garden. We stood on the flat stretch of lawn where our tree had once towered, and gazed at an unfamiliar kidney-shaped swimming pool and a green covered garage, trying to conjure up our corner Wendy house which had occupied that site.

On my third visit, I was met with a rebuff: 'Close the gate on your way out,' an angry man told me. 'It upsets us when you come here.' I had no choice. I turned and closed the gate. At the same time as I wondered at his anger, I also thought that he was right: it was no longer ours.

It was ours then, back in the fifties. But even so, each year at Christmas, we would leave it behind so that Joe could drive us non-stop to Cape Town for our summer holiday. Each year there would be photographs of umbrellas on the beach festooned by rock candy, of *braais*, where red meat, gin and oysters were consumed beside the fishing lines, and of three dresses, two of them identical sailor suits, lying on the white sand as we three girls ran screaming joyfully into the freezing Clifton seas.

There are other photographs as well of that period of our lives, each telling a different part of the story. One, taken in 1956, is of us three chubby-cheeked sisters around a table, eating rice crispies. It was our second breakfast of the day. The newspapers had come to snap us eating because the night before both our parents were among 156 others, rounded up and taken to a police station to be charged with treason. Six-year-old Shawn was our spokesperson:

'Mummy's gone to prison,' she said, 'to look after the black people.'

Joe and Ruth were soon released on bail but the trial that followed, the Treason Trial, was the government's attempt to stop the Congress Alliance – a mix of African, Indian, Coloured and White organisations – from planning mass protests against apartheid. During the proceedings, a specially constructed cage framed the most brilliant of South Africa's activists (seated in alphabetical order so that for once in South Africa, blacks and whites were legally seen side by side) who doodled and dozed their way through tedious months of prosecution evidence. My father defended himself and caused a near riot after the magistrate tried to convict him for contempt of court.

While the trial went on, Tilly once again stepped in, looking after us while Ruth was trapped in court. Was it at the moment of her arrest that Ruth wrote her undated note to us: 'I send you all my love. Be sweet, happy girls and help granny ... Granny will look after you till I am home and you must look after Pandy [our black Labrador].'

So Tilly now had three young granddaughters and their animals to guard. But that's not all she did. Abstinent Tilly who, under protest, forced an annual birthday sherry down, was in her element: she would be found on the doorstep of the Treason Trial offices, waiting for the less-disciplined, and infinitely more hung-over, volunteers to open up so she could give them the money she'd been up since dawn collecting.

Treason – it has an ominous ring. And yet in those days they were almost casual about it. While my grandmother worried about what might happen, it didn't seem to concern the others. They would be driven up to court in closed vans, their hands stuck out the bars in a thumbs-up salute while crowds waited patiently outside, singing the ANC anthem of *Nkosi Sikelele i'Afrika* and holding up placards. The photos of those days show my parents as two glamorously dressed, confident people – him in suits, her in beautifully tailored dresses, with matching shoes, make-up and jewellery. They look as if they could be socialites, stepping, smiling, from some glittering occasion. And they were right to be so confident. The trial seemed endless but eventually, after four years, the prosecution was forced into an ignominious backdown.

I was four when the Treason Trial started. I remember it only as a double breakfast, the first of a confusing number of occasions when my parents would fade out of family life. Perhaps, without the photo, even that would have passed into the drifting cloud where one experience merged into the confusing next. We lived in a world beset by contradictions. We were three close, squabbling sisters who played fantasy games in the garden, swam in the next-door neighbour's pool and staged grandiose cut-out doll weddings. We were privileged white South African children, serviced by servants, attending whites-only schools, driven from one safe haven to the next, and our parents were plotting to overthrow the state.

My memories of those years are mainly of exclusion. Of hiding under the table at nursery while the teachers laughed at me and of my first, big, jostling school where I was supposed to play the cymbals in a band whose practice rooms I could never manage to locate. I solved the problem by developing delirium on the night of the performance; that night comes clearly into focus in the image of my sweet-smelling, ravishing mother coming to my bedroom to blow a kiss my way before wafting out.

And I remember, as well, my mother's anxious face framing the background of a bathroom mirror. It was in the middle of one of their parties when I tripped down the two stone stairs that separated the open-plan living room from the dining area. I somersaulted on the crazy paving, twisting through a forest of trouser legs and landing hard. Before I had time to scream at the blood pouring from my eyebrow, I was in the arms of one of my parents' black comrades and rushed to the bathroom. I remember the whisky on his breath, his callused hands wiping at my skin, his curly hair framing my straight bob, and in the background my mother, seeing I was all right, shifting from horror back into abandoned gaiety.

We children played out fantasies in the garden while around

us the world moved fast. The images of those times come to me sporadically; the sound of neighbourhood dogs barking as black dustbin men hefted huge trash cans on their backs and ran down the road after the dustbin lorry whose driver's white skin stopped him from slowing down for them; the sticky crimson blood oozing out of the black newspaper deliverer's skull, seeping on to strewn newspapers as we waited for the black ambulance to come and pick him up; the black women who ran up our driveway seeking sanctuary from the men who had robbed them in the *veld*, the fear in their eyes turning to dulled acceptance as the police, hearing that the victims were black, refused to come round.

And all the time while this was happening we were lifted in our freshly pressed uniforms to school, sitting in small whites-only classes, directed by kind white teachers whose ample bosoms were cossetted in fluffy, wool twin-sets. And then we were driven back again to that garden of our imagination to feel the first, faint echoes of what was to come.

Chapter Seven

In the forward rush of my childhood years that bled one into the other, there are occasional moments of pause. One is dated 1959. I was a gawky seven year old (my hair bobbed long enough to cover the prominent ears I'd inherited from my father), standing by the front door, watching my mother's car move slowly towards me up our long driveway. When she braked and turned off the engine, the slope-backed Citroën sighed and sank down into the ground. I saw her leg tilting out and was mesmerised by the sight of her high heels clipping their way towards me. She stopped in front of me: my eyes moved up to her face. She was beaming.

'Let's celebrate,' she said, reaching into her soft leather briefcase and pulling out three packets of crisps.

I grabbed at one of them, ripped it open and began crunching greedily through the packet. I hardly tasted anything but that didn't matter: I was satisfying a desperate craving, a lust which had been fuelled by deprivation. For the past few months crisps, like all potatoes and their by-products, had been banned from our household in line with a countrywide ANC organised boycott. This was not the first time the outside world had impinged in outlandish ways: our childhoods were punctuated by incidents which were the life blood of South African protest. But this one stuck particularly fast not because crisps were so dear to me, but because of the jubilation on my mother's face.

Now I know that she had good reason to be happy that day. She'd been in at the very beginning of this boycott: its seeds, in fact, were sown in the office of the tabloid *New Age* which she edited.

It had all started some months previously. Wolfie Kodesh, the friend who had blessed my parents' first date, had just shut the door on Ruth's inner sanctum in an attempt to drown out the sound of her machine-gun fingers banging at her typewriter, when an African walked in off the street. He was dressed in filthy rags and his eyes were red rimmed. He'd escaped, he said, from a prison farm, moving secretly at night to reach Johannesburg.

He'd come to *New Age* because, in the midst of general indifference, movement journalists, and in particular, Ruth, had a courageous history of investigating the treatment meted out by white farmers on their black labourers. Some years before a set of exposures on conditions in the farm lands of Bethal by churchman Michael Scott, and by Ruth (then aged twenty-two), caused a furore. Now, a good ten years later, this stranger brought with him a story that was horrifyingly familiar.

In the days of apartheid all Africans were forced by law to carry freshly stamped passes which would prove their right to live and work in particular areas. The visitor to *New Age* told of men arrested on minor offences, mainly incorrectly stamped passes and handed over by the police to farmers who worked them mercilessly. He told of being shut up at night in cement bunkers so dirty that lice fell from the ceilings, and of beatings which ended, on several occasions, in death. The sentences the courts passed on the men might be relatively short, but once they were taken to the farms, they found that there was no escape. The man in front of Wolfie had been held for more than nine months, only managing to get away on this, his second escape attempt. But he hadn't come to *New Age* to complain: he'd come to plead for help for a friend who'd been too weak to get away.

Wolfie showed the man into Ruth's cubicle. She didn't look up – once Ruth was concentrating, she was almost impossible to distract. While their visitor took in his surroundings, Wolfie walked round Ruth's desk which, like all the other furniture, had been supplied courtesy of the First factory. The office displayed all Ruth's ferocious energy. There would have been teetering piles of newspapers waiting to be cut, jagged-cut paper, glued and pinned together with Ruth's comments scrawled over them which were her articles in progress, and two poster-sized photographs – one of Moses Kotane, the first black general secretary of the Communist Party and the other, Bill Andrews, a British trade unionist who had been, when he was alive, Ruth's father's mentor.

But there was no time, suddenly, for any further observation: Wolfie had got Ruth's attention. She pushed her typewriter aside and, staccato-style, started firing off questions, mentally cross-indexing these new tales of men arrested for minor offences and traded for slave labour with the old. By the time the man had come to the end of his story, Ruth was on her feet. In her Pugen exclusive suit she was up and hurrying Wolfie and a young African journalist, Joe Gqabi, into Wolfie's black Chevrolet.

Wolfie drove Ruth and Joe Gqabi out of Johannesburg, past fields of corn and into the long, flat expanse of the potato belt where Mr Potgieter's farm was located. Some distance from the farm's main buildings, he slowed down. Ahead, they could see Potgieter's land dissected by the road on which they'd come. In the fields was a vision straight from Hades: scarecrow men, shoeless and dressed in sacks, working with hoes along rows of potatoes while *baas boys* – black overseers – stood ready to lash at them with *knobkerries*.

Wolfie stopped the car and Joe Gqabi stepped out. Joe was an ex-boxer who'd been trained by Ruth in journalism. On that day in 1959, he disguised his boxer's swagger under the practised cringe that was part of every black South African's camouflage. He went to the farmer, cap in hand, and asked the *baas* permission to deliver a message to one of the labourers. Another black face, the farmer barely looked at him, just nodded briskly. Keeping his pace carefully even, Joe began to walk towards the line of men. Wolfie and Ruth sat waiting in the car. While Ruth talked of the next issue of their newspaper, Wolfie looked out of the window. He saw some dirt mounds by the roadside. They seemed vaguely familiar, he wondered why.

He stopped wondering when he heard a distant shout. Looking around, he saw Joe Gqabi running through the field with a farmer's *bakkie* (a pick-up truck) following close and closing in. Ruth made sure the back door was open: Wolfie headed straight for Joe. When they came up abreast, Joe dived in, shouting at them to get out fast. The farmer's son, he said, had grown suspicious and had come chasing after him.

'Get a move on,' Ruth called and Wolfie put his foot down hard as three *baas boys* on bicycles, wielding whip-like *sjamboks* drove straight at them.

As he turned the wheel, Wolfie's mind flashed back to the time when he had landed with his army unit in Ethiopia. He remembered how he had run along the beach, dodging bullets, and how he'd tripped and kicked against some dirt mounds, only later to discover that they were the hastily dug graves of dead Italians. Now, speeding towards Johannesburg, Wolfie realised that the oblong mounds on Potgieter's lands were identical in shape to the ones that had obstructed his progress on that Ethiopian beach.

Back in Johannesburg Ruth bullied a writ of habeas corpus out of the courts, leaving the farmer with no choice. He arrived in court with one of his black farm workers who, dressed in torn blue overalls, was caged in a *bakkie*. When Ruth turned up, she was accompanied by the missing man's wife who, not knowing what had happened to her husband, had given him up for dead. The wife walked over to the *bakkie* and looked inside and what should have been a moment of jubilation was turned to disappointment. After a long moment, she shook her head, saying no, this painfully thin, beaten wreck whose skin was covered in ugly weals, was not her husband.

The first glimmerings of triumph showed on the farmer's weather-beaten face: these bloody 'commies' had made a mistake, now he would teach them a lesson. He turned, ready to give reign to his indignation. At that moment, the man in the *bakkie* smiled, and in that faintest hint of a humanity which had been almost annihilated by nine months in hell, his wife saw that it was really him.

The court freed James Musa Sadika and ordered an investigation into the mounds that lay on Potgieter's farm. They found skeletons so disintegrated that nobody could tell who had died, or how. But the ANC boycott, the resultant stockpiling of potatoes in all of South Africa's major cities, and the fury of other farmers who could no longer sell their wares, meant eventual victory for *New Age*. Government departments and farmers' unions each started separate commissions of inquiry and, six weeks after the original article came out, they suspended the forced-labour scheme.

No wonder then, that on that day in 1959, Ruth was smiling. Camelot had triumphed. The ANC campaign of protest which had dominated the fifties was building to a peak. Next year, the beginning of the new decade, it would be more successful, might even, perhaps, bring the government to its knees. Those people like my parents who had been part of a movement which every year gained in strength, those people who had planned and partied hard, were at a peak of optimism. They were making a revolution: soon the people of South Africa would reap its benefits. Or at least that's how it felt in 1959.

One year later and the old certainties were all rapidly being eroded. In that year, 1960, in one of the wealthier northern suburbs of Johannesburg, an architect came home to find a house guest sitting in his kitchen. Her name, his wife told him, was Ruth Gordon. She was from out of town, from Cape Town, knew very few people in Jo'burg, would be staying for an indefinite time, and would not be going out much.

The woman, initially at least, seemed to be a hermit, keeping herself very much to herself. She worked in the spare room, emerging into even the dullest light wearing sun-glasses with lenses which were almost pitch black. Occasionally she would have visitors. The man who had brought her there would call on her and the two would go up on to a roof terrace to talk in soft but urgent tones. Very infrequently, she would pull a scarf over her curly black hair and run out to a waiting car, to disappear for a mysterious few hours. After she had been there some weeks, the architect began to get to know her better. Eventually she trusted him enough to tell him that her surname was not Gordon – it was First – and that she was on the run.

It was less than a year since the successful end of the potato boycott but the atmosphere in South Africa had irrevocably changed. It had all started in March 1960, in a township called Sharpeville. As an unarmed crowd marched to the police station, intent on burning their passes, a policeman opened fire.

Humphrey Tyler, the editor of the magazine *Drum*, described what happened:

The crowd seemed to be loosely gathered around the Saracens (armoured cars) and on the fringes people were walking in and out. The kids were playing. In all there were about 3,000 people. They seemed amiable. Suddenly there was a sharp report from the direction of the police station. There were shrill cries of 'Izwe lethu' (our land) – women's voices, I thought. The cries came from the police station and I could see a small section of the crowd swirl around the Saracens. Hands went up in the Africanist salute. Then the shooting started. We heard the chatter of a machine gun, then another, then another. There were hundreds of women, some of them laughing. They must have thought the police were firing blanks. One woman was hit about ten yards from our car. Her companion, a young man, went back when she fell. He thought she had stumbled. Then he turned her over and saw that her chest had been shot away. He looked at the blood on his hand and said: 'My God, she's gone!'

Hundreds of kids were running, too ... Some of the children, hardly as tall as the grass, were leaping like rabbits. Some were shot, too. Still the shooting went on. One of the policemen was standing on top of a Saracen, and it looked as though he was firing his sten gun into the crowd. He was swinging it around in a wide arc from his hip as though he were panning a movie camera.[1]

By the time this policeman and his colleagues had downed their guns, sixty-nine people lay dead.

Pictures of the Sharpeville massacre and the mass burial that followed were beamed out of South Africa, shocking the world.

Inside the country, the ANC swung into action with countrywide protests. The government was defiant: it upped the stakes by declaring an Emergency. In the middle of one night, in a huge co-ordinated swoop, police knuckles beat a tattoo on a myriad doors. It was an event that activists had long anticipated. As the flashlights of police photographers went off, freezing images of the half-asleep captives climbing into black police vans, phones started ringing. My grandfather was one of the people whose fingers were busy dialling. Friends of his, asleep in bed, picked up their receivers to hear his voice speaking a language that came from deep in his childhood. '*Ze zuchen,*' he said. They are looking.

They came in vast numbers. In the days that followed, the ANC, like the Communist Party before it, was banned. Twenty thousand people were arrested. They came to our house, although they almost did not get in. The officers whose car had screeched up our driveway in the early hours, couldn't locate our front door. Having wandered aimlessly about, they ended up tramping across a flower-bed and knocking at my parents' bedroom window to ask, embarrassed, which was the way in.

Despite the barbarity of Sharpeville, the security branch had not yet fully removed its gloves, particularly in relation to whites. That night, Joe, and not Ruth, was on their list. She knew, however, that she would be next. As had already been agreed between her and Joe, she didn't sit and wait. She went to the bathroom, pulled a red wig over her black hair, packed us three

---

1. Edward Roux, *Time Longer Than Rope*, University of Wisconsin, 1964.

children into the Citroën and drove across the border into Swaziland.

We lived in a rented apartment in the Swazi capital of Mbabane, in a block which housed a whole group of radical exiles, my grandparents amongst them. The transformation was almost seamless. One moment we were running three-legged races in the lush gardens at our suburban Johannesburg school, the next we were catching ball in the brown dust of our new Swazi school. Venison took the place of casseroled chicken, communal story sessions the nuclear family's bedtime regime. For entertainment we strode in groups across the Swazi landscape and came back afterwards to sit high upon an expansive balcony and watch life passing by; thin doors separated us from other families, other lives as we lived out our strange limbo. And all those months Joe sat in gaol.

I have a memory of that small package of time in Swaziland, of us three, our grandparents, and Ruth, preparing to go back home. And although I cannot remember the return journey, I was convinced that when we eventually made it, we did so together.

But, more than thirty years later, rifling through correspondence and talking to my parents' contemporaries, I realised that here was another secret I must once have known but which I had somehow managed to conceal from myself. We didn't go back together. When the first flush of the Emergency died down, our grandparents travelled with us children back to Johannesburg.

Ruth was not with us, but she did make the trip. She went separately and secretly, going underground to the northern suburbs, to help reform the opposition. She was in hiding because she was still a target for police pick-up. There was talk of fixing her up with a disguise which would give her freedom of movement, but Ruth, hearing the suggestion that she should be made up to look like an old woman, vetoed the idea. Red hair was one thing: if, however, they were going to age her, she was definitely staying indoors!

No one can remember exactly how she ended up in the

architect's house – that time was the beginning of a serious and ongoing quest for new safe houses. A friend of a friend would have a cousin, perhaps, who had a room somewhere. A sympathetic acquaintance who was not herself directly involved, would be prepared to vacate her house for a few hours while a meeting was hurriedly convened. Secrecy, which had been part of our lives for as long as we could remember, now ran riot.

Even after the government had called an end to the Emergency and the last of the incarcerated, including Joe, walked through the high gate that studded the walls of Pretoria gaol, Ruth stayed in hiding. For a while Joe would visit her, both of them waiting to get a more accurate sense of how vindictive the government would be to those who had left the country. In the end, they decided it was safe. Ruth came home unmolested.

We were already back at our regular schools. Now our family was reunited and the sun continued to shine. And yet, from that time on, the government had shown what lengths it was prepared to go to in order to hold on to power. The innocent fifties were over and Joe and Ruth must have known that nothing would ever be the same again. Even then, however, they couldn't have guessed that, of the three friends who'd travelled together to Potgieter's farm in 1959, only Wolfie Kodesh would escape a violent death and live to see the birth of the new South Africa.[2]

---

2. Joe Gqabi, who spent years in Robben Island for his involvement in the formation of the ANC's army, Umkhonto we Sizwe, came out in time to be a guiding light for the youth of 1976. Forced by constant police persecution to leave the country he became the ANC's Chief Representative in Zimbabwe. In 1981, a year before they got Ruth, Joe was walking down a main street in the Zimbabwean capital of Harare, when a car passed by, blazing gunfire. By the time the car had gone, Joe, the last member of his entire family to have survived apartheid's onslaught, was dead.

Chapter Eight

Once again my memory fast forwards, this time to New Year's Eve, 1962. It had been so hot that night in Cape Town that I had drifted off to sleep with the melt of ice cubes dripping down my neck. And then, suddenly, it was the middle of the night and I was awake. Dazed I looked around, trying to figure out what it was that had wrenched me from sleep.

I saw a woman's figure framing the lighted doorway. She was speaking softly, in an angry whisper. 'Who would be so inconsiderate as to hide beneath a child's bed?' she hissed.

I blinked, adjusting my eyes to the gloom. The curtains were half-open and I could see moonlight slanting across my friend, Margaret's, unmade single bed. It was empty. I looked again towards the doorway. This time I noticed Margaret standing behind her mother, peering in.

I heard a noise, coming from the end of my bed. I sat up in time to see a policeman's peaked hat emerging from beneath the bed frame. Another sound, this time from the wardrobe: there were two of them in the room, searching desultorily.

When the second pushed his way out of a forest of girlish clothes, I saw that he'd been cloned from the same block as the first. He had the same stubbled brown hair moulded to the back of his head, the same stiffly creased trousers which ended in gleaming black shoes, the same brown jacket wide at the shoulders and tapering in to a waist pinched by the tight plastic black belt which served a double purpose of containing his holstered gun, and the same edgy defiance working overtime to toughen his callow face. Seeing me, he used his head to gesture his colleague towards the door. Within minutes, both men had gone.

I was ten years old and holidaying in our family's regular

summer venue of Cape Town. That year, however, with my sisters elsewhere and my parents served with banning orders that stopped them leaving Johannesburg, I was in Cape Town on my own. It was the first time I remember being so completely separated from my family. I remember lazy days spent cooing over a clutch of month-old puppies or trudging the steep eighty-four steps from the high point of Cape Town's Kloof Road down to the white sands of Clifton's Fourth beach. Our expeditions were mostly unfettered by adult company since Margaret's parents, Sonya and Brian Bunting, long-time comrades of my parents, were both subject to another one of the government's growing pot-pourri of despotic laws – house arrest. Brian was on night-time curfew while Sonya was completely restricted, given permission only to leave the house for three hours out of every twenty-four in order to look for work.

Work: there was not much chance of that. The world had closed in on us: all our friends were similarly restricted and no stranger would have been prepared to take the risk of hiring a named communist. So Sonya would occasionally use her 'time off' to sneak out to the beach with us. That night, when I saw the policeman floundering around our children's room, I wondered guiltily whether Sonya's transgression – made, I was sure, for my benefit – was what had sent them in.

But of course even in South Africa the security establishment didn't have sufficient manpower to check on every dissident's hourly movements. Their visit was mere routine. Every year since I, and presumably the police, could remember, the Buntings had thrown a huge New Year's Eve bash. This year, because of their banning orders, a gathering of more than three people in their house would constitute a crime. Which is why the police had burst in at midnight, to check for reds hiding under the Buntings' beds.

The raid was one amongst the many all of us experienced in that year, part of our new normality. After the police left, that early dawn of 1963, Margaret and I didn't even bother chewing it over. She got into her bed and I lay down in mine and we drifted back to sleep.

Within days my holiday was over and I was flying back to Jo'burg. It was my first time in a plane and I was on my own. A ferocious storm, the like of which seemed to keep thundering through the whole of my 1963, jolted at the plane's metal body. I sat rigid, the seat-belt cutting into my stomach, trying to pretend that I didn't notice that after each rearing up of the plane, it appeared to fall by an even larger distance. I breathed in the collective queasy silence as streaks of jagged lightning lit up the sky.

The storm was too ferocious, we couldn't get through. The plane really was going lower. Within minutes it had reached ground level and we landed on a small airfield somewhere in the middle of rural South Africa. Holding tightly to the slippery rails, I followed a line of passengers down the steps and through the pelting rain to an airport building which looked more like an old warehouse than a terminal. There weren't enough chairs to go round: we huddled on the floor, the other passengers in their family groups, me on my own, waiting for the storm to blow itself out.

But the storm was stronger than us and eventually we were grounded for the night. With an air hostess as our guide, we were siphoned off into a coach which drove slowly out into the darkest night. I was a lone, unaccompanied child. When a couple sitting opposite, heard me give the air hostess my name, they exchanged a meaningful glance. Experience had taught me all the possible interpretations: I knew that what had passed between them wasn't the most extreme of the possible reactions – horror that they were sitting so close to a notorious Slovo – but rather the equally predictable and more liberal response that managed to imply sympathy for my parents' goals with distaste for their means.

In the three years since Sharpeville, the battle for South Africa had been irrevocably changed. If Sharpeville showed the world what apartheid really involved, it also heralded the end of legal protest within the country. By declaring an Emergency and banning the ANC, the government had demonstrated that peaceful protest would no longer be tolerated. Only one option faced the activists – give up or raise the stakes. How could they give up? It wasn't possible. They turned from passive to active resistance.

In his unfinished autobiography my father describes the decisions they took:

> The first phase of armed action in 1961 was a sabotage campaign directed against government installations. Instructions were issued to avoid attacks which would lead to injury or loss of life. No one believed that the new tactic of sabotage could, on its own, lead to the collapse of the racist state. It was the first phase of 'controlled violence' designed to serve a number of purposes. It would be a graphic pointer to the need for carefully planned action rather than spontaneous or terrorist acts of retaliation which were already in evidence . . . And it would demonstrate that the responsibility for the slide towards bloody civil war lay squarely with the regime.
>
> The point was strongly featured in the proclamation accompanying the first sabotage acts which expressed the hope that 'even at this late hour' the actions would awaken everyone to a sense of realisation of the disastrous situation to which the regime's policy was leading, and would bring the government to its senses before it was too late and before matters reached the desperate stage of civil war.[1]

A sober assessment this, written by my father, in hindsight of their early military plans. And yet I know that he believed more than that then, and that, caught up in the excitement of the shift to action and of the Boy's Own adventure on which they had all embarked, the end of injustice in South Africa still seemed to be imminently within his grasp.

---

1. Joe Slovo, *Slovo: The Unfinished Autobiography*, Hodder and Stoughton, 1996: p. 152.

He was so central to what was going on. In 1961, he, along with Nelson Mandela, became the initial high command for the new army – Umkhonto we Sizwe – MK for short. A small group which included my mother's journalist friend, Joe Gqabi, were sent to China for training while internally a sabotage campaign, aimed at government installations, was launched. Amateur bomb-makers slipped chemical bombs into buildings that were the visible symbols of apartheid: Bantu Administration and pass offices. In the countryside railway lines, telephone wires and overhead electrical cables were blown into mangled pieces. The photos in the papers momentarily shook white South Africa out of its complacent daze.

The government responded with a mass of repressive legislation, cracking down so fiercely that it became apparent that there was no longer any turning back. Their Camelot was well and truly dead.

As the stakes got higher, secrecy drifted over every section of our lives. It reached such a pitch that my mother no longer made even the most innocent arrangements by telephone. If I wanted to go to a friend, she would write a special note which she made sure I delivered only once I was inside the school gates. We put on uniforms and went, scrubbed and polished to school, but it was getting harder to pretend our daily routine was following the same, uncomplicated path as all our nice white friends.

Many white people wholeheartedly backed their government. There were others who disliked apartheid, who would have wanted it all to be different. But the early sixties in South Africa was a time when it was no longer viable to sit on the fence. Commitment carried penalties – sides had to be chosen. As the terror deepened, a gulf opened between 'them' and 'us'. That year, 1963, was the time I noticed it.

I was used to sidelong glances darted my way when people thought I wasn't looking. I was a well-trained child who'd learned the dangers of indiscretion. I sat in the airline coach, silently polite, enduring the journey down a country lane and into one of those orderly, methodically laid out, sterile *dorps* that dot the South

African landscape. We were driven from one small hotel on to the next, unloading passengers at every step. I was a victim of a South African Airways Catch 22. As an unaccompanied child, I had to stay with the air hostess but since the air hostess couldn't go to bed until all the passengers were safely tucked in, neither could I.

It was gone four in the morning by the time we learned that every hotel room within a radius of twenty miles was full. There were only three of us left in the bus – the driver, the air hostess and me. We did a u-turn and drove back to the airport.

In a hangar we found a group of men – white airline crew and white airport engineers – lounging by a large wooden work-bench, playing cards while two half-empty bottles of cheap brandy did the rounds. When we entered – me and my tippy, tappy uncommunicative, beehived companion – ribald jokes rose to greet us. I can still hear them, those gruff male voices echoing in the sawdust-encrusted space. Even then I couldn't make out their meaning – they were speaking in Afrikaans, a language that a childish intransigence had stopped me from learning. I was a waif, standing in the huge empty space, in enemy territory while manly suggestiveness was countered by womanly guile.

Eventually one of the engineers took pity on my exhaustion and suggested we stay at his house. But my ordeal wasn't over. There was only one bed available and so we had to share. I will never forget that night. I spent it lying stiffly beside an air hostess who was dressed in a light blue nylon shortie nightie, her teased blonde hair splayed out above her on the pillow. Between her world and mine was an immense and widening gulf. I hardly slept. I was so conscious of what she didn't know – that I was the child of parents who were working to bring the downfall of everything she held dear. Perhaps something I muttered in sleep might give me, and them, away. I lay the whole night terrified she might find me out.

Or at least that was how I saw it then. But now as I look back at my childish self so stiffened by proscription, I wonder whether it wasn't something else that had kept me awake: not moral rectitude but jealousy, not fear of discovery but a craving to be like her. That air hostess with her blonde hair was a living example of someone with a normal, carefree life. In my imagination the thing that caused her to worry was whether her lipstick matched her nail varnish not when the police would next come calling. Somewhere deep inside of me, I lusted for that kind of normality. I had built a wall of defiance around myself, placing my dazzling parents at its invulnerable centre. Only in the darkest night, alone, in the middle of South Africa could I allow myself a twinkling of desire for ordinary life.

I think of my mother then, of her French perfume and her carefully straightened hair and I wonder whether it was like that for her as well. She was, to a stranger's eye, a defiant communist, quirky enough to care about her appearance but willing to break every one of society's conventions. And yet when I look at her in the photos of those days, with her neat suits and her carefully constrained hair I see a woman whose secret ambition might have been to be Jackie Onassis.

From mother to daughter and down again. Tilly transformed herself from a Yiddish-speaking child into a fearless dowager whose English accent was crystal cut. My mother was utterly defiant and yet struggled almost her whole adult life to disown her unruly Jewish frizz. And I, her growing daughter, lay beside a sixties Barbie doll pretending to despise what my heart desired.

Back to Johannesburg to normal life. I was in my last year of primary school and the starting gun had just been fired on the competition for the end of year prize. In my own way I continued passing for white, pretending that my life and my school friends' lives were on par. It was easy to pretend. I knew how different were our realities but they did not. Their days were played out in an immutable childish paradise, insulated from harsh reality. The history they learned started in the seventeenth century with the arrival of Jan van Riebeeck and ended in a white victory over the savage hordes. The black people they met emptied their garbage, made their beds, mowed their lawns and cuddled them when they were sick, and all of this with a smile. The anger that was brewing in the country couldn't really touch them. They must have seen the occasional picture of a policeman peering at the remains of a blown-up phone box, but all this was so very far away. Big brother, their government, was watching: it would take care of them.

We three children of Joe and Ruth pretended, for as long as we possibly could, to be like them. We listened, as we always had, to radio plays and afterwards, we'd creep down the corridor to our bedrooms, keeping our backs to the wall because, for reasons we never analysed, we were scared someone might stab us from behind. The front door would go; it would be one or other of our parents returning from a mysterious outing which we all pretended hadn't really happened. The next day the lowered voices and the soft clicking of the front door, would disappear from our memories. In the brightness of each new morning we ate our breakfast and were driven to school. With Shawn already at secondary school, Robyn and I turned up brightly in our short-sleeved blue and white gingham dresses, surreptitiously donning our reviled white panama hats as we moved through the school gates, ill-matching brown shoes polished to a gleam by our Elsie at home.

I learned fractions that year, taught by Mrs Bowskill with her ring of pearls resting on her fluffy pink bosom, her thick black-rimmed glasses and her sheer white hair. She was a teacher who had the light of knowledge shining from within, instantly believable, especially when she spoke of God. That was the year that, for a few months at least, I turned to her God, a Christian one who would watch over everything we did and, we hoped, over our parents as well. In the bedroom we shared, I forced Robyn down on her knees beside me and I told her how to pray to Him for forgiveness. Mrs Bowskill's God was stern but fair. We were sure that He would understand why we could not tell our parents about our religious conversion. They had their secrets – well, now we had ours.

1963: it was the year when disaster struck my parents' political movement and we were at the centre of the storm. Our teachers must have got a hint, even in the early months, of what was coming. Nothing was said but when Ruth came to pick us up they smiled meaningfully at her in a way I always thought was friendly.

How little I really knew of what was going on in those adult heads. Many years later, in 1989, my publishers forwarded a letter which was post-marked South Africa. When I slit open the airmail envelope, a wad of densely written A5 pages slid out. The prose started affectionately enough with the information that my correspondent, who had just finished reading one of my detective novels, had taught me at school. She put in a few fond memories of what I'd been like as a child – shy, clever, polite – and said how hard that last year must have been for me.

But when I had finished one page and went on to the next, I did a double take. The letter was no longer friendly, it was vicious. In one long uninterrupted breath, my old teacher wrote that she had heard about my mother's death, that she was sorry for me but that the pity she felt was savage: she felt sorry, she wrote, because my parents were both terrorists whose hands were stained by the blood of innocents. And that wasn't all: my father, she continued, had killed my mother and the South African police had proof of it. Not that the writer objected: she was glad Ruth was dead, and glad that they would soon get my father too.

My vision tripped over words which crawled angrily one on top of the other, making the last few pages almost indecipherable. I thought I didn't want to know. I crumpled up the letter and chucked it away.

In 1963 we kept on smiling although our life was in the process of splintering into pieces. It started innocuously enough with Joe leaving town. He told us he was going on a short trip and that he'd soon be back and then he drove, illegally, across the border.

At the time he wasn't lying. He expected to be back. He had gone to organise the training of MK recruits throughout Africa, and to plead for guns and arms from sympathetic states. When that was accomplished, he was due to return: to operate underground.

Many years later, I asked him how he could ever have believed that the plan could possibly pan out. Mandela had gone underground and had been caught. Later, Bram Fischer tried it too, and he was also caught. 'How long,' is what I asked Joe, 'did you think you'd last?'

He answered with a slight, ironic smile and a question, 'It does seem crazy now, doesn't it?'

Crazy, because even the newspapers were following his every move. In June they reported that Joe and fellow communist J.B. Marks had gone to Southern Rhodesia where they'd both been arrested. Two days later the same newspapers spotted the two men at liberty in the neighbouring Bechuanaland capital of Francistown, staying in a local hotel. On 8 June the *Cape Times* informed its readership that Joe had, the night before, telephoned his wife.

The furrows on Ruth's face, grew deeper. One day she packed us in the car and drove us through the Johannesburg suburbs. We sat in the back seat, licking our fingers for the last taste of the hamburgers in baskets we'd bought from the Charcoal Oven and singing songs. The Beatles were a faint whisper from the mysterious 'overseas'; we stuck to local products, singing that early sixties jokey, whiney, favourite '*Ag* (pronounced gutturally as in the German Ach) *pleez* daddy'. We sang out gustily:

Ag pleez daddy, won't you take us to the drive-in,
All six seven of us eight, nine, ten.
We wanna see a flick about Tarzan and the Apemen,
And when the show's over, you can bring us back again.

Ag pleez daddy, we sang, pretending that our father was like the others, out at work earning money to buy us our hearts' desires, not somewhere in Africa, bargaining for guns. We loved the song's words, the demands of insatiable childhood for zoos and aquariums and South African boxers who would 'donner' Yankees to the floor. But best of all, we loved the chorus. We belted it out:

> Popcorn, chewing gum, peanuts and bubble gum
> Ice-cream, candy floss and Eskimo pie
> Ag daddy, how we miss, nigger balls and liquorice
> Pepsi-cola, ginger beer and Canada Dry.

If our mother, usually so fast to pick up on racial insults, noticed our shouting out the word nigger, the knuckles on her steering-wheel did not visibly tighten. Or perhaps I just didn't notice. They were already almost translucent with tension as she steered the car through the northern suburbs of Johannesburg to the Liliesleaf farm in Rivonia. At a farm gate she peeped the horn and a black man appeared. He peered into the car, smiled in recognition and opened up.

A gabled mansion stood at the end of the driveway, its front half opening up on to a rolling lawn. But when my mother stopped the car and we all got out she led us away from the house past the garage and to a set of low concrete buildings, the servants' quarters.

I climbed two low steps up to a concrete platform from which the bare rooms ran off. It was dark inside and each room seemed to be crowded with serious African men. The low mumble of their various meetings was drowned out by the endless back-ground clatter of a duplicating machine. My mother's special friend, and our family favourite, Walter Sisulu came out and hugged us and then he took Ruth off to one side and started talking urgently in her ear. And all the time, we hung about, unable to understand a word of the conversations going on around us, only sensing that our fates were tangled up in that makeshift place.

Chapter Nine

For many years I nursed an embarrassing secret. I had no idea what I was doing on the day President John Kennedy was assassinated. It seemed almost impossible: every member of my generation was supposed to know so why didn't I? It wasn't as if other world events passed me by. I can remember driving with my mother through Jo'burg during the Cuban missile crisis, for example, convinced that the gas-works we passed was about to blow up. But the impact of Kennedy's killing and the aftershocks that remained firmly lodged in most living memories, were lost forever in mine.

Only now, in hindsight, can I find an explanation. For on the day, 22 November 1963, when Kennedy was shot, my mother was enduring her 106th successive day of solitary detention. Nothing else mattered to me then.

I remember almost every minute, frame by frame, of that 9 August when they picked my mother up. I was eleven years old and on a constant weekly round of visits to orthodontists and opticians. I remember a ninth-floor office with lime green blackout blinds. I sat on a high-backed chair in the dark, cold iron frames wedged against my nose, struggling to answer the insistent questioning as to which of two sets of circles — red or green — was the clearest. Each time I blinked the focus would change. I could feel the eye doctor's exasperation rising at my indecision, which only made me hesitate more. But finally the ordeal was pronounced over. I walked out of there as I always did, clutching the spectacles that I refused to wear, sure that it wasn't the optician's halitosis but my failure to give him what he wanted that had made things end so badly.

My grandfather was waiting in the entrance hall. Mild-mannered, unassertive, gentle Julius. As a child, I adored him, this one member of our adult world who seemed content to stay calmly in the background. As an adult, I marvel at how little of himself he left behind. There's a passport, a plaque commemorating his eighty communist years and a handful of black and white snapshots. In many of the photos, Julius seems frozen by the camera. He stares out, unblinking, at an unlikeable world – like a man from a strange, unknowable culture trapped in the photographer's unfriendly gaze.

On that day, however, in the optician's foyer, Julius was his usual, calm, silent self. We went out to his car to join my waiting sisters.

He drove us through Johannesburg's business centre and into the suburbs, an ordinary route on an ordinary day. Even today, if I concentrate carefully I can hear a faint echo of my sisters' voices as they ganged up on me, rhyming 'Gilly' with 'silly', 'Jill' with 'ill' and 'pill' in one endlessly unchanging lilting poem. I was almost lulled into sleep by its monotony when Julius suddenly stamped his foot down hard on the brake. By the time I looked up he was already out of the car. He was such a careful man yet he left us skewed at an angle to the pavement, the engine ticking over, while he strode across the road to a corner café. I can guess now what must have caught his attention – a newspaper billboard with my mother's name on it. At the time, however, I didn't spot the headline. I just knew that there was something wrong.

Julius emerged soon after that. Clutching a newspaper, he walked towards us and got back into the car. I remember clearly the sound of Shawn and Robyn teasing each other. Julius folded the paper and threw it near my foot. I wanted to pick it up, to read what it was that had turned his face so white. Julius started the car. I left the paper where it lay and looked at him. He didn't seem to notice. Staring straight ahead, he pulled out and drove, faster than he ever had, to our house in Mendelssohn Road.

When we got home we found the iron garden gate open and, in the driveway, a stranger's car. The front door was also open and there was a stranger waiting there. Silently, we walked towards him. I don't remember Julius with us. Perhaps he wasn't there: perhaps he'd dropped us off and fled.

Inside the house every drawer and cupboard, every nook and cranny, was being turned over by policemen. I saw my grandmother and our nanny, Elsie, hovering in the background, their hands hanging uselessly by their sides. My two sisters and I walked down the corridor, conscious of alien faces watching with expressions we couldn't fathom. I held my chin high and felt an illicit childish thrill at the attention.

Ruth was in her bedroom, packing. A man, leaning nonchalantly against a wall, was watching her every move. She greeted us, her face immobile: almost everything she did showed her iron control. I remember her tapered fingers painstakingly folding each piece of clothing and laying it carefully on top of the one that went before. Half-way through, she fetched a book from the dressing table – Stendhal's *The Charterhouse of Parme* – and put it in the suitcase. As I watched it going in, I heard the policeman snort. My mother heard him too. She turned to look at him, her eyes blazing. He couldn't hold her gaze. He pretended to relax, folded one arm into the other and leaned heavily back against the wall.

The suitcase closed with a final click. My mother picked it up and started walking. Men went with her to the door. I followed them. They put her in the car, in the front seat, one on either side of her. Three jovial burly men squeezed themselves into the back seat. My mother looked at me, almost as if she didn't know who I was. I stood, waiting for her to say something. Finally her eyes seemed to focus on me and, leaning closer, she tossed a few loving reassuring words my way, topping them up with one last injunction. 'Look after Robyn,' she said.

The man beside her pulled the car door shut. The driver on her other side turned on the engine and started down the drive. I didn't wait while they reversed carefully out into the sharp bend at the bottom of our drive and then drove off. Instead, I went inside the house in search of Robyn.

I found her in the kitchen, standing close to Elsie who used to wake us, feed us, dress us and paint mercurochrome across our cuts and bruises. Shawn was in the garden and my grandmother kept walking in and out, opening her mouth to say things that had no meaning. I stood by Robyn in the kitchen, helping her make apple fritters.

After we had come to England, Ruth wrote a book about her prison experiences. In it, she sketches the three visits we made to her during her 117-day incarceration. She describes each of her daughters in a well-turned phrase. Shawn, is 'the vulnerable thirteen-year-old', Robyn, the 'jolly' one who brought Chappies bubble gum so Ruth could read the cartoon joke written on the inside wrapper and as for me, I was 'serious, wide-eyed considerate Gillian [who] exerted her usual tight control'.

In those phrases are encapsulated the roles each of us was assigned. Shawn, the first born, 'daddy's favourite' was the one who kicked out the path ahead; Robyn was the youngest, cheeky, cheery, troubled while I, wedged between the other two, was the clever, responsible one. I would have preferred a more exotic part but it didn't matter what I did to kick against this phantasm, I was stuck in it.

I remember clearly how once I stepped outside my role. It had started as we three sisters were playing in the garden. The French doors that led to the living room opened and Ruth emerged, beckoning to me. I went to join her and listened as she told me, *sotto voce*, that the doctor would soon be arriving to give us all a top-up inoculation. 'You're the sensible one,' she continued. 'You go first and show the others it doesn't hurt.'

Nonchalantly I nodded and went back to my sisters but I soon found that the game we were playing had lost its pull on me. I'd been picked out to participate in much more seductive, adult entertainment, full of tantalising secrecy. I knew the rules: I mustn't warn my sisters. I didn't. I hugged the precious knowledge of our impending doom to myself.

But as the secret grew inside me I became increasingly aware of time closing in. Images of the sharp point of the needle piercing my flesh threatened to overwhelm me. With all my reserves of tight control, I told myself I was being silly but the conflict soon grew unbearable. The sensible part of me disappeared until, by the time I saw the doctor's car turning into our driveway, I was hysterical with panic. Screaming an incoherent warning at my sisters, I took off.

I remember scrambling through the bushes that stood in front of the wire fence that lined the garden's limits. An African man passed by on the pavement, ignoring me entirely. I kept on going, running to the house's back courtyard, through wet, hanging sheets, and beyond. I ran in circles, away from adult grasping hands. Panic made me so speedy that it took the combined cunning of three of them – my mother, the doctor and Elsie – to trap me under the Citroën and to drag me out. I was taken inside, my arm held firmly as the injection went in. My sisters watched, puzzled by my behaviour because of course it didn't really hurt. Or at least, the inoculation didn't. I saw something in my mother's eyes, however – disappointment – which I had never seen before. I'd not do that again, I promised myself, never again.

Perhaps in the run-up to her arrest, Ruth might have remembered what had happened and understood the dreadful anticipation that had me clinging, trembling, to the Citroën's chassis. For she, too, had experienced what it was like to be forewarned. In that year, some weeks before the police came to get her, she knew she was a sitting duck. And the question was, *Why didn't she run?*

Her world had collapsed on a Thursday afternoon in mid-July, when a bakery van drove into the grounds of the Rivonia farm we had so recently visited. Following closely behind it was another van, this one with the name of a dry cleaner's painted on its side panels. The vehicles had a common purpose: as the front van stopped outside the house, a voice called out, '*Ons slaan toe*' – 'Let's get cracking'.

That was the signal. Both vans' back doors burst open and

forty policemen started swarming through every crevice of the property. For the occupants hiding out in the servants' wing, it was clear what was going down. The night before they had decided at a meeting that it was too dangerous to have so many of the movement's leaders concentrated in one location, and they should disperse to other hiding places. Now it was too late.

My mother's special friend, Walter Sisulu, sporting a Chaplin-esque moustache and chemically straightened hair, was stopped from climbing out of a back window by a snarling police dog named Cheetah. When Ahmed Kathrada refused to let the police handcuff him the police held him down until they succeeded. One man who tried to run was brought down by a police dog.

There was nowhere to run. No one got away. The police swoop was deadly effective. Fourteen people were taken, along with duplicating machines, leaflets, maps of potential sabotage sites, nitric acid, 'mechanical devices' that the police said were primitive land-mines in the making and evidence that Nelson Mandela, who was then beginning a five-year gaol sentence, had been a visitor to the place.

For the police it was a major coup. They had busted the very nerve centre of the opposition: they must have been ecstatic. But for Ruth the raid was a devastating blow, both personal and political. Some of her closest friends were in gaol soon to be charged with offences which carried the death sentence. Her anxiety for them must have been dreadful, made worse by the fact that it would have been tinged by self-interest. She must have wondered how long it would be before the police had a record of her almost daily visits to Rivonia. And she must have known, as well, what the raid meant for Joe. In Rivonia the police had uncovered Operation *Mayibuye* (Come back), a plan to train soldiers outside the country and send them armed, back in to start the insurrection. *Mayibuye* was partly Joe's brain child – he had gone out of the country to prepare the way. Now he would never be able to return.

There are letters Ruth wrote to Joe in that July of 1963. They make strange reading, written as they were in the expectation that they would be intercepted. In them, Ruth's reference to the Rivonia raid makes it sound almost like an event of no concern.

'This place not so restful,' she wrote. 'One wakes every day to startling news. *The Transvaaler* this morning: arrests of Sisulu, Kathrada, Mbeki, Rusty ... Dennis Goldberg, A & H Goldreich. To be held for 90 days, *The Star* says. God knows who isn't held for 90 days!' She ended the letter with a cryptic, 'Am still sitting here wondering what it's all about. It could be anything.'

Joe must have had a pretty good idea how far her 'wonderings' stretched. And he must have read between the lines again when he received her letter of 12 July where she wrote, after providing a list of fresh ninety-day arrestees, 'These men disappear behind cell doors and that's the end.' She wrote to him again on 2 August, a mere five days before she was picked up, 'So many people are absent, one way and another ... People disappear behind barred doors and then???'

That said it all. Her 'and then' with their alarmed question marks. She was soon to be among the disappeared. And then?

Why didn't she run?

Ninety days – it was an arbitrary sentence that could be endlessly prolonged. Anybody could be picked up and held in solitary, without charge or recourse to legal advice. The period of ninety days itself was a euphemism. At the end of it, the prisoner could be summarily rearrested and held for another ninety – on and on and on, as the then justice minister Vorster put it, '. . . until eternity'.

In its first six months of existence 500 people were held under the Ninety-Day Law. Friends and relatives were allowed to bring in food but had no access to the prisoners. In early September, the first of the detainees, Looksmart Solwandle Ngudle, was killed. At his inquest, a policeman was asked:

'If a detainee ... says "I am not under any circumstances prepared to give you any information whatsoever" do you leave him alone or do you take further steps?'

The answer came, '*Well, he has got to be asked again.*'

'And again?' '*Yes.*'

'And again?' '*Yes.*'
'And again?' '*Yes.*'

Ruth knew that her name too, would soon be amongst the growing list of the detainees. She and her soon-to-be parentless children would be completely at the mercy of the police. *Why didn't she run?*

She continued with her life. She was banned from practising journalism and so she enrolled in a librarian's course at Wits university. She was banned from having more than two people at home so she saw friends in solitary succession. She was banned from speaking to any other banned person and, as the stakes got higher, most non-banned people avoided her, so she went to Johannesburg's weekly film society showings and sat there on her own.

The playwright and director, Barney Simon, got to know Ruth at that moment of her life. He watched her at the movies, alone, waiting for the film to start, an empty seat on either side of her. He was attracted to the intensity in her face and the starkness of her loneliness and he went to sit beside her, thus beginning a lifelong friendship. Barney would later speak about Ruth's vulnerability that seemed to fill the space around her. He knew what was coming, he said. He tried to persuade her to run. But she wouldn't. She went through the motions of everyday life, waiting, always waiting. It was as if, Barney would later say, Ruth, who had never turned down a challenge, saw what was coming as the greatest challenge of her life. Though common sense told her to avoid it, she could not. She had to prove that what others had suffered, she too could endure.

It was the times, as well, I guess that sucked her into their tightening web. Ruth had been born into a family whose central obsession was universal justice. She had joined a movement which had given her a life of danger, daring, and achievement – and all of this with right on her side. During the Emergency, when Joe was in prison and Ruth in Swaziland, she wrote to him, 'I expect it's sheer hell to be a hero ... and the ones born bad, rogue, or heroic are flukes.' But, she continued, 'Those who achieve heroism by struggle, sheer tenacity and unflagging determination, spurred on by unwavering and unbreakable spirit, those ones are the real heroes. It needs an experience like this to sift us all out, I expect, and put us to the test.'

This Ruth wrote in 1960.

But it was different then. In 1960, when Joe and others were imprisoned, there were nationwide protests against what was happening. In Cape Town alone, 30,000 marched on Caledon police station. The newspapers' front pages show photos of the crowd of African men, their trousers sharply creased right down till their turn-ups, wide-brimmed panama hats sitting jauntily on their heads, as they filled the streets around the police station. There is a dignity about their protest and a sense of quiet confidence as well.

By 1963 the landscape had been dramatically changed. The arrest of so many leaders was a fatal blow. The 'sifting' experience was to be much more testing than anybody had ever dreamed. Ruth's time had well and truly arrived.

Chapter Ten

The five police roughs joked in Afrikaans on the ride that led to Marshall Square Police Station [Ruth wrote in her book about her time in solitary] Only once did they direct themselves to me, 'We know lots,' one said. 'We know everything. You have only yourself to blame for this. We know...'

It was about six in the afternoon when we reached the police station. The largest of my escorts carried my suitcase into the *'European Only'* entrance. As he reached the charge office doorway he looked upwards. 'Bye-bye, blue sky,' he said, and chuckled at his joke.[1]

She was searched and taken to the single cell which was to become her home. The book she had packed had already been removed. She was a ninety-dayer, which meant no company, no reading material save for the Bible, no talking to other prisoners or the warders and no access to the outside world.

For the first fifty-six days of my detention in solitary [she wrote] I changed from a mainly vertical to a mainly horizontal creature. A black iron bedstead became my world. It was too cold to sit, so I lay extended on the bed, trying to measure the hours, the days and the weeks, yet pretending to myself that I was not ... Left in that cell long enough, I feared to become one of those colourless insects that slither under a world of flat, grey stones, away from the sky and the sunlight, the grass and people.[2]

---

1. Ruth First, *117 Days*, Bloomsbury 1988, p. 13.
2. Ibid., p. 9.

Alone in the cell, she tried to prepare herself for what was to come. When the police had searched our house they had found a copy of the banned *Fighting Talk* on which Ruth had once worked. Possession of that one newspaper would have been enough to send her to prison: she knew however that the danger she faced was much greater than this. She'd been present at many of the crucial meetings at Rivonia where sabotage was discussed. It didn't matter if she had been the one to place an incendiary device or not: if she had even written a leaflet justifying this turn to arms, then she would be judged equally guilty. If somebody had talked, if they found out and charged her with treason, as they were soon to charge her friends, she could get not only life but death as well.

This she knew, and she also knew that the police could keep hold of her indefinitely. She was powerless to do anything about it. She, a woman who had never let anything stand in the way of what she wanted to do and who had played an active part in every major anti-apartheid campaign since the forties, now '. . . embarked upon a campaign to accommodate myself to the prospect not of 90 days in a cell, but years.'[3]

While Ruth was isolated, our lives were open to anybody who cared to pry. Not that most people did. My teachers' smiles just grew more mysterious while my school friends greeted the news of Ruth's arrest with a mixture of silence and incomprehension. How could they have understood? I lived in a house where the desks were fitted with secret compartments; I went with Tilly to deliver food to Ruth and watched a policeman poking tangerines, checking for smuggled notes, smelling asparagus, almost holing Ruth's stocking by the roughness of his handling: such a contrast to my class mates' serene, ordinary world. 'Is your mother a kleptomaniac?' was how one of them tried to get to grips with what had happened. A kleptomaniac, she explained, because compulsive shop lifting was the only reason she could

3. Ibid., p. 57.

conjure up for the gaoling of that precious South African jewel – a white woman.

One of my teachers was also the mother of my best friend, Susan. She helped my grandmother by occasionally taking me home to spend the night. I knew why she was doing it and so did she. We never discussed it. I never even found out what she'd told Susan. Everything continued as if nothing had happened.

In their care, I paid a tourist's visit to their safe white duplex, to ordinary life where the trouble Susan and I got into was about being polite enough to adults, or cleaning up after a glove-puppet performance. Not that I was a target for reproof. On the contrary, I was a model guest, impeccably behaved. With a kind of desperate gusto, I threw myself into normality. My fixation reached a climax during our school's end-of-term play where I'd been given the minor role of gypsy dancer. My mother wasn't there to watch me: no matter. All my will power went into articulating each successive step. I stamped the ground, tossed my head, grinned wildly, my body calling on the audience to notice me.

A refrain kept echoing in my head:

Notice me,

notice me,

don't notice me.

I didn't know which I wanted.

While my mother was in prison another school friend, Carol Sutton, had a birthday. Our classes were small and the parents well off and the custom was to be invited *en masse* to each other's parties. Not this time however. With rising apprehension, I watched moon-faced Carol doling out her invitations. When I didn't get one, I tried to pretend to myself that it was the result of some kind of mad bureaucratic error which would soon be remedied. Even after she had carefully folded the paper bag in which she'd brought them, and dropped it in the waste basket, I remained optimistic. Tomorrow, I promised myself, she'd give me one tomorrow.

No invitation came, not then, not later. At first, I feigned nonchalance, pretending it hadn't really happened. But then, in the days that led up to her party, I broke. I played it extra specially nice, flirting my way into her affections. I knew I'd been struck off not because she didn't like me but because her mother didn't like my mother. I should also have known that there was nothing I could do to change that, but I guess I was my parent's child doing battle against the odds. Somehow I thought that if I could only demonstrate how wonderful I was, Carol would force her mother to reverse her ban.

The weekend of Carol's party came and went. On the Monday afterwards she offered me a selection of sweets, beautifully packed in a cellophane wrapping and tied up with a pale blue bow. I almost refused them. I knew that this was what self-respect demanded. But then another memory, more than two years old, stopped the 'no' escaping from my mouth.

It had happened in 1961, in May, a year after Sharpeville when the South African government left the Commonwealth and proclaimed the country a republic. While most white people applauded this declaration by the apartheid state that it no longer cared what the world thought, my parents helped organise the general strike which was the ANC's response. I had a foot, as usual, in both these worlds.

As the Republic Day celebrations reached their climax, I knew each white school child was to be presented with a pocket-sized model of the new flag and a gold commemoration coin. I thought about it often. I didn't want the flag which was a symbol of everything my family despised. But as for the coin, boy, how I coveted it, so much so that I convinced myself that it wouldn't do any harm to take it. Besides, a little voice informed me, if I did take it, no one need ever know.

Aged nine, I stood in my school's line, waiting for my turn, nervous, not that I'd take the coin but that my refusal of the flag would bring censor on my head. At last, I arrived at the front of the queue. The flag was proffered, I shook my head, no. While I'd been preparing myself for this act of rejection, my teacher had already anticipated it. She smiled and held out her hand to the girl waiting behind me. To ask now for the coin would have been humiliating. I had no choice. I walked off, coinless.

How I coveted that shining, fresh-minted, Judas coin. How I regretted not asking for one. And so, two years later, I wasn't going to make the same mistake. Instead of knocking the Alice band off Carol Sutton's mouse-brown hair, I took her offering.

There was no way I could win. The package sat like poison on my desk. When I got home, I threw it away untouched.

Not that anybody at home noticed. Our world had gone quite haywire. One day, not long after they'd taken Ruth away, I saw a police car heading up our drive. I ran inside, shouting out a warning. Like a cartoon character, my grandfather panicked, moving frenetically this way and that. I couldn't understand what was the matter with him. I followed his jerky progress down the corridor and to the bathroom where he jumped, fully clothed, into the bath pulling the shower curtain round him as if its opaque plastic could ever have protected him. I remember standing outside the bathroom door, anxious to protect him, and anxious also that he was so unable to protect himself that he'd chosen a hiding place which even a three-year-old could easily have uncovered.

I needn't have worried. The curtain was never put to the test because this time at least, the police had not come for Julius. They were there because my grandmother, doubly tyrannical in Ruth's home, had sacked one of Ruth's domestic workers.

I think of Tilly now, of her sharply raised voice and her censorious tongue. I cannot understand what drove her on. She had started her working life in a shoe shop, and yet when we were children we hated going shopping with her because of the offensive way she addressed the staff. Looking back, I wonder what it was that fuelled her stern contempt of them, and where on earth had she learned to throw her voice like that. I never got to ask her. All I know is that Tilly could, with one blink of her heavily lidded eyes, intimidate the most articulate of Ruth's friends. No wonder that she was altogether too much for an impoverished, and now unemployed, black woman that Tilly had summarily dismissed. The woman had gone to the police and asked for protection while she collected her belongings. I guess they were only too happy to oblige.

After the squad car drove away, my grandfather vanished from our lives. When I gave him the all clear, he emerged, shamefaced from the shower, got into his car and drove away. I never saw him after that, not in South Africa that is.

Since Tilly's lips sealed over his departure with characteristic tightness, I made up my own fiction to explain Julius's absence. Tilly was living with us, I decided, therefore Julius must have gone to look after their house. As an explanation it didn't hold water – they lived too close for that – but I stuck by it because this was, at least, some way to fill the void of not knowing.

As much as I wanted to, I knew there was no point in pushing Tilly on the subject. She had far too many other preoccupations. Her day was book-ended by a drive to Ruth's prison, where she delivered food and clothes. She went, morning and night, in brightness and during thunderstorms, between the unrelenting school runs and the uncomfortable meal-times where she concentrated on getting us to sit up straight. Her spare time she used to harass senior policemen, demanding that they release her daughter or, at least, provide her with books to read.

How trying she must have found us three, with our stormy quarrels and our menagerie. We had cats and dogs and white mice, and something was always going wrong with one of them. During Ruth's stay in prison the mice went first, developing some fateful rodent virus that slowed their breathing and eventually stopped it altogether. We laid the dying out on flannel-swathed hot-water bottles and used an eye dropper to feed them brandy, but even as we were doing it, I could see the barely concealed amusement in Elsie's face. Not only did she think we were mad to care about those unlovable white things, she knew a lost cause when she saw one. And she was right. Within days the whole mouse colony was dead.

They went the same way as the silkworms we'd pulled from deep within our neighbour's mulberry bush and carefully placed in holed cardboard boxes. Each day, we'd look inside the boxes to see the worms' manic handiwork and imagine the silk we would soon possess. But nature was too slow for us. Gradually we lost interest until finally Tilly would demand permission to throw the moth corpses and their ratty spinnings out.

Our animal disasters did not end there. Our dog Pandy, the black Labrador, had been with the household long enough to rate a mention from Ruth in 1956, the last time she'd been imprisoned in Marshall Square. Now he started breathing laboriously as if in sympathy with the moths and mice.

Tilly couldn't cope with three of us: Shawn went off to boarding school. Meanwhile, despite my mother's parting words, I wasn't doing such a great job of looking after Robyn. She was continually in trouble. I remember sitting in my classroom, in the sweltering heat, and hearing the sound of breaking glass. My heart sank. I knew it was something to do with Robyn. It had to be. And of course it was. She'd put her hand, accidentally, through a window. The teacher's response was to scold and use elastoplast to staunch the blood. Four hours later, after Tilly had picked both of us up at the usual time, a doctor used three stitches to bind the wound.

It wasn't the only mishap Robyn had. She was on crutches, immobilised by a pain that was probably emotional, that day in Zoo Lake when we were having afternoon tea. While Robyn limped off to feed the ducks, I sat in the restaurant by the lake, comfortable between my grandmother and her stylish friend, Annetta, my thoughts drifting in the heat haze that had enveloped me.

Many years later, Shawn and I were to take Tilly to that same restaurant. She was over ninety then and her memory, both long and short term, had almost entirely gone. We sat at a linen covered table, watching silver-service waiters wafting through white suburbia's luncheon hour and as time passed, Tilly's mind slipped back momentarily into focus. She had talked little in the days before – I had doubted, sometimes, that she even knew who we were – but now she started making connections with the past, volunteering information, cracking those biting, half-funny jokes that had always been her speciality. It was the restaurant, I'm sure of it – that place where she had spent her rare moments of calm.

But in 1963, at Zoo Lake, I was watching Robyn using her crutches to scare the ducks when I heard Julius's name. I was immediately alert. Maybe now I'd find out where he was. I looked up, just in time. Tilly and Annetta were both staring at a newspaper. They were so caught up in what was written there, they didn't seem to notice when I leaned over them and it too.

Police want Julius First, the headline proclaimed.

I stared at the snap of Julius, his face stiff as if he were already lined up for an identity parade. The police security branch, the article said, was asking for information on Julius First, now South Africa's 'most wanted man'. His photo had gone up at every police station, airport, harbour and border post along with instructions to arrest him on sight.

Julius? What could he possibly have done? I never did find out for sure. Never a talkative man, Julius took his secrets to the crematorium in London's Golders Green. Of all the people in my family, he was the most elusive. I've had to dig deep to uncover even the faintest of glimmerings of his involvement.

Poor Julius. He had the soul of an accountant and the convictions of a revolutionary. He could have made a lot of money – there were times when he was on the brink of doing so – but his conscience always put a stop to his acquisitiveness. He built up his business and then turned away from it to concentrate on politics. He had a factory running smoothly and he spent the weekends patrolling the grounds, serving as a personal early warning system for the illegal gatherings inside. In the end the incongruity proved too much for his partners – he was driven from the business.

But by the sixties Julius had found a way of resolving his nature's contradictions. He was retired yet he continued as he always had, inscribing tiny, spidery numbers in neat columns of in- and out-goings. No matter that these figures referred not to iron converted into bedsteads but to money for explosives which had been laundered through sympathisers in Britain or in Sweden, Julius was happy.

He seemed the least macho of men but in 1963 he threw himself into a Boy's Own dream. For a man with little imagination, nothing seemed too surreal. Acting on instructions, he bought a ship with movement money, its aim to ferry recruits out of the country for military training. Its captain was Ronnie Fleet, chosen perhaps for his surname since his real-life job was general secretary of the hairdressers' union. One night Ronnie, waiting for instructions to leave, held a party on board. It went on for so long and was so raucous that his boat-yard neighbours called the police. Which was the end of Ronnie Fleet's naval ambitions and my grandfather's cover. The police searched the boat, found the plans and tracked the ownership back to Julius.

The fact that it was Julius's picture in the paper, rather than him facing a long prison sentence was a combination of luck and swift thinking. When the police came after Julius, he was working in the office of his friend and comrade, Mannie Brown. He was at a desk, doing the accounts when two security branch men entered. Julius was not the only possible suspect: all four occupants of Mannie's office were members of one or other now illegal organisation and thus liable for pick-up. Four heads went down.

The police identified the boss, Mannie, and walked over to him. 'Is Julius First here?' they asked.

Quick-witted Mannie realised the policeman didn't know what Julius looked like. 'Mr First only works part time,' he said. 'He's not in today.'

A rash of sudden coughing broke out amongst the office workers. The policeman didn't seem to notice. 'When do you next expect him?' one of them asked.

The coughing was redoubled.

'Tomorrow, perhaps,' Mannie said.

The policemen left, returning dutifully the next morning.

By which time, of course, Julius had gone into hiding first at his sister, Bertha's flat, and then masquerading as a patient at a nursing home. Eventually with Eleanor Kasrils and her husband, another Ronnie, then wanted by the police for his part in the sabotage campaign, now South Africa's deputy Minister of Defence, Julius took a back route out of the country.

How hard it must have been for Tilly. First her beloved son-in-law had left the country, and then her daughter was picked up. After Julius skipped, she suffered another blow: the arrest of her son, Ronnie, whom the police held out of a combination of vindictiveness and mistrust that the apparently apolitical Ronnie did not know where his father was. Tilly withstood all this with a strength that bordered on the fanatical. When the police questioned her about her husband, she told them a barefaced lie – that she hadn't seen him since the day of Ruth's arrest. Us, she told nothing. In her care I grew more alert, learning to perfect my eavesdropping technique.

Which is how I heard her on the phone to the butcher, cancelling the dog meat. I knew what that must mean. Pandy, who'd been taken to the vet because his breathing had grown increasingly heavy, was no longer with us.

Three down, and Pandy as well. Only one to go. No wonder Shawn and I were convinced, when the thunder pealed, that our granny was dead.

Chapter Eleven

In November 1963, when Ruth was in prison, a man called Johannes Jacobus Viktor, a dapper policeman whose short-cropped hair and rigid posture gave him a military look, walked into a chemist's shop in the white Johannesburg suburb of Mayfair. Viktor, then aged thirty-four, was a lieutenant formerly of the fraud squad; a fastidious, methodical man who always kept his matches in the same pocket because he couldn't stand the sight of men patting themselves in search of a light.

Although the chemist's was frequented by people from the left, it was owned by Johannesburg's then-mayor whose wife was on the board of the police rugby squad, so Viktor felt quite at home. A career policeman who had recently been transferred into the security branch – that section of the police that dealt with 'politicals' – Viktor's most important prisoner was a woman who was rapidly reaching the status of a legend, Ruth First.

In the claustrophobic atmosphere of middle-class Johannesburg, where the uncommitted watched their former bridge partners being carted off to gaol, gossip was rife. And Ruth was especially fascinating to those who expected their communists to come dull and deadly serious. She was as 'red' as they made 'em but with her soft smells and expensive attire, she broke the mould. No wonder tongues were wagging. Viktor, people said, had been seduced by Ruth into providing her with privileges which included books. It was the romantic coup of the decade – a gaoler who had fallen in love with a beautiful communist – and Viktor did nothing to subdue it. His eyes shining, he admitted he'd fallen for her.

Ruth was nearly at the end of her first ninety days when Viktor walked in on her. She was in Pretoria Central Prison where she'd been taken at the beginning of her third month's imprisonment. She described how:

> . . . it was like being sealed in a sterile tank of glass in a defunct aquarium. People came to look at me every now and then and left a ration of food. I could see out of my glass case and the view was sharp and clear, but I could establish no identity with what I could see outside, no reciprocal relationship with anyone who hove in view. In Marshall Square my sooty surroundings and the general air of gloom about the old police station would have justified melancholy, but I had been buoyant and refractory. Pretoria shone of bright polished steel and I grew increasingly subdued. My imprisonment was an abandonment in protected time. I reflected on the new-found skill of the Security Branch in subjecting people to an enforced separation, a dissociation, from humanity. I felt alien and excluded from the little activity I saw about me: I was bereft of human contact and exchange. What was going on in the outside world? No echoes reached me. I was suspended in limbo, unknowing, unreached.[1]

'Unreached' and yet she knew that, since the Rivonia detainees were all in the men's prison down the road, her relocation to Pretoria might mean that she was to be charged with them. She couldn't afford to let the worry of what might be drive her mad. She created her own routines, stretching time and, at the same time, trying to pretend to herself that she still retained some measure of control:

> I made the bed carefully several times a day, I folded and re-folded my clothes, re-packed my suitcase, dusted and polished everything in sight, cleaned the walls with a tissue. I filed my nails painstakingly. I plucked my eyebrows, then the hair from my legs, one hair at a time, with my small set of tweezers (When I got into the sun I pulled out the strands of grey hair

---

1. Ruth First, op cit., p. 71.

growing at my temples). I unpicked seams in the pillow-slip, and then, using my smuggled needle and thread, sewed them up again, only to unpick once more, and sew again.[2]

But none of this dented her increasing isolation. The only news she got came either deliberately from her interrogators or by her interpreting the slightest deviation in routine. On 7 October, she found, along with her laundered clothes and a thermos of soup, a smart navy-blue dress and matching coat with red silk lining. She guessed, rightly, that this was Tilly's way of warning her that she'd soon be taken to court.

Except they never took her. On 9 October, as the Rivonia Trial began, Ruth paced her cell. Nine men, including the already-gaoled Nelson Mandela, were charged with 222 separate acts of sabotage and with organising an armed uprising. Fifteen other people, all of them now out of the country, my father and grandfather amongst them, were also named as co-defendants.

Who knows why Ruth never stood alongside the others in the Rivonia Trial dock. Perhaps they didn't have enough evidence against her: perhaps they were still hoping she would turn state's witness. Or, most likely of all, perhaps they didn't want the world to see a white woman standing in the dock accused of crimes that carried the death sentence.

Four days before her ninety were up, Ruth was taken back to Johannesburg. Just before she went, Viktor introduced himself. He was different from the other interrogators, less bullying, much cleverer, the archetypical soft cop in fact, who, or so he told Ruth, had been reluctantly seconded to the security branch and was counting the days until he could return to fraud.[3] At their first meeting he did everything to put Ruth at ease. He told

---

2. Ibid., p. 73.

3. Lieutenant Viktor was eventually to rise to the highest echelons in the South African Police. He officially retired as a Major-General, having been the Divisional Commissioner of Soweto. He also served time as the Commissioner of Police of the Ciskei

her that he had met her husband, that he had in fact saved Joe from a gang of stiletto-wielding prostitutes who were determined to get Joe for proving in court that they'd paid the police to prosecute his client, a rival madam. As Joe fled down the court corridors, it was Viktor who had opened an inner door and showed him a new way out.

Ruth had spent three months in almost total isolation save for a succession of uncommunicative prison warders and a group of alien, bullying Afrikaner policemen. How tantalising it must have been to meet somebody who related to her in a way she understood. In her book, she described the journey back from Pretoria: '. . . between Viktor and me there was an atmosphere of bristling animosity. He was provocative; I was waspish. And felt all the better for it.'[4]

She had four days to go before her ninety expired. She fought to subdue her rising expectations. She fought even harder when, the day before the ninety was up, we were allowed a visit. She wrote:

> I had no time to consider what they were planning. The three bright faces rushed at me as I entered and we had a fevered session of hugging, with the three taking turns to sit on my lap with their arms around my neck. I don't know why I permitted myself to say out loud what we were all thinking but I said to the detective, Sergeant K–, who sat in on the interview, 'Tomorrow my ninety days is up. Are you going to prosecute me?'[5]

I don't remember being with her in that cell, nor her talking to the Sergeant, nor the fact that he did not answer her question. All I remember is going to the police station, eyeing its enormous gate, and then, afterwards, going back to school. As Robyn and I walked into the packed assembly hall, all eyes

---

4. Ruth First, op cit., p. 88.
5. Ruth First, op cit., p. 105.

swivelled round. Our headmistress used a curt nod to discipline the school. We sat down and she returned to giving details of the sports day soon to come. I breathed out: visit over.

For Ruth, facing the uncertainty of what was to happen, our visit must have been an agony. But it got worse. As our allotted time neared its end, Tilly whispered in Ruth's ear that an imprisoned comrade was talking to the police. It was the worst possible news: the man in question knew most of the things Ruth had done. She was taken back to her cell, her mind awash with anxiety, as she tried to plan out her response. They didn't leave her time to think. Within minutes she was called again, this time to a room where one of her interrogators was waiting.

But this was no interrogation. The man was smiling. 'I've come to tell you to pack your things, Mrs Slovo,' he said. 'I'm releasing you.'

She didn't believe him. She told him as much, shouting that he was being unnecessarily cruel to raise her hopes. He denied this. He was, he said, really releasing her and eventually with the wardress chipping in encouragement, Ruth was persuaded. She went back to her cell, put on the navy dress with its splendid coat of red silk lining that Tilly had brought for her court appearance, and carried her suitcase out.

She was in a phone box, trying to phone and tell us she was free, when two policemen rearrested her for a second period of ninety days.

It was almost unbearable. She wrote:

Left to face my second round of ninety days, I was filled with loathing and bitterness against the Security Branch detectives who had stage-managed my humiliating phoney release and then rearrest; but I was also overcome, for perhaps the first time since my initial arrest, by a wave of self pity. I had said barely a word throughout the cruel pantomime, because I didn't want to give the detectives the satisfaction of an outburst that would reveal my feelings; my instinct told me to keep a tight hold on my emotions and to let no sound of them escape me, but it was more than I could manage. I sat on the edge of the bed, still in my navy outfit, and shook with sobs.[6]

Humiliated and demoralised, she made a couple of crucial mistakes, the first by protesting against her rearrest by stopping eating, the second a decision to give a statement she thought she could control. Instead of sitting around waiting to see what happened, she would pretend to give them information as a catalyst to finding out what they knew.

One terrifying session in a room full of policemen panting for what she had to give, and she realised the full extent of her misjudgement. She had told them nothing of value – she talked only of herself and her own past, naming activists who were either dead or out of the country – but she knew that once she started talking there might be no stopping her. Her interrogators had all the time in the world. They could call her in, day after day, waiting to pounce when she made the slightest slip.

At the end of that first statement, Viktor left the room. That's when one of Viktor's colleagues, Swanopoel, the 'hard' cop started raging at her, using his bulk to intimidate her, promising that he would break her.

By the time she got back to her cell, she knew that she could not give her statement without implicating friends. What she'd done had been a terrible act of hubris, to think she could wrest control from them. Hunger and isolation had affected her judgement. She would eat again, she resolved, but she would not talk.

The next day she refused to go with Viktor to headquarters. His response was to tell her that her mother was waiting to see her there. How could she resist? She went. The visit was to prove almost the last straw. Tilly, seeing Ruth without lipstick, asked her in a whisper as they parted, 'Are you cracking up?' When Ruth nodded, Tilly added only one more thing, 'We're depending on you.'

We're depending on you – how those words must have stabbed

---

6. Ruth First, op cit., pp. 112–113.

at the demoralised Ruth. Outside were people who relied on her and yet she was on the verge of talking. Ruth wrote:

> I was persecuted by the dishonour of having made a statement, even the start of a statement. Give nothing, I had always believed; the more you give the more they think you know, and the more demanding they become. I had never planned to give anything, but how could I be the judge? It would be impossible to explain such an act, to live it down.[7]

I used to sit and stare at that last sentence and wonder how Ruth could ever have believed it. *Impossible to live it down?* But she had told them nothing. In solitary for months on end, deprived of everything she loved, she had made a mistake and then pulled back before it was too late: how could any of her friends judge her for that?

But now I know that she was right and that it was I who'd got it wrong. She thought her friends would judge her, and she was right, some of them did. Those were macho times: those who talked at all were ostracised. If Ruth had not written her book, no one would ever have known that she had said anything, however trivial. Yet, once the book was published, instead of applauding her courage, some of her closest comrades judged her for her weakness. She must have known, before the book came out, that this was bound to happen and yet she let it ride. She was a brave woman, my mother.

She was a brave woman and yet, with the full force of revolutionary morality weighing down on her in gaol, she faced the abyss.

She began imagining the rumours that must be circulating. She thought about the journey from Pretoria, how she had sat in the back laughing at what Viktor had said. What if someone had seen her in the car? What would they think? She knew now what was her greatest fear: that her friends would believe she had betrayed

---

7. Ruth First, op cit., p. 129.

them and she feared that Viktor had understood this and would exploit it. Only two things remained to her – her self-respect and the good opinion of her associates in the political movement.

While she struggled with her growing anxiety, Viktor hovered in the background, manipulating her. He was present in the room when his boss, Colonel Klindt gave Ruth a Penguin book of crossword puzzles that Tilly had long ago brought in. On their way out, Viktor told Ruth he had never known the colonel bend the rules so generously for a detainee. At the same time, in the outside world, Viktor let the lie stand that he was the one who had stuck his neck out by providing Ruth with books.

The truth, in fact, lay somewhere else – in Cape Town where in November a judge had ordered that another ninety-day detainee should be allowed books and writing materials. Colonel Klindt had tried to argue that this ruling applied to the Cape and not the Transvaal, but soon other ninety-day prisoners were given books to relieve the monotony of their isolation. Ruth was one of them.

It was too late for her: the crosswords only made things worse. She was suffering from one of the most well-known side effects of continuing seclusion – lack of concentration. For Ruth, who didn't understand what was happening, this must have been a terrible blow. After all, she was the woman with the whiplash mind. Anything anybody could understand, she could under-stand faster. Or at least she could have once.

Worse than all of this she realised that, in giving the beginnings of a statement, in pretending to herself that she could control what came out, she had forfeited her own sense of esteem. All that remained was the good opinion of her comrades outside, 'whose understanding and succour I most needed'. She could think of only one way to keep that and that was to kill herself.

On the fly-leaf of the puzzle book she wrote a note, apologising for her cowardice, saying how much she loved us – her children and Joe – and indicating that she hadn't talked. And then she swallowed down every one of the sleeping pills that a visit from her doctor had provided.

*

She woke up knowing that her suicide attempt had failed. She never resumed her statement: after a few days of hysterical crying, she was calm, resigned to a life in solitary. She was given more books, the first being the *Charterhouse of Parme* which she had packed while I stood watching. When Viktor summoned her, she appeared. She was drawn into talking to him, hating herself for enjoying his company and yet wanting to believe that he was different from the rest of the security branch. He came so close. He watched her talking to her mother, her sister-in-law, he watched her reaction to our third visit when Shawn sat on the ground and 'howled her heart out'.

And then, on the 117th day of her incarceration, Viktor told her that he was releasing her. This time, it was the truth.

After she was out, Viktor continued to dog her. Was it he whom Ruth's friend Barney saw one night in the street outside our house, skulking in a darkened car, waiting? It was certainly him who visited her after her release, bringing with him a book. She'd laughed in his face, she told a friend: the cheek of the man, presuming that they had a relationship to continue.

But there is no doubt that of all of them, Viktor had hurt. He had been clever and he had almost got beneath her skin. He had got a hint that for this apparently invulnerable communist there was one real chink – she cared, deeply, what people thought of her. It was fear of what her comrades might think that had driven Ruth to the brink of death. It was Viktor's treating her like a woman that had almost allowed him in.

Viktor seems to have enjoyed the game he controlled. A year or so later, he was present at the interrogation of a friend of Ruth's, and he was still boasting of how he had made Ruth First fall for him.

I tried to see this man, Viktor, decades afterwards, when I was in South Africa. He was retired by then, and ex-directory but he agreed that a police press officer could give me his fax number. I faxed him many times, asking if I could come and interview him about my mother. Eventually, I got a phone call. He refused to tell me where he lived. He didn't think the time was right to meet, he said. There was too much happening, he didn't want to talk. I asked again, said I was leaving South Africa and that I would like to meet him.

'I will ring you before you leave,' he said. 'That is a promise.'

It sounded more like a threat than a promise. It turned out to be neither. Despite the fact that I faxed him several more times, I never heard from him again.

I remember that day when Ruth returned from prison. I see her, in my mind's eye, far away from me, climbing from a car and hugging our nanny, Elsie. I remember also how jealousy engulfed me, jealousy either because Elsie was the recipient of such easy joy or because that embrace, given by our nanny, belonged to me. I didn't know which. I didn't know either, how to be with her. Not that it much mattered. Behind her uneasy pretence of joyfulness, it was clear that her mind was elsewhere. I remember her going through the motions of a greeting but I remember also that feeling that her arm wanted to ward me off at the same time as she hugged me to her.

I withdrew into myself, using a visual trick to take away the hurt. It worked. She got smaller, almost as if I were looking at her through a reversed telescope. In the distance she sat while I hovered at the peripheries, keeping her in my sight, and myself in hiding. I watched from afar as she talked of her experiences to her friend Moira, not to me. I was on full eavesdrop patrol – I heard Moira say that it was Barney Simon who had helped two of Ruth's friends who had escaped from gaol into hiding. It was the kind of secret that, if uncovered, would have sent Barney to prison for a very long time. Guiltily I hugged the knowledge to myself, too scared even to tell Ruth what I had overheard.

Family friends, the few who had stayed faithful throughout her incarceration, continued to visit and to take us out to Zoo Lake and lunch at Killarney. But now instead of proving a distraction, I felt that what they were doing was keeping us from

Ruth. Yet what was there to say? Ruth needed it that way. All that was left for us to do was bide our time and wait to see what would happen next.

Chapter Twelve

On 7 December, the day Ruth came out of gaol, she wrote to Joe who had reached London by then:

It is over. At least so they say. They say no re-arrest. No charges. At last the nightmare begins to recede. Perhaps as time passes and there is a return to normality, which is as normal as things can be at home in our present circumstances, I will forget too much. Was ill at the end, but now all I need is a holiday and to learn how to sleep. Yes me! I can't sleep!

She desperately needed to get away from Johannesburg but, vindictive to the last, the police wouldn't give her permission to go beyond the city limits. So she sent us off instead. By Christmas, we were all dispersed. Shawn was with friends in a game reserve, Tilly back in her home, and Joe and Julius in London. Meanwhile Robyn and I and Ruth's Citroën were all holidaying with Hilda Bernstein, whose husband was one of the nine Rivonia Trialists, and her two children.

So my year was book-ended by two parentless holidays. We celebrated the new year in the resort town of Port Alfred in the Eastern Cape. A few miles down the road, in 1705, the white Afrikaner settlers first encountered the indigenous Xhosas. But by 1963 Port Alfred, and the Grand Hotel where we were staying, was a kind of Butlins, packed with nuclear families, all white, who rushed about by day, yodelling happily, and gathered by night in a huge, garishly decorated hall to play communal games. To us they seemed like aliens from outer space.

It was midsummer but it rained a lot. I remember grey skies when we wakened, which grew darker as we punted on a lake, getting ourselves wet enough to go home and change again. I also remember loud fights between the kids and loud laughter, horse riding on the beach, fishing without success and an exhibition of heavily muscled life-savers hauling thick cables from the sea. On New Year's Eve, dressed as cavemen, our faces smeared with dirt and carrying lethal-looking clubs, Robyn and I won the hotel's fancy-dress competition. We all got sick drunk in our imaginations as we gazed admiringly at our prize of cheap South African champagne.

But more than anything I remember witnessing a conversation between Hilda's daughter, Frances, then twelve years old, and a hotel guest. The man, intrigued by our entourage of one anxious-looking woman and four sulky children, asked Frances where her father was. I knew immediately why Frances's face turned bright red, and why she mumbled something inaudible. I stood, close by, knowing also what was next. I was right. The man asked another question. 'What's your father's name?'

Frances's father was called Lionel but, because of his shock of red hair, everybody knew him by his nickname of Rusty. 'Lionel,' Frances said, as softly as she could.

The man had good hearing even if he did seem a trifle simple-minded. He frowned. 'Lionel?' I watched the monicker ringing a distant bell. 'Lionel? Lionel Bernstein?' Now he'd got it. An expression – embarrassment? distaste? admiration? something in between? – crossed his face. Whatever it was, he needed confirmation. 'Do you mean Rusty Bernstein?'

At which point, Frances turned and fled. I followed as she ran crying to her mother and asked whether it had been an act of betrayal to tell a stranger her father's name. I understood exactly what she was going through. I carried the same unbearable sense of responsibility and guilt with me.

But I could not deny that the sympathy I felt for her was only half of what I felt. The other part of me was possessed by an emotion which surged despite my attempt to elbow it away: jealousy. Jealousy at the way Hilda hugged Frances, and at the way Frances had her mother and all the attention too.

If I could not be carefree, I guess, I must at least be recognised.

The litany kept going round: 'Notice me, notice me, don't notice me', changing occasionally to: 'Notice my parents, don't notice them' and the one almost unthinkable addendum, 'Notice me for what I am, not for what my parents do'.

Many years later, I was to go to lunch with Mac Maharaj, an old friend of both my parents who was then in his first year as the new South Africa's minister of transport. We met in his fourteenth-floor suite in the building on Cape Town's Plein Street where, while Parliament is in session, all the ministers have their offices. With bodyguards massing, we took the lift down to the basement, got into his car – a standard ministerial Mercedes – and drove to the restaurant. The room was all rag-rolled walls and oversize white plates, a far cry from the tack of that old Port Alfred hotel. We sat down, ordered quickly, and got down to business. I had asked to see Mac because I wanted to talk to him about is work in the ANC underground with Joe. But before we got on to my father, Mac leaned across the table and told me something else.

He told me how, some years previously, he had watched, in the company of other ANC people, *A World Apart*, the film my sister, Shawn, wrote about Ruth's imprisonment. The film deals poignantly with our last year in South Africa, a wrenching account of the impact on a child of her mother's political involvement. Mac said he had enjoyed the film but then he added something different: some of his African comrades, he said, had decided that what the young girl in the film needed was 'a good slap'.

A good slap – it felt like that to me. I read behind the words and breathed in their implications. They conjured up a judgement I knew only too well, that we were white kids who indulged ourselves in whining. Legions of other renowned whiners, white South Africans all, who'd been brought up with black servants to wipe their noses, make their beds, tell them when to walk, massed behind us. They were still very much in evidence in 1995, those whites who stood about helplessly when there was something to be done. A nation of the over-indulged having trouble growing up and we three white kids were being ranked amongst them.

Mac said quickly that of course he disagreed. Our childhoods were particularly difficult, he said, for the very reason that we were white and therefore isolated in our community. Not so the kids of African comrades, he continued. They all knew the score. 'Africans lived in a community that warned you,' he said, 'that was with you, even if only in spirit. You didn't.'

A good slap – it stayed with me long after the main course was cleared away and I was spooning through an extravagant chocolate dessert. It was part of my inheritance anyway, that inner voice that asked how I dare protest when so many Africans had suffered so much more. 'Mummy's gone to prison to help the black people,' the six-year-old Shawn had told the newsmen. It was second nature to us, this owning of black South Africa's pain. Even as children we carried internal scales of justice which we used to weigh up 'their' needs – the needs of the impoverished masses – against ours. How could we win? Compared to the poverty, degradation, discrimination they endured, our suffering was negligible. When it came down it, the scale was weighted permanently against us.

We were brought up in a political culture which used self-sacrifice as its fuel. It never went away, this conflict between the demands of 'one' and the needs of the 'whole'. Our parents were rebels, they saw a wrong and they fought to make it right. To do that they had to turn away from the subjective. Their eyes were on a greater prize than self – they were fighting for humanity.

But we were only children. We knew enough about what our parents were doing to realise that we couldn't ask them to make another choice. But could we also find a way to hush those inner voices which cried out for safety, security, normality – all those things our white school friends had?

Amongst the letters that my family kept was one written in 1964 by a great friend, Bram Fischer, to my grandparents. Bram was writing in response to a condolence letter that Tilly had sent on hearing of the death of Bram's wife, Molly. Bram wrote:

During the past twenty years, we have had to make many important decisions which might have had grave consequences for ourselves and our family. I know that there was no single occasion when Molly ever let herself be influenced in any way by possible personal consequences. She had the rare quality, supposed to belong to judges, of being able to exclude entirely from her mind what the consequences of a decision might be to her and – what was perhaps even more remarkable – what such consequences might be to her family.

There it is, that almost biblical conviction that what matters is not the person but the cause. And yet Bram was the least impersonal of men. I remember him with such affection. I remember his warm, unassuming presence by their swimming pool on Sundays and the brief squeeze of his hand that one time in London when, already suspect and threatened with imprisonment, he had been given permission by the South African government to go abroad on legal business after promising he would return. This was the last occasion I was to see him. He kept his promise and went back and was imprisoned.[2]

He was one of the most heroic of men and the kindest and here is his accolade for the dead wife he had adored: that she thought not of herself, or of her family, but of others, less well off than them. I read through the letter again and I think perhaps what Mac's comrades had said was true – perhaps a good slap would have sorted us out.

And then another, contradictory voice, rises up in protest. We

---

2. Bram Fischer, a member of one of South Africa's foremost Afrikaner families with the most dazzling of careers ahead of him, threw in his lot with the ANC. Heavily involved in all that was going on, he risked his own freedom to act as barrister for the Rivonia Trialists. After the trial was over, he went underground, determined to keep the resistance going. Shortly after Molly's death, he was caught and given a sentence of life imprisonment. It proved to be for life – in 1975 Bram died of cancer. He had been let out of gaol for the last few weeks of his life but, after he was cremated, the prison authorities insisted on reclaiming his ashes.

were not asking them to stay silent, that voice says, or to put our needs before the needs of the oppressed. All we wanted was a simple acknowledgement that no political movement can ever fight for justice without there being casualties.

Between these two polarities I am endlessly caught, swaying between my needs and theirs, between the self and the community to which, because I was a white child, I never fully belonged.

In Johannesburg Ruth was isolated. She had spent Christmas and New Year almost entirely on her own. When she spoke to Joe on the phone, she must have told him something of the way she felt. She must have told him, as she wrote eventually from England, to a nameless friend inside the country, 'I found myself very nervous when I came out about intruders and hearing walls ... My spell [in gaol] brought all kinds of things closer to skin surface and some popped uncomfortably out.'

Still completely disoriented and unable to work out her next step, she worried about taking the exams in librarianship her incarceration had made her miss. 'You might think I am being bogged down in a trivial matter like exams,' she wrote to Joe. 'But I can't suspend myself here in limbo while you and I work out plans for a new life.'

There spoke that one Ruth, the independent woman who was busy bridging the chasm that had almost swallowed her. And yet immediately after that, she added, 'I need to talk to you. There are things I must tell you because you are you and I can tell no one else. And when will I see you to tell you?'

The strain was beginning to show. She was banned from meeting with most of the people who mattered to her and there is tension evident in her communications with Joe. 'You moan about Xmas,' she wrote to him. 'Mine has been hell. Empty, deserted house – no swimming ... and anyway no one to swim with – no parties. You've forgotten what these bans can be like?'

Nobody, however, would accuse *Ruth* of ever needing a good slap. Stoical to the last she took away the sting of her complaint by adding, 'Never mind, I'll survive.'

There it is again, the censorious voice, which elevates stoicism above private pain. And yet how useful this must have been in those days. There were big decisions to be made. The country was gripped by terror. Most of their friends were either banned, in gaol, or out of the country. 'God only knows how those left inside still cope,' Ruth wrote to Joe. 'Don't know how many there are, even, but pressure has been *tremendously* effective this time.'

Her Christmas had been miserable and, perhaps without us to keep her going, her collapse went further than she'd anticipated. And she had other problems: Joe's side of the correspondence did not survive, but from what she wrote, it's obvious that he was nursing his own insecurities, the most pointed of which was that she might not want to join him. On 30 December she, who had spent her working life shaping words, wrote,

> . . . am afraid my letters haven't been good enough and may have given you the wrong impression and upset you. You must make allowances of difficulties in communication; some degree of disorientation (which crept in later rather than immediately after release, curiously) and acute difficulty of making decisions without you to help me. *I want to come very much.* I can't see this half-life for you and me going on much longer . . . I'm anxious about the future – I don't see how I can last even ticking over at one eighth of my former capacity for living and working for this former year. *But* I don't want to be indecently hasty for reasons you will understand. Rushing ahead oblivious to some local considerations will be sad and misunderstood. I feel so split and divided against myself . . . I think I must have an overdeveloped and oversize conscience. *And* I am also apprehensive about a new life in a huge unknown world.

They knew that Joe could never come back, not unless he was prepared to spend the rest of his life in gaol. If they were to be together, Ruth would have to join him. Yet still he felt she was holding back. She insisted she wasn't, breaking into capitals on

2 January to reassure him that '*THERE ARE NO FACTORS OF WHICH YOU ARE UNAWARE*'. 'Put all that out of your mind,' she continued. 'My ailment is overdevelopment of conscience . . .' And of course being Ruth, she was honest enough to admit, as well, to her apprehension at having to live without a cook. Later she really got down to business, voicing her enduring concern by asking plaintively, 'Can they straighten hair in London?'

What the South African government did in 1963 was to be deadly effective. For more than a decade afterwards, the opposition in South Africa was completely quiescent. When the new generation rose up, it turned on those who had gone before accusing them of betrayal because they fled the country and left behind a vacuum. This is what tugged at Ruth's conscience: that she was somehow a deserter.

But there was no life remaining for her in South Africa. She had to go. She applied for a passport, which meant at least that she could come back. The police kept touring the block, sometimes hourly, checking on her movements but from the government administration offices in Pretoria where her passport request had gone, came only silence. While she waited she continued to see people, but 'not the right ones'. She went to the movies, 'five nights running' in one week. For her first movie after prison, she made Barney Simon go with her to see Cleopatra because she thought Elizabeth Taylor was so beautiful. She came out sorely disappointed though: Taylor had not lived up to expectations.

'For the rest,' she wrote, 'I lunch in town sometimes, sit about in cafés a bit, eat three meals a day, go to the hairdresser once a week and rejoice that I have decided not to swot.' The occasional piece of good news − like hearing that the black workers at Julius's old factory had cheered when they were told he had escaped − was overwhelmed by a sense of doom that she had barely escaped. 'A third suicide inside a cell,' she wrote to Joe in January, 'this one a 30-year-old African in Port Elizabeth. Horrible.'

The pressure was building. We returned from holiday and went back to school. Months passed and nothing was settled. She and Joe argued on the phone. On 3 March she wrote: 'Your call tonight made me sad. Jilly noticed it and remarked on it. We've been parted a long while and the sound of your voice made me feel sorry for myself and us.' Things got worse: Joe continued to press her until she gave vent to her irritation:

> You seem to think I'm responsible for the delays in my getting papers [she wrote]. I ring the Pretoria passport office repeatedly – get nowhere. I've put in for an exit permit and expect the same cat's paw game on their part. And I don't have influence in those circles! . . . Now you write and tell me how to persuade the Special Branch to give me an exit permit in my time, not theirs. Perhaps a letter from you to Colonel Van du Bergh will tip the scales. ha. ha. ha.

I can just see her, clicking her way to the post office, shoving the letter briskly into the post box. Soon afterwards, however, she regretted it:

> Tonight of course [she wrote] I have remorse over the sore letter I wrote you yesterday . . . I know there are difficulties and involvements your end . . . but there are difficulties here too. We need to talk actually and be together and all will work out, I know. I really haven't been able to help the delay and if you discuss 'delaying tactics' they are not of my free choice. I'm not really frightened of us being together. Much more frightened that you'll be away from me . . . miserable at the prospect.

We knew we were soon to be going to that mysterious overseas, that land we viewed through the old-world lens of Charles Dickens and Jane Austen. The signs of our imminent departure were all around. The house had been painted, its woodwork varnished and it was finally sold. The bird, the only one of our animals left alive, was given away. Shawn was booked to leave on a boat with friends on 13 March and Tilly was to follow at the end of the month.

At the last moment Ruth's papers came through: not a passport but an exit permit, one way only. We were to leave on the 14th, the day before my twelfth birthday. In my school's back garden, a hurried party was convened. I came away with a gift of a tiny teddy bear and a feeling of things forever unfinished. And then we were off.

There was a car waiting in the road as we drove down the driveway. The faces of the two behatted men inside it didn't seem to register our going, but they fell in behind and followed us all the way out of Johannesburg. At Jan Smuts airport, Ruth's goodbye to cousins was made farcical by her attempt to avoid the policemen who planted themselves behind pillars, observing her. Our flight was called. We went outside.

As we began to climb up the steps, a news photographer shouted out. We turned, Ruth, Robyn and I, and were caught in the camera's eye on our way to the unknown. On Ruth's left is Robyn, grinning cheekily. Ruth is centre frame, not one hair out of place, her make-up immaculate. On her right, I stand, half-turned away, staring back – caught, carrying a Tintin book, between confusion and blank incomprehension.

Chapter Thirteen

Heathrow airport: Ruth, Robyn, and I walked down the steps into the greyness of an unusually cold mid-March day and the glare of television lights. We were taken straight from customs to a TV studio where someone stuck a microphone in my face and asked how I liked England. What stayed with me afterwards was not the inanity of the question but the way I had stood, stranded with my mouth agape, no sound issuing out.

The interviewer turned to the real attraction, Ruth, and questioned her about her time in prison. As she answered, articulate and to the point, I counted the minutes until release. Finally, it was over and we were let loose on the scrum of people who'd been waiting for us, Joe amongst them. I remember not him particularly, but the clamouring of everybody for Ruth's attention. And I remember, also, the disappointing drive into London. Jane Austen had let me down: instead of beautifully cobbled streets leading on to quaint tea shops I saw endless rows of terraced red brick; instead of the luxuriant whiteness of satiny snow, dirty grey specks floated sporadically down from an unrelenting dull sky. There was one other sight to surprise – a woman on her hands and knees polishing at her doorstep's metal grating. Coming as we did from a world where manual labour was a blacks-only occupation, what amazed us was not the old-fashioned nature of the woman's task, but the fact that she was white.

A year later we were eating our first meal in the house that Ruth and Joe had bought in Camden Town. As supper neared its end, I leaned across the table, meaning to put my plate on the pile of others. An unfamiliar cracking sound startled me. Like the rest of the family, my eyes were drawn towards the uncurtained window. I saw the dark outline of the building yard whose boundaries ran from the end of our small garden down to a particularly murky section of the Regent's Canal. The place looked utterly deserted.

Another crack: this time, as something flew through the air, a small hole blossomed in the window pane.

Joe's reaction was almost instantaneous. He shouted a sharp 'get down', and, doing just that, he pulled Robyn down with him. Another crack. We all dropped to the floor. 'Stay down,' Joe said, crawling along the carpet, grabbing for the phone. I was still trying to work out what the hell was going on when he dialled 999 and asked for immediate police assistance because somebody opposite was shooting at us.

To get out of range, Joe was on the stairs: the rest of us were crammed together under the table. Silence, but not for long. It wasn't funny, but we started laughing. How could we not? We had travelled 6,000 miles and a whole culture away from our pasts, and yet, on our first night in our new house, somebody tried to kill us. It wasn't funny – it was ridiculous.

Which is precisely what the police must have thought. They took a long time to arrive. For twenty minutes we sat in partial darkness, bathed only in the neon yellow issuing from the street. Joe phoned the police again. 'We're coming,' they assured him. No new bullet had been fired. In single file we crawled out from under the table and went to join Joe on the stairs.

Eventually an old-fashioned bobby came by. His sceptical look remained in place as Joe described what had happened. Desultorily and without success he searched for the bullet. Giving up, he stared at the neat hole in the middle of the window pane. 'Probably an air pistol,' he said.

He was right. It was an air pistol: the two teenagers who had fired it were foolish enough to be lurking by the canal when Joe and the policemen finally went over there. Thus, to Joe's great embarrassment his first encounter with the British courts was not as an attorney but a witness to the night when we, weird South Africans, had panicked.

★

My father had reacted so fast because like Ruth, his whole concentration was on the country we'd been forced to leave. It was a South Africa wreathed in suffering: the letters Ruth received give vocal testimony to the terror that had descended. Not one of them is signed, not one addressed to Ruth. They were sent variously to a D. Mercer in Compayne Gardens, the road where we temporarily lived, to 'The occupier' of that same Compayne Gardens and c/o Barbara Castle at the House of Commons.

The secrecy my parents had practised over so many years was paramount. To one regular correspondent, code named Johnson, Ruth signs off as 'Rob(ert Browning)'. He replies with long descriptions of how he finally got the book she had sent him after it had travelled from one safe address to the next. It was getting more difficult, he wrote, to find anyone prepared to take a risk, since it is 'so easy to break friendships these days and no one will talk to me'. To emphasise the dangers, he ended his letter with, 'NOW VERY IMPORTANT please send all my correspondence to ... AND DON'T USE MY NAME'. He had good reason to be worried. In South Africa then, and for the foreseeable future, contact with either of my parents was dangerous. Even the words they uttered from afar were banned. And there were few voices in that wilderness willing to protest. Those who did were picked off and brutalised. One of Ruth's correspondents describes how in a single family – the Weinbergs – Eli had been imprisoned for a year for refusing to testify against his friends, his wife Violet was held incommunicado under the 180-Day Law, and their eighteen-year-old daughter, Sheila, was sentenced for nineteen months for the crime of painting an anti-government slogan.

For me this South Africa, with its strange conspiracies and its deathly intensity, seemed a million miles away. I wanted to keep it that way. My first task was to negotiate London, to do things like crossing a road, catching a bus, getting to my friends without my parents' intervention, activities I'd not done before. My second was to ditch my unlovely, hick-town South African accent.

To most of my new English peers, South Africa was the jungle, and that was the end of it. I let it end there. What had the old country ever done for me, but cause me pain? I embraced the new, and as my uneasy adolescence progressed, South Africa did become progressively more distant.

When it was required of me I walked round Trafalgar Square holding anti-apartheid posters or I licked endless stamps on to unending requests for money to keep the cause going, but my heart wasn't in it. That place, that my parents persisted in calling 'home', was gone for me. Okay, some things would never change. Joe, who soon worked full time for the ANC, would probably always be spotted by my new friends opening his parcels out on the balcony, or he'd be away and I wouldn't know where, or he'd be sitting at a desk painting across an apparently blank sheet of paper to reveal words written in invisible ink, but that was only Joe. I had been given a break from the pain of South Africa. I had my own life now, I was going to seize it.

I was really quite successful. I was much more English than South African by the late seventies when I visited my parents in Mozambique, and much more English when I went there after Ruth was killed. And yet I was to discover that my escape was far from absolute.

Amongst the people who came over to Ruth's house in the days before her funeral was a grey-haired black South African. A well-built man, he sat with us, legs planted wide apart on the long bench that ran under one of the sitting-room windows. For hours he stayed there, motionless, his eyes focused on some distant point as if he had come to endure rather than condole. But then, in one rare moment's calm between one set of people leaving and the next arriving, he turned and looked at me. He spoke. 'Your mother has been forced to drop the spear,' he said. 'Now you must pick it up.'

The spear was the symbol of South African resistance. The ANC had used it to name its army – Umkhonto we Sizwe – the spear of the nation. And here was a stranger telling me to pick up my mother's. How could I? I was English not South African, I was myself, not Ruth. Her shadow was too large, her spear too heavy. When my parents had grown to adulthood back 'home' they'd been forced to choose between black and white, not I. I was brought up elsewhere in a different time; I had got away.

And yet what the man had said continued to reverberate. I looked at the crowds who had come to mourn Ruth, I read the tributes, I saw the pain of her death in others' eyes and I recognised something that I had too long denied – I couldn't walk away. The place wouldn't leave me alone. If nothing else, I would have to work out what South Africa meant to me. From that moment, I would have to face my past.

But in 1965, in London, that moment was still a long time coming. Ruth was launching herself on her new life. The ANC paid our mortgage, Joe's food, clothes and travel costs. For the rest Ruth was the family breadwinner. She was also the one with the growing reputation. While Joe worked behind the scenes, desperately trying to rebuild the smashed opposition, Ruth was in demand as a fiery public speaker, often the lone woman in a sea of men who stood on the platform in front of the stone lions in Trafalgar Square and addressed the increasingly more populous demonstrations. Not everybody was a fan: there were those in the 'movement' who found her constant embracing of new ideas galling. And sometimes it got worse than that. Many years later, Joe was to tell me that, if it hadn't been for him, Ruth might very well have been expelled from the Communist Party for the accumulated crimes of heresy against accepted truths. Ruth must have heard the tongues wagging but, by the time she got to England, she'd stopped blindly following lines. And there were compensations. Her willingness to question brought her respect from English activists. For many, she became the acceptable face of South African communism.

For money, she worked as a freelance journalist and author, travelling Africa. She and Joe, at least initially, ran the family with their own version of serial parentage. If Joe was not somewhere in the world on some mysterious mission, Ruth would be – researching the books she wrote on Libya, on sanctions, and on military coups in Africa. Her CV grew, reflecting both the breadth of her interests and her bravery. No subject was too large or too macho for her to tackle.

The lines etched on her face were laid down in those English years. It cost her dearly, worrying about money and jobs and her children's futures. But did she at the same time also feel a kind of freedom to remake herself? Just as Tilly had once chosen to switch her accent into another social class, so was there a part of Ruth that had disdain for the new world, immigrant brashness that pervaded South Africa. In England Ruth had money problems and the burden of three adolescent daughters but she also had access to an intellectual world she had always craved. And her timing was so perfect: in Paris, London, New York, there was a rebellion stirring. Ruth threw herself into the thick of it. Not for her the old certainties by which old communists like her parents had lived and died. She wasn't satisfied with an idea unless it continued to work. If it didn't, she would discard it.

Those first years in England were stormy times for Ruth and Joe. Her life was a round of new ideas, of her growing confidence in the world, of international conferences and late-night exchanges and of new ideas. His was full of secrets and of disappointments, of trips to the Soviet Union for 'consultations' or abortive attempts to kick start the rebellion in South Africa. At home they argued passionately, fiercely, bitterly. They argued about money, about why his only contribution to the house-hold's domestic labour was to make the salad dressing, about his continuing and urgent calls away which disrupted almost every holiday we took, but most of all they argued about politics.

I remember one of their fights. I started it or, more accurately, I brought the news that launched this, perhaps the most relentless of their confrontations. I had got up early, intent on doing some piece of leftover homework, and was eating breakfast to the sounds of Radio One when the 7.30 am news came on. It was May 1968 and the bulletin I heard was a harrowing description of Russian tanks rolling into Czechoslovakia.

I rushed upstairs to tell my parents. They were side by side in bed, still half asleep. Not for long. Within a few minutes they were arguing: Ruth protested about the invasion while Joe defended it, using all his lawyer's tricks to imply that Ruth was speaking out of ignorance. The fight went on for weeks, over family breakfasts, over the television's blare and through dinner parties they gave. They never cared who saw them arguing.

I see now, in hindsight, that their political disagreements served a double purpose. They were conduits for the resentments that built up between them but, at the same time, they were used by each to hone their intellects. They each had their roles: Ruth was the critic, the outsider who questioned orthodoxy while Joe was an organisation man, biting back criticisms of the system that supported him, biding his time, his eyes always focused on a greater, distant goal.

In the last few months of his life, Joe talked about how much Ruth's razor-edged tongue could hurt him. And yet I knew he had also relied on it. I remembered how in 1983, a year after Ruth's death, Joe and I had gone for a walk along the beach in Ponta do Ouro. He told me that there was pressure on him to become the chairman of the South African Communist Party, and he asked me what I thought he ought to do. I was so flattered. It brought back that image of my parents walking that same beach, their heads close together as they talked of things forbidden to the children, and now he was consulting me! I told him that I thought the military struggle and his place in the ANC was much more important. I advised him to turn the job down.

He didn't take my advice. He'd used me, as he often had used Ruth, as a sounding board. A canny politician, he always liked to find out what the opposition thought. Soon afterwards, in a *dacha* on the outskirts of Moscow where the Party had its conference, he was elected chairman. But after the voting was over and he'd smiled his way through ebullient congratulations, he went back to his room, set amongst the pine forests, and cried. To a friend, who'd come to join him, he explained, 'Today I really needed Ruth. I needed her for her criticism and I need her to keep me honest.'

It didn't always seem that way. In England the choices they made meant they were often separated. In the beginning it was Ruth who travelled most – going to Africa to do her research – but after a while it was Joe who took up the long-distance baton. How that must have galled Ruth. She was every bit his equal, in fact, within our family Ruth was the star, more than Joe's equal, and yet hers was increasingly the domestic role: another provocation for their arguments. She felt Joe had it easy, that because he was so often away, his children would let him off the hooks which they used to strangle her.

They'd started out as equals on a road that they had always known would be arduous. And so it proved. It was harder, in fact, than they could have guessed, young and optimistic as they were in the beginning. But now had come the parting of the ways: there were no servants to help and Tilly was too old to take over. Someone had to stay and look after the children and that someone was Ruth. She didn't find it easy to let Joe forget the fact.

There were other strains between them as well. I can't remember when it first dawned on me that my parents were not monogamous. I do remember how, when I was in my late teens, Ruth laughingly told me that Joe had accused her of having an affair with a mutual friend. I looked at her and said, 'And are you?' and the shock that crossed her face was the first acknowledgement between us that I knew that sexual faithfulness was not part of the bargain that she and Joe had struck. I walked out soon after that. I was a teenager, struggling to come to terms with my own sexuality. The last thing I needed was to know about theirs.

As the decade rolled by, my parents' bases were increasingly separated. The ANC had got a toe-hold in Africa and Joe started spending longer periods in what was all-embracingly referred to as 'down south'. His life was a round of mysterious meetings, of flying visits to the eastern bloc countries, of plans and, at least until 1976, of continual defeats. How tenacious he must have been to stick out those years: how far, in that bleak time, he must have stretched his optimism to stop himself giving way to despair.

Meanwhile Ruth was finding that though her outspokenness might annoy her comrades, her red affiliations made it difficult for her to get a permanent job. In the end, she took a lectureship in Durham. We had all but left home, Joe was increasingly in Angola, why not? She packed up and went, ready to remake herself again. England might have given her undreamed-of intellectual opportunities, but it was also hard work. She had battled for acceptance amongst the English – now she was going to a city she didn't know in order to get a job.

Ruth in Durham, Joe in Zambia: were they in the process of going their different ways? It's possible: their constant separations might have eventually proved too much even for them. They might, perhaps, have drifted more permanently into other's arms.

But in the end that's not what happened. They were people whose lives were shaped by history and at a crucial point, the bell tolled again.

Chapter Fourteen

It was a sudden and unanticipated turn of history that changed my parents' lives. It began, of all places, in Europe, in Portugal's capital of Lisbon, travelled from there to the southern African countries of Mozambique and Angola, and further south again into South Africa. What happened was that in 1974 the Portuguese army deposed their ageing dictator Salazar. In 1975, anxious to rid itself of its unwinnable colonial war, the new Portuguese government vacated Mozambique and Angola and, finally, one year later, driven by the example of these recently independent black states, tens of thousands of young South Africans rediscovered the power of anger.

In Soweto in 1976, black children came out on to the streets protesting against the use of Afrikaans in school. Nobody knew it then but they were the first wave in what would eventually become the storm that annihilated apartheid. My father told me at the time that Soweto taught him that it is the young who change history because only the young have the courage to defy death. So it was in '76. As ships and guns and tanks were aimed their way, the children kept on coming.

The long, quiet, frightened years were truly over. Once again, the South African police and army patrolled the townships in an effort to drive this next generation into submission. But this time, without effect: the ANC's army, Umkhonto we Sizwe, which hadn't, for more than fourteen years, fired a single shot in anger, was suddenly transformed. Young people flooded out of the country, demanding weapons so they could go back and fight. They were funnelled through Swaziland into newly liberated Angola where Joe and his comrades were there to meet them.

Ruth wasn't far behind. A year after the Soweto uprising, she found a job across the South African border, in Maputo University's research institute. She had no idea what her new life would be like: she was heading out into the unknown.

Initially she took just one year off from her teaching post at Durham University. Her main concern, she said, was not the risk to her, but the possible damage done to us. 'I don't know why,' she wrote in her first letter to me, "cos you're all old enough and so am I, but I don't really like leaving you all behind.' It's a refrain that continues throughout her time in Mozambique.

Joe thought she took it all too far. She wrote that he 'keeps on about how I should let you go, all three of you and you're grown up and all that'. Joe's great strength was the way he single-mindedly directed his energy at events he could affect, but Ruth was different: she railed continually against the things that bothered her even if she couldn't change them. She tried to justify her involvement with us. 'Worrying about your problems,' she wrote, 'doesn't make me see you as any less resourceful and grown up, just that the problems are real.'

Real or not she went to Mozambique. On her way, she stopped off in nearby Angola to visit Joe who lived, she wrote, 'in a big house covered with exotic house plants, smooth tiled bathrooms, in company with a horde of young students fresh from Soweto all glowing with rebelling, and some older, tireder men, and [he] misses his telly, hot baths and other London Luxuries but is looking happy enough and is too busy to notice much else'.

She continued on her way and reached Maputo. She didn't know it, but she was nearing the end of her life. Those, her last years, were not witness to a slow decline into sickness and then death: instead they were a period of exciting change. Ruth and Joe were both in their fifties but they relaunched themselves into lives which were unequivocally youthful. They were modern nomads, driven on by revolutionary zeal.

By August, Ruth was settled in Maputo and Joe was on one of his increasingly frequent visits. 'Looking fatter,' she wrote, 'than after an Angola stint but then he came here directly from the pleasures of socialist sausage or something and with a pair of new white sheets in his baggage to raise the living standards of Luanda when he gets back there.'

They made new friends, closer to their children's ages than to theirs. They were engrossed in a kind of frontier living which must have reminded them of home. The rhythm of past revelries before their enforced slow-down in the northern hemisphere, reverberated in the letters Ruth wrote. On Joe's birthday, she described how they held a celebratory meal in a taverna. The variety of the food might not be up to Jo'burg standards, but the entertainment was just as frenzied. In the middle of their meal, the doors were locked and a huge neon sign demanded silence for three serious, guitar-strumming artists.

It was soon obvious how much at home Ruth felt. Her letters are full of her new life, of descriptions of research trips into the countryside, of prawns and lobsters, socialist delegations, her frizzed-out hair and of course, shopping lists given to friends to carry into neighbouring Swaziland. But these were different lists: Mozambique changed her requirements from Italian shoes and chunky silver jewellery to '2 pin plugs, mop for kitchen surfaces, thermos flask, desk diary, hairbrush and Vim'.

She never lost her love of fine objects and yet, slowly, even her passion for shopping was dimmed. I remember how once, having picked her up from the airport, I took her to a London delicatessen because she had written to tell me how much she had been craving fancy cheeses. She stood in front of the counter looking at the selection for a long, long time. I stood beside her, thinking that she was frozen in admiration of the variety. But then suddenly she turned to me and told me that it was all too much, she wasn't used to it, would I mind choosing for her. Having got the question out she was almost proud. It was as if Mozambique had somehow freed her of acquisitiveness.

Her letters were packed with news. She wrote, half-mockingly, of visiting Chinese delegations, of red flags flying, of Mozambican President Samora Machel's twelve-hour speeches.

She was in her element. As head of a unit which was training future leaders by getting them to do practical and much-needed research on their country's economy, she was respected and in turn she had a coterie around her whom she respected and who gave her confidence. Mozambique, with its food shortages and its dearth of trained personnel, offered a challenge to which Ruth could apply considerable talents – a challenge that she was winning.

Yet her old responsibilities continued to tug at her. She had to learn a whole new language and a new way of life as well, but the miles that separated us did not make her communications to us any less intense. In June 1982, three months before she died, she wrote to me, encouraging me to press on with my novel which, at that time, I had almost given up. In case I took offence, she quickly qualified her counsel. 'Jill,' she wrote, 'this is not advice, only correspondence about your book which is dear to your heart, and to you, who is dear to mine.'

I sit at my desk, her smiling photograph behind me, and I stare at her letter, the last I was ever to receive from her. It speaks to me even now, over all the long years past. In that one loving, apprehensive sentence lies the nub of our impasse, the reason why we ended our final meeting with an argument. I was in my early thirties then, had been living independently since I was eighteen, and yet Ruth still worried about me, still felt she had to bolster up my life from afar, and, at the same time, still feared my rejection of her efforts. We were far apart and we were enmeshed – tied by family, by our different needs, and, more than anything else, by our pasts.

She was a difficult act to follow, was Ruth. She was the kind of role model our generation was searching out, a beautiful, well-dressed woman who had made an impact on the world and who was fighting for a cause that was indisputably just, but she was also our mother. She was both the best of mothers and the worst. When she turned the full light of her attention our way, she could dazzle. And yet, so often, her mind was elsewhere. When my younger sister Robyn was eleven, she launched an offensive to try and get Ruth to be like other mothers, to be there at breakfast and at supper too. Robyn soon gave up. What Ruth did was so obviously important – how could our petty needs compete?

A difficult act to follow. She was ahead of her time, a path breaker who though beset by guilt towards her children, carried on. We were different from her. If life had not demanded from us the same sacrifices then neither had it provided the same highs. We faced an unrelated set of hurdles. While she had fulfilled all her mother's thwarted ambitions, we had a mother who, in contrast to Tilly's passivity, was not only prepared to give everything for a cause worth fighting for but who'd also made a genuine impact on the world. Some competition that, especially for children who'd been brought up amongst such fiercely competitive parents.

Towards the end of her life, she grew confident enough to acknowledge the way she operated. She wrote in 1979 about a friend who'd complained that her husband could not tolerate weakness, even in his wife. 'I reckon,' Ruth wrote, '[that] I'm another of those male chauvinists: I cannot stand weakness either.'

She couldn't stand weakness: not in other people, not in herself. The one time in her life she had made a bad mistake it had driven her to the brink of death. We, her daughters, tied her to what had gone before. In the letters that passed between she and I can be traced the thin thread of a conversation that we had started many years before and that we never got to finish. She wrote to me asking why, when she had always taught her daughters that we could achieve anything we wanted, we still felt inadequate.

I wondered how she could even have asked, she who was the most competent and the least secure of people. And how could I explain to her that although, unusually for a woman of her generation, she had encouraged us to fulfil our potential, her choices had at the same time removed us from South Africa – the source of her heroic life's work.

We see-sawed, she and I, caught in mutual misunderstanding. Part of her wanted to see me as an equal, but another part wasn't quite convinced that I was yet a grown up. Did my demands make her impatient? Was I too weak for her as well?

When she got back from London, only weeks before she died, she told a friend that she had finally worked out that what I wanted from her was to be left alone. I didn't want that, not really. I wanted what most daughters ask of their mothers: that she should see me for who I was.

And perhaps she might one day have done that. Who knows? Her death slashed through our process. We were struggling, both of us, for an equilibrium that neither had yet fully understood. Maybe Joe had been right: maybe all I needed was for her to do for me what parents usually did, earlier in life, for their adolescents: to help me go. Somehow, because our parents were the ones to leave, those bonds of interdependence became distorted.

She lived a life that her own mother had coveted. It cost her dearly and me as well. Sometimes, it was difficult to know which of the two of us was the mother and which the child. When Julius died in London in 1980, my sisters were also out of the country and so it was I who phoned Ruth to tell her. After I'd spoken, there was a small satellite delay before I heard her disembodied voice asking, 'Should I wake Joe?' *Should she wake Joe* – I didn't understand the question. Yes, I said, wake Joe, thinking that she was perhaps asking whether I wanted to talk to him. Only after I put down the receiver did I realise what she had really wanted was permission to get Joe's comfort for the fact that her father was dead.

She needed my permission at other times as well. When she was trying to decide whether to prolong her stay in Mozambique, she wrote to me, asking me what I thought. I acted my part to perfection. I, ever the good mother, wrote back telling her that she must make the decision for herself no matter what it cost us.

It was the advice she'd wanted. Year by year, she took another leave of absence from Durham and renewed her Mozambican contract. It was only in May 1982, five years after she'd gone to Mozambique, and six months before her death, that she finally committed herself by giving in her notice to Durham.

The longer Ruth stayed in Mozambique, the more frequent did Joe's visits become. By the end he was with her permanently. They continued to fight out their political disagreements, but gradually there was an easing in the atmosphere between them. The transformation was not absolute. Ruth would still find herself barking resentfully at Joe but, at the same time, safe in her new life, she seemed finally able to acknowledge his.

As the battle for South Africa accelerated and as Joe was drawn increasingly into its forefront, my parents lived with constant danger. It seemed to suit them both. I remember how in 1981, watching them, I realised that something had been lightened. The arguing had grown almost jocular. I understood then that what had helped fuel Ruth's venom was a feeling that while she had struggled for everything she achieved, Joe's path had been much easier. She was a woman in a man's world, forced continually to prove her capabilities. Now finally she had found a home that would accept her talents, her brilliant mind, her fierce commitment, her long experience. She felt validated: she could be herself.

She was only fifty-seven when she was killed. It shouldn't have come then, the end of her life. And yet, those last few years were perhaps her best. In Mozambique, she was wanted and, at the same time, she and Joe had finally achieved a kind of equality. He was rising in importance in the ANC and had notched up a series of military successes as the ANC's Chief of Staff. She had her university work, her students, international recognition and the trust of many high up in the Mozambican government. They would never be a couple who would talk when they could shout or who would bite down on an acerbic reaction for the sake of the other, but in their own way, they had found their own version of peace.

Peace: but their enemies would not leave it that way. They had failed previously to get Joe, now they came for Ruth.

My childhood in South Africa taught me a useless lesson – that if you constantly anticipate bad things, chance will some day make your prediction come true. But it wasn't chance that killed Ruth: it was men with names and faces.

She had always, partially, expected it. The final sentence in her book about her 117 days in gaol, reads, 'When they left me in my own house at last I was convinced that it was not the end, that they would come again.' For many years, she lived her life as if they would.

The irony of it was that when she finally found another home, when finally she relaxed, that was when they came.

Part Three

Chapter Fifteen

In 1983, a year after Ruth's death, Andy and I went to visit Joe in Mozambique.

I don't know whether Andy even remembers what he thought he was getting into when we met in 1978. He knew, of course, of my background and my parents' involvement, but in '78, no matter how much my childhood dogged me, neither of us could have predicted what was to come. And yet, we quickly both accepted it as normal: the accidental glimpse of an AK47 lying at the bottom of my father's cupboard; the glance, far too cursory for us, that Joe would give his car's undercarriage before getting in and switching on; and the wall of silence that would be erected after each of my tentatively proffered questions. Andy also swiftly learned how to ditch the way we operated in London and embrace this strange new world where rhetoric and practice met.

Joe had moved again to a house somewhere in the Maputo suburbs. Without Ruth to make life seem familiar, he lived in a way I could barely comprehend. He had no office that I knew of and no set routine. Years of stealth had given him his own unique way of operating. He had no address book but used the back of his pocket-sized, disposable diary to store the most innocuous of telephone numbers – the rest he must have committed to memory. For a man who was always busy, his diary was a joke, with its empty pages, save for the occasional mention of a dentist's appointment or a time scrawled in a margin without a hint as to what it might denote. His only other piece of equipment was a set of cheap, lined notebooks, accompanied by a Heath Robinson rubber band to mark the current page, which we bought for him, in bulk, in London. In his cramped, curling, almost childish hand, he would use them for domestic lists or incomprehensibly cryptic comments. As soon as one of the books was filled, he'd throw it away and start on the next.

He lived by secrecy, it was second nature. Although he used the phone often, he never identified himself on it. Even now I can hear his characteristic long-distance words of jovial greeting, 'Hello, how are you' – the only clue he supplied to the person on the other end that they should fall into step and answer without ever mentioning Joe's name.

He had a job description – Chief of Staff of MK – which told me nothing. He would not talk about what it meant. Not that I ever asked. What I gleaned from the newspapers, or from snatches of conversation about the military operations that Joe had planned, the bombs that went off at oil refineries or army buildings, I did not discuss with him. All I could do was watch and wonder. I would drive beside him, at dusk, around Maputo and hold my tongue as he, seeing another car coming in the opposite direction, would stop, get out, meet its driver – inevitably a young, black man – in the middle of the road and talk intently, before returning, starting up again, and driving off. All without a word of explanation.

We drove a lot during those weeks of our stay. We would meet at night and Joe would take us on his rounds. We went from one household of *corporantes* to the next, always in a different order, sometimes to eat, sometimes to drink tea or alcohol or to merely chat, always to move on afterwards. I thought this ever-rotating safari was Joe's way of dealing with his aloneness, of getting easy contact that did not demand too much of him. Later I learned it had a double purpose.

I have a photograph that was taken during that year's stay. We had invited the members of Joe's circle to come and share the Stilton that we had brought from England. As the remnants of the cheese liquefied in the heat, we chatted of everyday things – of children, books and movies – and not of guns. And yet now, when I look at the picture, at the circle of people leaning casually on the clear white Mozambican marble table top, I register Klaus de Jonge who, a few years later, was arrested in South Africa for smuggling in ANC guns and who managed to run and take refuge in the Dutch embassy. There are a couple of other people as well – the man who went into South Africa to buy for Joe a vehicle big enough to carry the launching tube for a rocket-propelled grenade back into the country and another, a woman, who spent many years as a courier, travelling between Joe and his operatives inside. Staring at the photo, I reinterpret our evenings' constant movements and remember how, during Joe's casual drop ins, there was always a moment when he and one of his hosts would be talking too softly for the rest of us to hear.

There was so much I didn't understand and so much that remained unsaid. Like the time when we went together to the cemetery where Ruth was buried. It was a day when members of the ANC in Mozambique had gone to commemorate their dead. I don't know why Joe took us with him because when we got there, he made us wait while he went to speak to somebody by the cemetery's iron gates. They stood together, in a pose I knew so well, their heads bent and almost touching as urgent words passed between them. When it was over, a frowning Joe came back to the car and curtly ordered Andy and I to stay put. There was no arguing with him, he was fiercely, determinedly resolute. He went in, alone, to lay his flowers on my mother's grave, while we sat outside, and waited.

Many years later I read an account of an attempt on Joe's life. A former policeman told a journalist that they had put a bomb on Ruth's grave, planning to detonate it when Joe visited. It might have worked, except that some bright cadre had spotted the South African agent lurking in the cemetery, and arrested him.

Was that why Joe kept us out that day? Because the plot had been uncovered then?

Perhaps it was. He never told us and, true to form, I never asked. The only tangible result of the incident was that when I went to visit Ruth's grave, I went in the company, not of Joe, but of a friend of Ruth's.

I needed a guide to take me there. I had no idea where the

cemetery was, and even if I'd used a map to find it, once I got there I would have been completely lost. During her funeral in 1982 the crowds around us had obscured all the landmarks. And on that first visit back in 1983, there was nothing to indicate the spot where she was buried. There were only mounds of fine, dry, red dust, set to one side in the arid cemetery.

Thirteen years had passed before I returned to Mozambique. This time was very different for 1996 had seen a summer of ferocious, pelting rain and the cemetery was elegant and green, long avenues of dark green trees marking out each grave side aisle. I walked past mini-columned mausoleums and slabs of engraved stone to one end of the cemetery where Ruth lay. Her name was now in evidence: Ze Forjaz, her friend, had designed simple headstones to commemorate each of the ANC dead.

I found her, her name, her date of birth and of death, surrounded by the graves of ANC soldiers who had been killed in Mozambique. The dirt that covered her was now held at bay by succulents that someone had planted on every ANC grave, by tall grass seedlings that had taken root since Joe's last visit, and by the dry yellow pods of the plant that he had dug in there. I sat by her, and as I pulled out the grass, my hand kept brushing against something which had been pinned into the ground. Only when I had removed the worst of the spindly weeds did I realise what it was: an ANC flag, stiff with the buffeting of the sun and rain, whose stripes of black, green and gold had been bleached into an unfamiliar grey, blue and white. It looked all wrong but I couldn't bring myself to pull it out. When I was ready to go, I got up and turned away, leaving the flag behind.

More than a decade previously, in 1983, Mozambique had seemed so full of Ruth. Andy and I spent our days by the pool side of the faded grandeur of the Polana hotel and I kept seeing her, in my mind's eye, as she had once been, on a lounger, her face concealed behind the dark glasses that were her trademark. In England, which Ruth had long ago forsaken, her absence didn't seem so odd but in Mozambique I kept expecting to come across her. I was still struggling to come to terms with what had happened. She had gone so suddenly and so finally, and there was nothing I could do about the unfinished business that lay between us.

During that visit, Joe and I talked little of Ruth. The time for that seemed to have passed. Perhaps he was all talked out. In the year that had gone before he'd travelled often to London and, in the months immediately after her death, he had been different. He spoke about her incessantly, reconstructing their history as if he were trying to work something out. He had talked of her, not as the idealised martyr she had become to so many English anti-apartheid activists, but the real person she was to him: a feisty, competitive, brilliant, difficult woman. He talked of the good times and of the bad, dropping hints about the affairs that they had each once had, and finally of the peace that they had reached together, at the end, in Mozambique.

The one subject we never broached was the identity of her killers. We knew the kind of men they were, and the system they supported, but I, at least, had no real way of understanding what they were really like. From earliest childhood I had lived in the knowledge of a society divided between 'them' and 'us'. I could not put a face, a name, an individuality to 'them', and nor could I imagine how I would feel if that ever became a possibility.

But Ruth, and the manner of her death, lived on with us. I grew used to the shock in the faces of people who innocently asked how my mother had died, and the sympathy in the eyes of those who already knew. It became part of what I, of what we all, lived with, a constant source of friction that neither went away, nor changed.

The manner of her death arose officially in Mozambique in 1984. A high-level South African delegation had crossed the border in order to sign the Nkomati Accord, an agreement that South Africa had wrenched, with blood, from Mozambique. Amongst the visiting delegation was the then commissioner of the South African Police, Johann Coetzee, who found himself sitting beside a friend of Ruth's at one of the official banquets. When the friend demanded to know why Ruth had been killed,

Coetzee sighed and said that Ruth should not have been killed, and that her death had been a terrible mistake.

A mistake? What kind of mistake is that, when someone puts a bomb inside an envelope and someone else makes sure it is delivered? And yet that's where it lay for many years: an unknown, a mistake.

The signing of the Nkomati Accord 1984 was a moment of change for Mozambique, South Africa and for Joe. How quickly things had moved on. Only three years before, in 1981, a group of South African soldiers and mercenaries had crossed the border and driven into the Maputo suburb of Matola, attacking three ANC houses, killing twelve. The Mozambican President Samora Machel had been defiant. At a crowded rally in the centre of Maputo he thundered:

> We shall not allow our country to be transformed into a firing range. We do not permit our territory to be a transit corridor for every mob of murderers ... They say they attacked us because of our support for ANC. They want to divide us, to weaken us ... They want to come here. They want to come and murder. Let them come ... But let them be sure that the war will end in Pretoria, and that the majority will take power in Pretoria ... We are all the peoples of the world. We are millions and millions ... We will smash them one by one. Let them come. There will be nothing left of them.

Fighting talk, and yet in the end it was the Mozambicans who feared that, if they continued to support the ANC, there might be nothing left of them.

Perhaps that is one of the reasons why, the year after the Matola raid, the South Africans killed Ruth – to show the Mozambicans that they could, and that they would target anyone they chose. But they didn't stop there. They poured expertise and guns and money into Mozambique, feeding the members of the MNR who ranged the countryside, attacking at will, bringing the Mozambican economy to the brink of collapse. The Nkomati Accord was the end result, an agreement that the South Africans would stop supporting the MNR if Mozambique evicted the ANC.

And so it was that Joe was forced, once again, to relocate. It happened fast. One moment there were rumours that Samora Machel had been seen weeping in his sitting room, in the next Machel summoned ANC president Oliver Tambo to tell him that the ANC must leave. Soon afterwards, Joe was meeting with the Mozambican security minister who said, 'Even as we are talking, our army is searching your home.'

Within weeks, Joe had left. He went so hurriedly that the Mozambican government offered to store his belongings until he could send for them. And so the pictures, and the carpets, and the sheets, and cutlery and kitchen equipment that Ruth had painstakingly collected during her years in Mozambique were taken by the army into a warehouse. A year later, when a friend of Joe's went to collect them, they had almost all been looted. One piece of furniture remained, a round slab of marble resting on a makeshift stand constructed from a plough.

Joe's new house was too small for the table. He sent it to me, this last remnant of Ruth's life in Mozambique. It was so badly packed that when it arrived in London in 1985 on the day my daughter Cassie was born, although the black painted metal base was intact, its marble top was completely shattered.

By then Joe had settled in the Zambian capital of Lusaka, many miles away from the South African border. This enforced retreat had been a moment of disappointment and defeat, a time when revolutionary rhetoric was turned to dust. And yet within a year the sparks that Joe and his comrades had lit in the early eighties took flame and within five, it became obvious that the ANC would soon be able to cross officially into South Africa.

Chapter Sixteen

On 29 April 1990 my father was amongst a group of sixteen people sitting on the Boeing 737 provided by the then Zambian president, Kenneth Kaunda. The group had been together since early morning. They had met at Kaunda's state house in the Zambian capital of Lusaka, stood in silence as K.K., as he was affectionately known, said a prayer and then, exchanging a couple of nervous, off-key jokes, ate a breakfast of mealie-meal and coffee. By eleven they were at the airport and by midday their plane was in the air, taking them to a place that had been the focus of their dreams for almost three decades. They were going to South Africa, they were going home.

It was two months since the world had watched Nelson Mandela walking free. Now the plane flying towards the Limpopo, the river that separates South Africa from its northern neighbours, was carrying senior representatives of the exiled ANC into the country for its first ever formal meeting with its age-old enemy.

More that ten years before another delegation, this one made up of representatives from ZANU and ZAPU (the two Rhodesian liberation movements), had also flown out of Zambia for talks. They had headed north, to London and Lancaster House. On the day they left, ZAPU's Joshua Nkomo had followed his runway goodbye to Kenneth Kaunda with a casual, 'See you when we get back.' The legend is that Kaunda shook his head and said, no, no matter what happened in London, neither of the men would be returning, which is how they realised, at that final moment, that they had no other choice but to reach a settlement because they had irrevocably lost their Zambian base.

Things were not quite as stark for the ANC delegation. They were going, not for final negotiations, but for 'talks about talks'.

Nobody could have predicted how these would end. The then South African president F. W. de Klerk might have released their leaders and unbanned their organisations, but, with de Klerk's Nationalist Party still insisting on the need to safeguard minority (i.e. white) rights, everything was up for grabs. A few days before, in protest against a massacre in South Africa's populous Vaal triangle area, the delegation had even put off its trip.

Yet behind this apparent uncertainty lurked another reality. The course of history had changed again. It had started this time as it had in 1976, in a far away place – in Europe – with the collapse of communism. This, combined with dangerous instability in the whole of southern Africa, meant more than a mere change of scenery for the ANC. It meant that the guns and Acroflot flights and tinned corned beef and sanctuary that had sustained them throughout the long, bleak years were gone. Now the months playing footsie with the South African government were also over. In a very real sense, no matter what happened, there was no going back.

When the Boeing's pilot announced that the plane had just crossed the Limpopo, there was jubilation. The passengers crowded round the windows, staring out. It was a perfect clear blue day as they skirted over the reef area around Johannesburg. Below was laid out the patchwork country that they loved, the country for which they had fought and for which so many of their number had died. From their vantage point up high, they could see the sheer complexity of this place at the tip of Africa. They could see the white suburbs with their twinkling of swimming pools, the sprawling black townships, covered by a murky coating of smoke from a multitude of paraffin and wood fires, the long, flat roads radiating out to all corners and the bleak dirt mounds, the discarded debris of the race for South Africa's gold.

For four hours the plane kept going. The pilot called out each successive landmark to his passengers who had spent years infiltrating soldiers over this same terrain. Now they were seeing it for real. They flew south, passing over the dark red soil of the

Orange Free State, its jagged ravines broken only by thin tracks of blue water and the semi-desert of the Karoo, heading straight for Cape Town.

It was clear flying almost all the way but fifteen minutes before the plane was due to land, their vision was abruptly obscured. There was nothing to see now save for the monotonous grey of an overcast sky. The conversation, which had already grown muted, was abruptly stanched. When the pilot announced that they were about to land, each member of the delegation sat, immersed in solitary thought.

The plane taxied to a stop. The doors were opened. Still silent, the passengers filed down the stairs. It was a grey, drizzling kind of day, the kind that Cape Town does almost as well as any English city. In the place of the crowds they might have expected to greet them, they saw only a couple of bored looking flight attendants. They made their way slowly over to the terminal building. There were some TV cameras in sight, and they could hear a few 'Viva ANCs' coming from somewhere in the far distance but other than that, the place seemed utterly deserted.

But then, when an official opened one of the glass doors that led inside, they were swamped by sound. Behind barriers, stood crowds of people, cheering, shouting, singing. Each member of the delegation grinned foolishly, their uneasy silence severed. The moment they had been waiting for was finally upon them: they were home.

In the press conference that followed, the cameras zoomed in on the red socks that were to become Joe's trademark. Of all the members of the delegation, Joe was the one who fascinated. He was, in true South African style, a walking colour chart: the white whom blacks revered; the red whom whites demonised; the hero – JoeSlovo – sung like that in one lilting spurt in township streets; or the devil, Joe, reviled in white *braais* as a KGB colonel.

And now here he was in the flesh, a chubby, genial, 'teddy bear terrorist'. Journalists, who for years had not even been allowed to quote him, asked him how he felt. A consummate performer, Joe was ready with a quip. 'As I was saying twenty-seven years ago before I was so rudely interrupted . . .' he began, borrowing his words from the Irish revolutionary De Valera. He paused long enough to allow the laughter to die down, and then, his face serious, he did a quick one-two. First his personal reaction:

> '. . . for us who left by the back door and have now entered the very front doors of South Africa, it's a remarkable feeling . . .':

his conviction:

> 'We are here with our hearts filled with great hope, not for ourselves but for . . . all the people of South Africa. But we haven't come as petitioners we've come as claimants on behalf of a people who have been kept down for too long'

and, finally, he tempered his challenge with a description of how, flying into Cape Town, 'it struck us how big this land is, how beautiful it is and how much room there is for everyone'.

In London six years later, I sit and watch a video of that first press conference. I see Joe framed, first in close up and then in long shot, his broad face smiling above a gaudy blue flowered tie. As he finishes answering the first question, he looks around for the next. I see how nervously he swallows. I know that there is no need for worry, he could have answered the question that followed in his sleep.

Was he, a journalist enquired, concerned about his personal safety given that 'for many white people in South Africa you're probably their greatest single hate figure?'

The answer that Joe delivered was one I'd heard a dozen times before. If he had tailored his life around the threats generated by his involvement in the struggle, he said, then he would have given up long ago. But hopefully, he added with a smile, adequate security arrangements had been made.

*

Of course there were security precautions: the last thing the government needed was for some mad right-winger to take a pot shot at Joe. But for Joe, treading that uncertain line between the past, the present, and the future as well, the real question was: from whom did he need protecting?

After the initial talks in Cape Town, the site of action moved to the cities of Johannesburg and Pretoria. Joe followed it, his double life revving up. For his day job, government security personnel escorted him to the official talking grounds and back again. But when dusk fell, an ANC operative took over: his task, to give those protective, government eyes the slip so Joe could travel safely to a secret venue in the Johannesburg district of Berea, there to meet with members of one of the most important ANC 'underground machineries'.

An underground machinery – it's a phrase taken straight out of Joe's secretive world of danger, dlbs (dead letter boxes), fake passports and disguises – is a grandiose way, usually, of referring to a few secret operatives and their trusty duplicating machine. But in 1990 in South Africa, the group that Joe slipped out to visit was of a much higher calibre. It was one of the ANC's best-kept secrets: members of an operation, code named *Vulindlela*, which means in Zulu, 'open the road', soon referred to by its affectionate shorthand of Vula.

Vula, first mooted in 1981, was an answer to one of the ANC's biggest problems – the fact that, since 1963, its leadership had been either in prison or in exile. In the years that followed the defeats of '63, mass protest would be countered by an increasingly savage police force. Unfettered by the rules of habeas corpus or any other judicial controls, the police beheaded any nascent organisation by arresting all well-known activists. It was a simple formula and deadly effective. Waves of activists gained experience outside and then disappeared into gaol: for those left behind it was like continually having to reinvent the wheel.

Vula was the solution to this constantly created vacuum. It was a plan to have high-level ANC personnel living in secret inside the country, organising political and military resistance. Up until then, the external ANC had been engaged in what was effectively a series of hit and run actions: its soldiers, acting under external political control, would infiltrate the country, carry out their mission and then, if they were not caught, leave for more instruction. Vula aimed to change all that, for its leaders would be top cadre based inside South Africa, able to respond instantly to what was happening around them.

If Vula was to work it would have to be completely secret. Since it was widely acknowledged that the infiltration of the ANC by enemy spies had reached unmanageable proportions, the organisation's governing body, the National Executive Council, gave a mandate to the then ANC president Oliver Tambo and to Joe to run Vula without consultation.

Vula started in earnest in 1988. Mac Maharaj,[1] Siphiwe Nyanda[2] (who went by the code name of Gebhuza), Janet Love[3] and Ronnie Kasrils[4] were amongst the first of Vula's participants to set up shop inside the country. With a group of operatives from exile and some they recruited inside the country, they began to assemble their new network. Their success was astounding. Using computer-linked modems at a time before the rest of the world discovered the temptations of the Internet, Vula operatives were able to send instantaneous and detailed reports, via London, on to ANC headquarters in Lusaka.

By the time Vula closed down it had a mere three score and ten people as full timers and yet its tentacles had spread throughout the country. It had even managed to reach down into the murky cabinets of the South African government's

---

1. Mac Maharaj is now South Africa's minister of transport.
2. Siphiwe Nyanda is now a lieutenant-general and second in command of the South African National Defence Force.
3. Janet Love is now an ANC MP.
4. Ronnie Kasrils is now South Africa's deputy minister of defence.

National Intelligence Agency and pull out files on ANC personnel. And Vula had infiltrated the prisons as well: using the new communications, the gaoled Nelson Mandela was, for the first time since 1963, able to consult directly with his comrades in exile. At the same time, Vula stockpiled weapons, spiriting them away in secrecy from ANC arsenals in the front-line states.

But Vula had been planned in an era when the violent overthrow of the state seemed to be the ANC's only option. Times had changed, negotiations had started. The question was, should the Vula people dissolve their networks and come out of hiding?

The answer they were given was no. There was no cease-fire yet and the first negotiations were shot through with suspicion. De Klerk's police force and army were still intact and no one could even be sure that de Klerk himself, the man who had made the first move, was really acting in good faith. As masked gunmen peppered ANC strongholds and commuter trains with gunshots, the Vula people were told to sit tight and wait.

For them, it must have been a time of almost unbearable tension. Underground and isolated from what was happening, horrified by some of the compromises they saw their compatriots making, they felt abandoned. They needed to hit out and they did – at Joe. He bore the full brunt of their outrage. He sat in that safe apartment in Berea, engulfed by the anger of Mac Maharaj, Gebhuza and Janet Love who lambasted him for the way the negotiations were going and, in particular, for concessions they saw the ANC making over the question of indemnity for political acts.

At the beginning of the meeting, Joe protested that they were exaggerating but such was the force of their fury that, after a while he just sat, head bowed, as those with whom he'd had the very closest working relationships accused him of betraying their cause. The man who had driven Joe to the meeting said later that he had never witnessed such a harsh exchange, especially one directed at a leader of the movement. On the drive back, he said Joe sat shocked and utterly silent.

And yet it didn't take long for the spring to return to Joe's step. It was one of those rare moments of history, a turning point, not only for the opposing sides which were assessing the possibility of going down a peaceful road, but for individuals as well. In hindsight it all looks so smooth: at the time, nobody could have guessed how it might end.

It was Joe's finest moment: he survived the storm. His name, above all others, was bound up with the ANC's military struggle. He was a co-conspirator in the Rivonia Trial, the man who had tried to send a boatload of MK soldiers into the country in 1973, the man blamed for almost every armed attack in South Africa, and, above all, MK's Chief of Staff associated with the blowing up of the Sasol oil refinery in 1981. All that and he was a prominent communist and a white man to boot. And here he was in his adopted country, trekking between the centre of the negotiations and the secret underground. In that one crucial year, Joe kept his balance in these two entirely different arenas: the world of compromise and real politik, and the world of secrecy and heroism. He was buffeted by both.

When the newly released Nelson Mandela gave his first public speech one of the people to whom he paid tribute was Joe. 'I salute Joe Slovo,' was what he said. 'One of our greatest compatriots.'

The citation was an acknowledgement of one comrade to another of sacrifices made for the country they loved but it was more than that. It was a shot across de Klerk's bows. For, when he had heard that Joe was to be part of the ANC's eleven-person negotiating team, de Klerk almost backed out. To his mind, Joe was the devil incarnate. Even after he was convinced by his own side that the ANC must be allowed to pick its own delegation, de Klerk kept trying to persuade Mandela to cut Joe out.

All the time while this was going on, ANC activists were haranguing Joe for every concession granted. If he minded, Joe seemed able to override the effect of any doubts. It was as if his whole life had been in preparation for this moment. He had always carried inside that peculiar combination of lawyer and adventurer. Now he used both to keep himself afloat.

Chapter Seventeen

There were moments in 1990 when it looked as if Joe was going to sink. One such occasion began with a series of interlocking police coups: the discovery of some decoded Vula documents; the arrest of some of Vula's most important activists including Gebhuza and Mac Maharaj; and, at around the same time, the unrelated uncovering of the minutes of a local Communist Party meeting. The name of Vula, which the government labelled a communist conspiracy to overthrow South Africa by force, was suddenly on everybody's lips.

The story went like this. First two Vula activists disappeared[1] and then the police raided the house where Gebhuza was staying and arrested him. At the same time the police confiscated a set of minutes of a secret Communist Party meeting where a 'comrade Joe' had argued that, even if a cease-fire was agreed between the government and the ANC, those whose signatures were not on it would not be bound by its terms. The finger was pointed at my father, the newspapers arguing that if this is what he really said in private, then his public insistence that he would abide by any agreement reached was malevolent duplicity.

It was just what de Klerk had been searching for – the definitive proof that South Africa's arch-enemy was acting in bad faith. He sent for Nelson Mandela, demanding that Joe be chucked off the ANC delegation. How easily did the old rhetoric return: only days before the rally to relaunch the now unbanned Communist Party, the banner headlines proclaimed, *Red Plot: Joe Must Go.*

---

1. These two, code named Charles and Voyu never reappeared and are presumed dead by police hand.

The newspapers were brimming with speculation as to whether Joe could possibly survive the exposure. Journalists sought him out, trying to get a statement. But Joe was unavailable, sick in bed with flu and the only comment a spokesperson would make was that he'd answer the charges at the party rally.

As this drama unfolded, I was at Heathrow on my way to South Africa to promote my novel, *Ties of Blood*. For a moment there, it felt as if my timing couldn't have been bettered, my tour and the Communist Party launch were coincidentally in sync. All I had to do was climb on board and I would not only encounter my mother country for the first time in twenty-seven years, but I would also get to hear my father speaking in a Soweto stadium.

But it was not to be. A traffic controllers' slow-down delayed my flight, first for an innocuous three hours, then for twelve, and finally for a full twenty-four. As I sat by the telephone waiting to hear when the plane would leave, I knew I was going to miss the rally. I railed against the circumstances, and yet, somewhere in the back of my mind, the hitch felt almost appropriate: here was my ambivalence with that once familiar country externalised by BA. South Africa had fashioned my life and yet it was both remote and elusive. At the same time as I wanted to know it, I feared that it was not mine to know.

Eventually the departure time was re-set and I went back to Heathrow. But out troubles weren't over. Twelve hours later we were circling Jo'burg and listening to our exasperated pilot say that, since Jan Smuts was closed, we must go elsewhere. So it was that I touched down on South African soil, not in the city of my birth, but in a place I hardly knew, Durban.

I remembered going to Durban for a two-week break only once before. It must have been in the early sixties. We three sisters and another girl called Erica, who was the daughter of a friend of Ruth's, had been taken there by our grandparents. We all stayed in a tourist hotel somewhere on Durban's beach strip. What I remember of that time was daily trudges in the cloying, tropical heat to the water's edge; my screaming hysterically as I plummeted down a big dipper; the moment when Robyn was almost thrown through a sixth-floor window by a careless jostle; and the silence that settled on us all as the hairbrush one of us had thrown at Erica flew through the open window and landed on a woman passing far down below. That was all Durban meant to me, that, and the memory of the palm trees that I could see now, through the airport's glass exterior. An official windmilled his arms to get our attention. We were on South African soil, he announced, which meant we had to clear immigration.

I followed the line of passengers and when my turn came, I handed in my passport. In that cold, automaton manner so characteristic of white South African officialdom, the immigration officer punched my details into his computer. Because of Joe, and the rally that had just taken place, my surname was on the front of every newspaper. The man neither spoke nor looked at me as he handed back my documents. I was in, I was home.

Except was it home to me? When I gave my name to a BA official, I saw the nudge that started to my right and kept on moving, down a line of businessmen returning to their country. When one of them screwed up the courage to ask me if I was any relation to Joe, I was wrenched back into the past, back to that other time in my childhood when I had landed in the wrong airport.

'I'm a daughter,' I said, trying unnecessarily to stanch my voice's quivering. In the first intimation of the way fame had taken the place of infamy, I saw admiring interest cross my interrogator's face.

As we waited for a crew to bridge the last stretch of our journey, I stared at a bundle of freshly delivered newspapers. The front pages were full of Joe, his suit a shiny and slightly over-tight grey as he walked beside the ever-elegant Nelson Mandela and a radiant Winnie. There were wide grins on their faces and their fists were held up high in clenched salutes. In the background a mass of cheering Africans responded with their own clenched fists interspersed with a fluttering of red flags. The man who was

known by his affectionate shorthand of JS – the head of the only
Communist Party in the world whose membership was rising –
had arrived.

I bought a newspaper and read how during his speech, Joe had
answered the government charges of betrayal with a gesture: he
took out his passport and waved it in the air. On the page he was
holding open was a passport stamp, put there by one of de Klerk's
immigration officials, which proved that, at the time when Joe was
supposed to have been in South Africa betraying his promises, he'd
actually been in Zambia. The Joe who was minuted as speaking at
the meeting in South Africa was an entirely different Joe.

F.W.'s police had served him ill. Having accused Joe of something he could not possibly have done, the government now had to
drop its continuing calls to exclude him from the talks.

While Joe was bouncing back in style, I was trying to locate a
country that existed almost solely in my head. There were things
about South Africa that were so familiar: the crystal blue of
Jo'burg's clear sky; the burning reds of a sunset so abruptly
cloaked by dark night; the purple of low, sprawled jacaranda
trees in blossom; and, above all, the way, when I pulled out of
a line of traffic, the driver to my left yelled viciously, 'Who the
hell do you think you are?'

Who the hell do you think you are? It was a refrain that haunted
me. I was in South Africa to promote a novel I would never have
written if it were not for Ruth's death. The seeds of it were born
out of my grave-side realisation that if the country would not
leave me alone, then I would have to face it. But whose past was
I now facing: mine or my parents'? I was a stranger adrift in an
alien landscape, continually stunned by the things I encountered.

My publishers had booked me into the Sandton Sun, a hotel
in one of Jo'burg's most exclusive suburbs, perched above a
cavernous shopping mall. The complex was bedecked by gilt-
coloured walls and marble fittings and teeming with witless

looking white students who'd been drafted in to replace the black staff who'd all gone out on strike. I tried relocating but there wasn't another hotel room free in all the city and so I stuck it out.

One evening I accompanied Joe to a night club. He was the entertainment that evening, the red-socked communist who had come to answer questions. I sat on a plush chair, in a room full of crushed velvets, sultry purples and low lighting, sipping whisky and watching my father on stage, using charm on white suburbanites to dent their old age prejudices. When it was over and he walked off the stage and joined me, cameras flashed.

The next day I got up to find that the strike was over. I sat in the hotel's open-plan restaurant, muzak filling my cotton-wool ears, as the black waiter who'd seen my photo in the paper stopped and asked, 'Comrade, what on earth are you doing here?'

I wondered that myself when a friend drove me to our old home in Mendelssohn Road. The *veld* across the way was now crammed with low-rise suburban houses, a swimming pool occupied the space where our Wendy house had once stood, and the wire that had once separated our garden from the pavement had been knocked down, its place taken by garrison high walls. In answer to my ringing of her bell, a white woman emerged and grudgingly allowed me in.

The cliché that everything, including the driveway – the site of so many of my dramatic childhood memories – should have seemed so small was to hit me later. I could hardly take anything in. The driveway passed me by entirely. I came to, to find myself standing just inside the front door, staring at the French doors that led to a garden which was no longer familiar. It was so formal now, and bereft of the huge plane tree whose branches had once been our exclusive territory. I blinked and looked away, and my eye caught the mosaic-patterned stone floor on which I'd tumbled. And that's as far as it went. I was the most inept of witnesses. I was too conscious of the time that had elapsed since I had been there, of the woman's anxious twittering and the fact that I didn't know how I was supposed to feel in the face of a childhood that I had once assumed sealed up in this place, which was now able to come leaking out.

I parked my car by a low-rise housing block in the white district of Killarney. To one side I could see the ubiquitous mall, full of the identical brand name shops that can be found in even the smallest of South African *dorps*. On the other side, a wide, tree-lined street led to Jo'burg's imitation Oxford Road and access to the grander northern suburb shopping venues of Rosebank and Hyde Park.

I walked through the small parking lot and towards a cottage that stood to one side in the building's grounds. The purple bougainvillaea that covered its outside wall had a dusty, late summer look about it and the dark green fronds of the banana palm that peaked over the enclosed garden had been tattered by the beaks of aimless, passing birds. I put my hand through the grilled bars of the external door and rang the bell. When I got inside, I found my grandmother sitting by the round dining table, prodding apathetically at a plate of soft potatoes and grated beetroot. Seeing me, she smiled vaguely and put down her fork.

In 1985, Ruth's mother, Tilly had announced that she was going back to South Africa. She was eighty-seven years old and I could understand why she would want to swap Camden Town's unrelenting gloom for Johannesburg's blue skies. I said I thought it was a good idea. I asked her when she was planning to leave. 'In ten days' time,' she said.

I was more than eight months' pregnant then and she was going in ten days. I thought I must have misunderstood. I repeated my question.

'Ten days,' she said, her hawk eyes staring me down.

Joe was in Africa, Ruth was dead, Tilly was the only one still around. I wanted her to stay and see my baby. I asked her to delay, just for a short time. She said she wouldn't. I tried to understand: I asked her if she was going to South Africa to die. 'No,' she answered. 'I am going to live.'

With anger fuelling my abandonment, I pressed her for an explanation. Finally she produced one. She said, 'All my life, I have lived for other people. Now I want to live for myself.'

What a complex brew we all fermented. In the month before her death, Ruth had urged Tilly to start living for herself. Now, three years later, in the run-up to the birth of her first great-grandchild, Tilly was finally taking Ruth's advice. Nothing would stop her. Having made her decision she was going and fast.

And so, in 1985, I took Tilly to the airport, watching what I thought would be my last glimpse of her as she was wheeled through passport control. But I was wrong: my one-kidneyed, teetotal grandmother kept on going. She was still alive when finally I was able to visit South Africa.

In the time since I'd last seen her, stern, straight-backed, ferocious Tilly had ebbed into passivity. Getting up at my suggestion and walking to a sofa she hugged me because I hugged her. When we sat down, she said the name she had always used for me, 'Gilly', over and over again as if the repetition would remind her who I really was. She knew me and she didn't. She knew I was important to her and yet she couldn't find a way to slot me back into consciousness.

We spoke of my sisters – she recognised their names, she said, but memory of their faces seemed to be sealed up in a compartment she couldn't open. She lived only in the moment, dealt only with what was there in front of her eyes: everything else would just slip away.

I have a photograph dating from that time. Tilly's gnarled hand rests gently on the gilt frame of a picture of Ruth which someone has placed on Tilly's dining-room table. The whole thing, by some developer's eerie misjudgement, is tinted sepia brown. The photographer's skewed composition also adds to the poignancy. The image of Ruth is centre stage so that the eye is drawn to her dead elegance rather than to the badly cropped blur of Tilly's aged, but living, face. I wonder again how Tilly could ever have survived the loss of Ruth, the daughter who was her main achievement.

One year later, I was to visit Tilly in the old-age home where she'd been moved. Because she was cold, we climbed slowly up to her room to fetch a cardigan. Opening her cupboard, I found that same framed photograph of Ruth, discarded on the floor. I thought it must be a mistake and, seeing a nail above Tilly's bed waiting for a picture, I suggested that I hang Ruth there. She said I could.

Visiting her soon afterwards, I climbed the stairs and went to look. The photograph had vanished, back into the cupboard, I assume. This time, I let it lie.

Ruth had also disappeared from Tilly's memory. When I mentioned her, Tilly frowned and said, 'Oh yes, I had two children, didn't I? I know Ronnie: who's the other one?'

I told her, 'Ruth. My mother.'

'What happened to her?' Tilly asked. I hesitated, not knowing how to tell her. But there was no need for me to frame a reply. In that moment, she remembered. 'They killed her,' she said, distress taking the place of her habitual confusion, 'Oh Gilly, why did they do that?'

I held her hand, saying nothing, waiting until the one tear that streaked her soft face had gone. I was sorry for what I'd done. Old age had helped my warrior granny retreat from battle. I sat beside her and thought that my jogging of her memory had been an act of cruelty. She had forgotten for a reason, I had no right to remind her.

During that first visit, Tilly was still struggling to keep hold of her mental faculties. 'I'm befuddled and befogged,' she endlessly repeated, relishing the sound of the alliteration. I tried jogging her fiercely Stalinist synapses by talking to her of the changes in her once-beloved Soviet Union. She couldn't have been less interested.

'Joe's doing well,' I told her, thinking that news of her adored son-in-law must surely rouse her.

'Oh Joe,' she said. 'And what exactly does he do?'

'He's the general secretary of the Communist Party,' I answered.

She looked at me, half smiling and said in her acerbic voice of old, 'Not a very secure job, is it?'

Chapter Eighteen

When I met up with Joe later that evening and told him what Tilly had said, he roared with laughter. We were in Yeoville, a mainly residential district close to the centre of Johannesburg, which, although it was relatively close to Tilly's Killarney, felt completely different. Close to Johannesburg's high-rise city centre and bordering racy Hillbrow, with its street-side cafés, night clubs, sex shops and midnight spluttering of gunfire, Yeoville was, in its own way, unique. It was a path breaker with a new name – 'grey area' – used to describe its previously unheard of mix of black and white residents. It was also full of life. Within its boundaries were ordinary streets, not concrete malls, where shops and cafés and wine bars stood side by side.

Rocky Street was Yeoville's main road and it was there I went with Joe. He was a good twenty years older than most of Rocky Street's patrons, but he was moving into the status of a legend and everybody kept jostling for his attention. As we walked towards our restaurant, groups of strangers kept stopping us. For a man so easily identified, Joe's own recall of names and faces wasn't great. He'd developed a technique to deal with any possible memory lapse, an earthy, friendly all-purpose greeting which did as well for those he vaguely knew as those he'd never met. At first I thought that working on this was taking up all of his attention but soon I registered that although he replied to each salutation with a friendly, approachable hello, a smile, and a handshake if that was what was required, his gaze kept roving along the row of shopfront façades.

He found it eventually, the place he'd been seeking out. It was a narrow terraced three-storey building abutting the pavement, the premises of a bustling steak house. Joe pointed to the building. 'That's where I lived when I was a child,' he said. 'My parents had their greengrocers shop opposite but we slept there, in a flat upstairs. In the back yard,' he continued, 'is where my dog, Spotty, was buried.'

Spotty. Over a span of five decades and all that had occurred, Joe still remembered his dog's name along with the precise day – 8 April 1938 – on which Spotty had died. 1938 must have been a terrible year for the twelve-year-old Joe. It was the year he lost his mother. He wrote in his autobiography:

> I was not told of her death. I suddenly woke up in the middle of the night to find the mirror covered with a white sheet. The walk around the coffin, the hysterical wailing of women and, above all, the yellow, yellow face haunted me for years. But the shaft of horror and the shock which struck me on our return from the funeral still evokes a shudder within me. As we entered the dining room, staring at me from the mantelpiece was a large doll (a present for my sister Reina) completely wrapped in bright yellow cellophane paper. It was particularly horrifying since my mother had died in childbirth and I expected to see the still-born child in the coffin.[1]

It was a tragedy almost too traumatic for memory. Although Joe could continue to commemorate Spotty's death, he could not later recall either the day or the month when, in a Johannesburg hospital bed, his mother had died.

Is this what relocation and exile does to us all, this constant twisting with our memories? In Killarney, Tilly seemed almost wilfully trying to forget, while Joe and I were each, in our own way, bent on rediscovery. But in our search for the past, Joe and I travelled separately. I haunted the green suburbs and the house in Mendelssohn Road, where I'd spent my first twelve years. Though Joe's memories of that place must have been much more acute than mine – he had, after all, lived there longer –

---

1. Joe Slovo, *Slovo: The Unfinished Autobiography*, op cit., p. 16.

when he wanted to reinvoke his past, he went to Yeoville.

I watched the intensity with which he stared at the Rocky Street building. I saw the pleasure with which he shared a few memories, and I realised that to Joe, born as he was in Lithuania, separated from his father between the ages of two and nine, Rocky Street was the one remaining vestige of his early life. But it was more than that as well. In Rocky Street, for what must have seemed like a fleeting moment, the young Joe had experienced family life, sleeping under the same roof as his mother, his father, his two sisters and his dog.

His mother's death shattered all that. Unable to cope, Joe's father, Wulfus, disappeared leaving Joe in the charge of his eldest sister, Sonya, and the toddler, Reina, in an orphanage. Wulfus did eventually return but it wasn't long before he remarried a stepmother that the resentful, and now financially independent, Joe never got to know.

By 1990, Rocky Street was almost the last remaining landmark of Joe's childhood. Sher's boarding house in Doorn-fontein where, for a time after the loss of their family green-grocer's, Joe and Wulfus had shared an attic bedroom, had long been demolished. Yet even if Sher's still existed, I cannot imagine that Joe, carrying as he did such painful memories of the father with whom he could never really communicate, would ever point to it as home.

Joe did, of course, have another, entirely different home – his birthplace where he'd spent his first nine years. When we were growing up, Joe never talked to us about the village of Obelei, close to the Lithuanian capital of Vilnius. And yet he had not forgotten it and he never stopped trying to go back. In 1963, on his way out of the country to organise the ANC's nascent military wing, he had asked permission of his comrades to take a pilgrim's journey into Lithuania. He didn't manage it. The news of the Rivonia arrests broke too radically into his schedule. He would never have found it anyway: by adulthood he had forgotten the village's Lithuanian name and its exact location.

But he didn't give up. He tried again in 1968 when he was

in the Soviet Union. This time he'd found the village on the map and his Russian hosts had agreed to take him there. At the last minute, however, they cancelled the trip. Only after he had returned to London and was lying in bed on the morning that I brought the news of the invasion of Czechoslovakia, did he realise that it was probably troop movements on the border which had deprived him of his nostalgic journey home.

In 1981, Joe finally made it back to Obelei. Walking round the village, he remembered the smell of apple blossom and of the undergrowth where he used to scratch for wild berries, the one brick building in a sea of wooden constructions, the hill down which he used to sledge and a broken window on an outhouse which, forty-five years after he had left it, helped him identify his home. But there was no one there to help him remember more. He wrote:

> We strolled around the back paths chatting occasionally to old people ... trying to find someone who remembered the Slovo family and us as children. The old ladies consulted even older sisters, but we continued to draw a blank. 'The synagogue?' 'They burnt it to the ground.' 'The ritual bath house?' 'That also.' 'The people, are there any Jews?' 'Those that didn't run away were all slaughtered, even children.'[2]

In 1936, when Joe, his mother and his elder sister had made the journey south, they'd left behind a huge extended family. By his return, not one single member of the Slovo clan could be found in Obelei. Joe's father, Wulfus, had been one of six: he and one brother were the only ones to survive the holocaust. The rest, along with their six children, Joe's grandfather, David, David's three siblings, and most of their children, were slaughtered by their Lithuanian neighbours who continued to wear their clothes long after their deaths.

In that first visit to Obelei, Joe did manage to locate two

---

2. Ibid p. 6.

second cousins who had not been killed because, when war broke out, they were already on their way to Moscow. For thirty excited minutes, at a railway station, they talked in a mixture of his English and their Yiddish – Joe's mother tongue which he could barely remember.

So much change, so much loss. Is it this combination of circumstances that gave Joe his peculiar mix of flexibility, optimism and the ability to make difficult decisions? His belief in communism came early to him via an inspirational Irish teacher who had made him question the way the world was organised; an exiled community whose thoughts of home in the Baltic states were mixed with memories of programs and to whom the 1917 Russian revolution signalled a release from tsarist oppression; and a poor person's experience of the injustice of poverty. But was it also that communism offered to Joe a world view which was better than the one from which he'd sprung, that gave a meaning to his life that his early childhood had so cruelly denied?

Whatever it was, it was no wonder that Rocky Street, with its old buildings and its landmarks intact was the place Joe talked about as home, the place where, with his new family, he eventually chose to settle. Jo'burg was his town, and he was back.

A friend took me on a visit to Alexandria. Situated in a damp valley within spitting distance of wealthy Sandton, Alexandria is a township which sprung up in the days of apartheid to service the needs of the white suburb. I was shown around by an ANC women's group, taken to a community hall to watch a branch meeting, and then, when that was over, we travelled deeper into the township.

I had been born in South Africa. I was brought up knowing of its terrible inequalities, I'd gone to scores of meetings and watched dozens of documentaries about apartheid, but I was still unprepared for what I saw. It was, I guess, the fine graduations in the scale of deprivation which so appalled me. We moved away from the best of Alexandria's housing, small brick buildings complete with bathrooms and electricity, past smaller dwellings, lit only by paraffin, and then down into a valley of mud and slime. At its very bottom, beside a few cold water taps and some mobile bucket-based toilets which were the only sanitation, stood tin shacks in which thousands of people dwelt.

From the outside the shacks looked rudimentary. Inside they were unimaginable. Staring at the shell of one which had been destroyed by an accidentally overturned paraffin light that previous night, killing both parents of a young baby who'd received third-degree burns, I saw, finally, the real desolation of ordinary black South African life.

Back home, Joe dropped round again. He was ebullient – as he often was during those days of the negotiations – almost intoxicated by the high stakes, and the high risks, that they were taking. He told me then that he had proposed that the ANC unilaterally suspend their armed struggle.

I was stunned. No matter that the armed struggle, as it was grandiosely known, had never come anywhere near a full-scale war: it, through the ANC's army, MK, was nevertheless the stuff of contemporary South African legend, a psychological insurance policy, at least, against the terrible might of the South African state. And now, with the negotiations still at a preliminary stage, with the government making war rather than peace talk, with the escalation of armed attacks on ANC strongholds, Joe was proposing that they close down MK.

Still enmeshed in the horror of what I had seen that day, I argued with Joe. 'How could you?' I asked shrilly.

He didn't seem to mind. Happily, positively, self-confidently, he argued back.

Now in hindsight, I watch us in a suburban Johannesburg sitting room, engaging in a sparring match that was so familiar. Joe was Joe, and me? I had taken on Ruth's role of the sceptic who interrogated Joe's every move, who wondered whether he really knew what he was doing, who saw him as a party hack. And yet, at the same time, I know that the questions I asked must have been going through his mind as well. Alexandria was a first for me but not for Joe. He knew only too well the squalor of everyday South African life.

His passion was to make it better but the reality he was dealing with was far more complex even than the years of exile he'd experienced. He knew that if the ANC didn't make concessions, the violence that was already being unleashed throughout the country might escalate beyond the point of no return, but if they made too many, they might never be able to find their way back.

He was moving with lightning speed in those days, juggling these unknowns. And me? I was far behind. I took no notice of what he'd often said, that what the ANC had achieved was not an armed struggle but armed propaganda. MK, Joe would say, never had possessed the fire power to win a full-scale war: its purpose was to show Africans that they didn't have to be victims but could contest and fight. I hadn't taken that in: I was starry eyed. Joe was different: mythologised in MK songs, the beloved white chief of staff of a mainly black army, his strength as a politician was his peculiar combination of conviction and flexibility.

His strength as a politician – the legacy of our family's past still lived on in me. Within the four walls of our house, Ruth was the star, the difficult brainy one. In contrast to her, Joe was jovial and easygoing, a good-time man, witty and cheerful and slightly flabby. While Ruth's name was bandied about in the international arena, the place where Joe had made his mark was far away, amongst young fighters in the training camps, or in screamingly derogatory headlines in the South African press, far away from us and our experience.

No wonder I had never really got to know the other side of my father, the strategic thinker. While white South Africa was getting over its surprise at finding that this red, this enemy, was human, I was discovering that Joe was not the supposed klutz of my childhood, but a master politician.

Joe showed his mettle at a time when it was most needed. He

did what many would find supremely difficult – he turned away from the illicit, the secretive, the dangerous, out into the open. Two years on, when the negotiations seemed to have become bogged down in a place of no return, when it looked like the country might soon rapidly descend into a bloody civil war, it was Joe who, to a chorus of criticism from his own side, proposed the 'sunset clauses' which broke the deadlock and opened the way for South Africa's first democratic elections.[3]

With the sunset clauses came Joe's exoneration by the white South African establishment which had always condemned him. I took it all in my stride, but looking back I think of how quickly we can grow accustomed to changes which previously seemed unthinkable. It didn't take long, certainly, for me to get used to the special regard, the love even, that black South Africans had for Joe. Walking with him and his neurotic dog Simba in the old-style Afrikaner territory of the Orange Free State, I was touched, but unsurprised, when farm workers driving past on the top of an open lorry saw my father, clenched their upheld fists, and called out, 'Papa Joe'. But the change was more dramatic than that. Now ordinary white people who'd grown up thinking of Joe as a kind of bogeyman whose name was used to frighten naughty kids, also started jostling for his hand.

I should have known that it was coming. I should have remembered how in 1990, after that night when Joe and I had shared a meal in Yeoville, he drove me back to my hotel, or at least he tried to. He was in his old town, Johannesburg, which he had known since a child. Logic dictated to him, therefore, that he didn't need a street map. Never mind that it was almost thirty years since he'd last been here, he would find his way.

We got lost, mind bogglingly, waywardly lost. It was nearly

---

3. The sunset clauses gave guarantees to the mainly Afrikaans government employees that they would not lose their jobs after South Africa's first democratic election.

midnight and we were probably half-way to Pretoria but, map-less, we had no option but to keep on going. Twenty minutes later, we came across a petrol station. When we drew up and asked the way to Sandton, the grinning black petrol attendant pointed us back the way we'd come. We did a u-turn and we were about to pull out into the road when we crossed with another car. Its driver was a grey-haired white man, in a brown Terylene suit. Having sent a casual glance in our direction he stopped his car, his window close to Joe's. Slowly he unwound it and then, in a thick Afrikaans accent, said, 'Did anybody ever tell you that you bear the most remarkable resemblance to Joe Slovo?'

I sat beside Joe, willing him to say something innocuous and drive off. He grinned and answered, 'That's because I am Joe Slovo.'

I saw a look of amazement cross the white man's face and something else which I took for anger. I was wrong. The man stuck one broad hand out, and shaking Joe's said, 'Welcome back.'

Chapter Nineteen

His long years of exile over, Joe was on an almost permanent high. The movement to which he'd dedicated his life was on the point of victory. He was constantly in motion, rushing between the home he shared with his second wife, Helena Dolny and her two children (situated in the heart of Yeoville), and the conference rooms half-way along the road to Pretoria where the final political settlement was being hammered out. In between he could be found in Shell House, the ANC's high-rise offices in the centre of Johannesburg. He went there for meetings, to write his speeches, to pick up his expenses and to talk to the press.

He was there in July 1991, being interviewed by a French journalist. When the pleasantries were over, the journalist asked about the ANC's legendary inefficiency. Exaggerated, Joe breezily assured her, and their talk move into other territory.

Joe could be frustratingly tight-lipped – especially, I suspect, with his daughters – but given the right moment, and the right questions, he would loosen up, ricocheting sharp analysis off the back of wry jokes. That day in July, he was in an expansive mood. It was gone six by the time they finished. Leading the way to the door, Joe turned the handle. Nothing happened. Despite his earlier insistence on his organisation's competence, some passing comrade had accidentally locked them in. Joe hammered down on wood but nobody came. He tried the phone but he couldn't even get an outside line. Everybody, including the switchboard operator, had gone home.

Joe was fit, and his daily life had been the opposite of sedate. No barred door was going to faze him. He climbed up on a chair, used both hands to grip a high panel, levered himself up, squeezed his bulk through the small open space above the door, and out on to the other side. On the way down, he lost his balance and fell.

In a mid-July phone call, a slightly shamefaced Joe told me about his cracked rib, the result of this act of hubris. By early August he let slip the fact that his rib was taking an unusually long time to mend, and that, just to be safe, his doctor was doing tests. I could hear an uncharacteristic tightness in his voice. I thought the worst but when I tried to question him, he got angry and I backed off. I put down the phone, thinking he was right, that my childhood left me too easily expecting disaster. Helena was away from South Africa – perhaps Joe was merely missing her.

It took until mid-August before he was ready to tell his daughters the truth. He had multiple myeloma, one of the least common of the bone-marrow cancers. It was a painful debilitating disease, invariably fatal which hit the over sixty-fives. Joe was 65. He had been given two and a half years to live.

The terrible irony of it: on the brink of attaining an unthinkable goal, Joe's body had betrayed him.

I was away from home, sitting on a beach in Portugal, worrying. On 17 August, when I phoned to speak to Joe on this, the ninth anniversary of Ruth's death, we didn't even mention my mother. Joe was on his way to hospital for a blood transfusion and he was so weary that his voice was almost without expression.

Soon afterwards, Shawn and I flew out to see him. He was pale and drawn and thinner than I have ever seen him. His prognosis meant he didn't even know whether he would live to see South Africa's first-ever democratic elections. He didn't talk about it, but then he hardly talked at all. Pummelled by an almost lethal cocktail of noxious chemicals which were supposed to frustrate the cancer, he seemed to have shut himself inside a tight membrane which contained his pain. When he could he went to work: when he couldn't he sat, silent, stoic, unreachable.

One day, upset by the gulf that had opened up between myself and my father, I phoned theatre director Barney Simon for help.

What I got was one of Barney's beautifully folded morality tales which centred on his favourite poem by Rainer Maria Rilke titled *Orpheus, Eurydike, Hermes*. Either Barney kept the poem waiting by the telephone or else he knew it by heart. He quoted some of it to me:

> But now she walked beside the graceful god,
> her steps constricted by the trailing graveclothes,
> uncertain, gentle and without impatience.
> She was deep within herself, like a woman heavy
> with child, and did not see the man in front
> or the path ascending steeply into life.
> Deep within herself. Being dead
> fulfilled her beyond fulfillment. Like a fruit
> suffused with its own mystery and sweetness,
> she was filled with her vast death, which was so new,
> she could not understand that it had happened.

His recitation over, Barney began to talk. I knew already how, when Barney's measured voice revved up, there was no stopping it. I listened, trying to find my way through his complex, enigmatic, aggravating prose. It was difficult, at first, to work out what he was saying but finally, at the point when I'd become convinced that I'd definitely lost the plot, Barney cut to the chase. Which was that Joe, like Euridice, was 'pregnant' with his own impending death.

Perhaps Barney was right: perhaps Joe's remoteness came from his preoccupation with his mortality. Perhaps I was just enmeshed in childhood patterns when I assumed he didn't want me there either as witness to his suffering or as the source of demands he couldn't satisfy. Yet I watched the way he and Helena moved together into this most demanding of his life's phases and I found that I didn't know how to be. No matter how much I argued with myself, I felt as if I'd been cast outside.

But when the chemotherapy was over, those feelings also went. My father had returned to his skin. He continued delving away at a political settlement that would have tried a much younger and healthier man. He relished the pressure, pushing himself to prove he could still hack it, Once again, his voice, when we spoke, was warm, and once again, he used our calls to experiment with a batch of quips. These were new ones, designed to fend off unwelcome enquiries about his state of health. He came up with a succession of one liners like, 'life is a terminal disease', or 'I knew I was in big trouble when the doctor told me it was fine for me to carry on smoking'. He never said out loud that he had beaten the cancer – his doctors had made it clear that this was not really possible. But his test results were favourable (or, as he put it, dragging out his all-time favourite adjective, 'remarkable'): the flesh had returned to his face, the depth to his voice.

Chapter Twenty

Because Joe and I continued to live in separate countries, my memories of him then are fragmented, each one distinct from the one that came before. There's the time, for example, when I watched him walking down a dusty track in the vast desolation of an Orange Free State plateau. I close my eyes and conjure up the scene. His turquoise t-shirt looks brilliantly bright against the backdrop of a huge expanse of thunderous, charcoal-grey sky as he walks doggedly forward, a stick on one side, his cocker spaniel, Simba, on the other. He's heading for a set of craggy rocks, up which he will scramble in defiance of the encroaching brittleness of his bones.

His voice comes back to me, as well, over those years. His voice telling me that he'd been walking to his seat on a platform at an ANC rally when his foot had fallen through a gap in the hastily erected wooden structure. 'The bad news is that I twisted my ankle,' he says, 'the good, that I didn't break any bones.' It was to become a constant refrain: my father, whose eyes lost focus if you tried anything even vaguely technical on him, had retained his consultants' description of how, as time went on, his bones would become more fragile.

Not yet however: in 1993 when we took our break, Joe seemed fighting fit. He stood by the side of a muddy reservoir, and hurled a stick into the water laughing at the spectacle of poor, foolish Simba diving in and swimming ferociously past the object of his desire. Simba was Joe's dog. Rescued by Helena from a street trader who was casually mistreating him, Simba would growl at any kid who had the temerity to try and climb on to his loved one's lap. And if it's true that owners choose their pets to complement them, then Joe's form of a complement was contrast. While Joe was phlegmatic, Simba was excitable:

Simba's habitual neurosis becoming even more marked in the face of Joe's unending calm. During our four-hour drive from Johannesburg to our Free State hotel, I'd had to endure Simba's relentless digging of his nails into my leg as he stood on me, his head poking through a quarter open window, barking ferociously at the carload of bodyguards in front.

The bodyguards, all former MK combatants, were a new addition. They were there not by any choice of Joe's. Long ago he'd produced the theory that a bevy of muscled men with their pre-set routines were a gift to any potential assassin and he used this to justify his aversion to being guarded. Who knows whether he actually believed this, or whether he merely invented the argument because guards would have cramped his roving style, but he repeated it often enough to drown out the most insistent of his comrades' concerns.

But in 1993, a new 'Slovo Plot' had hit the front pages. Same headline, different story: this plot was aimed at Joe. In the aftermath of Communist Party general secretary Chris Hani's assassination, a group of right-wingers had set in motion a plan to shoot Joe from a nearby water tower. The plan was so tangible and provoked so much publicity, that the ANC decided it could no longer pander to Joe's prejudice. Which is how he ended up with his oddball unit of wiry black ex-MK soldiers, none of whom possessed a gun permit. Not that Joe had one either. To get him into South Africa and around the negotiating table, the government had granted him temporary indemnity from the old charges of murder, sabotage and terrorism. But then, in a country where suburban whites are amongst the most heavily armed in the world, and despite tangible evidence of a death plot against Joe, the police had used the pending charges to refuse him a firearm licence.

Not that his bodyguards were unarmed – they merely used shoulder-holsters to conceal their guns. The bodyguards were paid by the ANC to look after Joe but after the escort car had delivered us to our hotel and was ready to make its return trip, it came back to me how sharply political change was jostling with the past: one of the things the men needed before setting out was a letter of accreditation from Joe because the last time they'd made the trip back alone they'd been arrested by policemen who refused to believe that these three scruffy black men were legally in possession of a hire car.

That day, as we laughed at Simba's foolishness, we were in an empty landscape without any need for guards. While Cassie searched for another stick to throw to the dog, Joe talked about his recent visit to China. It was a first for him and he was brimming over with an almost boyish enthusiasm as he described the Chinese government's new market reforms. As I listened, it seemed to me that Joe was coming to terms with the failure of his once-beloved Soviet communism. But at the same time, I was preoccupied with memories of how, long ago, I'd been witness to a savage argument between Joe and Ruth. While he pushed the Soviet line, she heaped praise on the way that China, instead of opting for huge Soviet-style state factories and farms, advocated the development of small, locally based technologies. Ferociously they batted example and counter-example back and forth between them, neither willing to concede an inch. It was an argument that ran for weeks, months even, without resolution in sight. I guess there was no resolution to be had. History would prove that they were each, in their own way, wrong.

But that day on the reservoir, what I was registering was the way one of Joe's closest comrades described him. 'Joe's strength as a politician,' Mac Maharaj told me, 'was that if he hit a new idea, it didn't matter where it came from, or if it meant a 180 degree switch in his ideas, he would do it. But,' Mac continued, 'that was also what was so annoying about Joe the person: after he'd made the switch, he would never own up to it.'

I knew what Mac meant: all those years when Joe and Ruth had argued about Soviet communism, and now he'd grasped hold of a rationale similar to Ruth's and was happily using it against me in her stead.

By the time we'd let go of the 'China question', the sky was almost pitch dark. Walking fast, we made our way back in time for supper. In the small ranch-like hotel where we were staying a handful of guests ate at communal tables. Round most of them sat jolly family groups, swapping life stories. Not so for us. Our party comprised Joe, two bodyguards, Andy, me, our daughter Cassie, and two strangers who'd been allocated the task of breaking up the hegemony of our table. They were a fully bonded, gymned up white couple. He worked the diamond mines of Botswana, she styled the mine management's wives' hair, and they spent their Free State holidays getting away from it all, either bicycling through the mountains or sunbathing in matching swimwear.

Were they the only people in South Africa who didn't know who Joe was? Perhaps they were or perhaps they were deliberately playing dumb. What is clear is that our party perplexed them. There was Joe using his rare time off to subside into silence, Cassie chatting vivaciously, Andy and me, somewhere in between, and two mysterious and monosyllabic young black men who, occupying one whole side of the large, rectangular table, opted out of the general introductions. But the new South Africa was on its way. The woman bravely turned to the closest bodyguard and asked his name, but when he mumbled the name his parents had given to him, rather than the MK alias he'd long ago adopted, Cassie, yet to be inducted into the mysteries of nomenclature called out, 'You're not David!' The inexplicable silence that followed us through two meals brought home to me that question that continually dogged me: our world and theirs were so different, could there ever be a meeting place between the two?

Eventually help arrived in the form of two newcomers who, recognising Joe, asked whether they could swap places with our unhappy couple. It was soon arranged and for the first time, with the new arrivals much more at ease with us, there was animated conversation around our table. I couldn't concentrate on it. I was too conscious of the way our former companions sat, relaxed at their new table, and even the dark shadows of the flickering candlelight could not conceal their tangible relief at their escape.

★

I went back to South Africa one year later, in 1994. Joe's cancer had passed its two and a half year sell-by date by then and he was still going strong. I hadn't seen him for some time but before I left, I caught a glimpse of him on television.

I was sitting on my sofa in London, watching the TV news as a South African item, common in those days of the run-up to the election, came on. It started, as they so often did, with a funeral procession. Over a background of a white-robed priest walking in front of a coffin carried by t-shirted young men, solemn drum beats pacing them out, I heard, 'The day began the way it ended, with death dominating the lives of the people in Kathlehong.' At that time Kathlehong township was, as the reporter described it, 'South Africa's most violent square mile'. Since political violence was running out of control during those last days of a dying regime, that was saying something.

I watched as the reporter explained that the funeral was for a young leader of a local defence unit set up to combat attacks on the ANC community which the police did nothing to prevent. The first picture cut to the next. A group of men dressed in camouflage battle-dress marched in that stiff-legged gait of the MK camps, the camera focused on their heavy bok boots stamping on the dusty earth. When these para-soldiers had passed by, their place on the screen was taken by a group of women sweeping work-callused hands over their faces to mask their tears.

Another change of picture: this time it cut to Joe and Cyril Ramaphosa walking in the centre of a small group of Kathlehong residents. I registered his bodyguards close by, and was thinking vaguely that Cassie would be sorry to have missed seeing her favourite of them on TV, when there was an off-camera shout. The bodyguard's head whipped round. I was frozen as I watched him pulling out a gun. I knew that I should phone my sisters and tell them what was happening on our screens but there wasn't time. It went so quickly. There were the sounds of gunshot, pictures of bodyguards wrapping themselves physically around Joe, of journalists scattering, of young men doing impressively athletic dives for cover, and of a woman, gripping on to her white-frocked child, running for her life.

The shots had come from a hostel 300 yards away which housed members of Inkatha – Chief Buthelezi's organisation – which was implacably and violently opposed to the ANC. It was all over very quickly. I saw a man being carried, face up, by a running group of Kathlehong residents. His chest was a mass of sticky blood. Another followed shortly afterwards. They held him by his arms and legs in that crab-like, face-down posture that told me he, at least, was still alive. He was lucky. Two people, one of them a journalist, Abdul Shariff, who'd been standing next to Joe, died that day.

The news broadcast had skipped through time, moving to Joe and Cyril who were now a mile away, busy talking to journalists and haranguing a white policeman. 'That's why we're here,' Joe said, breathing heavily from his run, 'because this kind of thing has been going on and hundreds of people have been killed.'

That was it: item over – on to the next.

I phoned my sisters to tell them what I'd seen and then I picked up the receiver and called Johannesburg. The incident had taken place earlier that day and Joe was already home. He seemed ebullient, insisting jovially that nothing had really happened. It had been so quick, he said, there was no time to feel afraid, and besides, it was all over now. He set the tone for my reaction. I acted as nonchalantly as he, chatted for a while and then hung up.

Soon afterwards, in Australia, a man with a fake gun made an 'attack' on Prince Charles. I watched the footage of the prince's bodyguard shouldering him to the floor. It was an incident the news editors savoured, repeating it endlessly and in slow motion for days afterwards. I, who normally would not have given this non-event more than a second glance, was spellbound, a couch potato who clicked through successive programmes so I could rewatch the play. Only after I had witnessed this burlesque a half a dozen times did I realise that my interest sprang from shock.

I needed to hear the commentator's appalled reactions at the closeness of the encounter to validate those feelings in myself, those fears that could not be discussed with Joe.

The next time I saw Joe in the flesh there was little time for conversation. It was a few weeks before the April elections and I was busy, travelling with ANC personnel who moved at terrifying speed around the country. It was exhilarating stuff, going to rural areas with former guerrillas, soon to be cabinet members, who were canvassing the opinions of their future constituents.

But Joe was much harder to pin down than I. He was frantically preoccupied in tying up the last threads of a bitterly contested settlement, throwing water over a series of conflicts which threatened to ignite an already tense country, and sitting in on unending strategy meetings. There was a fraught feel to a country which seemed poised on the brink of an abyss. In the former 'homeland' of Bophuthatswana, apartheid's ruler, Chief Mangope, had provoked a series of escalating strikes by refusing to allow either voter education or election meetings; Inkatha's Gatsha Buthelezi had joined the white right under conservative leader Constand Viljoen, and none of them would say whether their parties would be standing in the elections. Throughout the country, violence was escalating.

In the midst of all this, the plans Joe and I made to spend time together were constantly put off. We had a last-minute date to go electioneering together, but instead Joe went to Bophu-thatswana which was on the verge of total collapse. The negotiations that he was involved in there took three days and three nights. My weekend had been spent in sporadic conversa-tions with Joe, who borrowed a stranger's mobile phone to keep delaying the time of our meeting. It went on for so long that I was convinced I would fly out without us saying goodbye in person. But in the early hours of the Sunday when I was due to leave, the negotiations ended. He flew home, snatched a few hours sleep and then phoned me to come over.

He had said he would drive me to the airport but I watched him dumping the bodyguards, telling them that he was staying in all day. As soon as they had gone, he led me to his garage and got in his car. He was completely exhausted but when I protested that this was dangerous, he said he was tired of being constantly surrounded.

He drove us to Bezuidenhout Park, a small grass-covered area where he would go, when he had time, to watch Simba running berserk with unaccustomed freedom. I'd been there with them before, but always in the company of Joe's guard and always I had been conscious of how much attention we'd attracted. This time, without four fit young black men to lace around the physical space of an ageing white one, no one took the slightest bit of notice of us. We chatted, inconsequently at first, of what had happened in the last few days.

And then Joe changed the subject. As a mud-spattered Simba weaved in and out of our legs, Joe said that he was feeling ill. He added that he was due to have a set of routine cancer scans and that he wouldn't be at all surprised if the results were bad. I reacted with a knee-jerk. He was sixty-eight, I thought, and he had been awake almost continually for fifty-six hours. I, who had for so long been frustrated by his refusal to broach the subject of his health, was doing an about turn. I looked at him and laughed off his concern: I told him that if I'd had as little sleep as him, I would also be feeling extremely ill.

I believed what I was saying and I thought it was what he wanted to hear. He seemed to: he nodded and became less pessimistic.

Now I look back and regret the words I used. It was so unlike Joe to volunteer personal information: I should have accepted this faint hint of vulnerability for what it was, and welcomed it. Instead, in laughing off his fears, I deprived myself of an opportunity that later I would crave. Only later was I to know that I had closed the door on his one attempt to share with me what he'd really been feeling. Only then did I stop and question myself as to why I'd cut him off. Was it, I thought, because I needed to stop my mysterious, dashing, all-powerful father from showing me that he was only human? Or was it something other, that although I wanted the truth, I wanted it on my own terms, and in my own time scale?

We dropped Simba off at Joe's home and then it was time for me to leave. Joe drove us to the airport, stopping on the way for petrol. He asked me to get the ANC petrol card from the glove compartment. It wasn't there: I found instead a small hand pistol. I reacted instantaneously: I pushed the glove compartment shut and pulled money from my purse.

When the petrol attendant had gone, I asked Joe whose gun it was. He shrugged, irritated at the question and said it must belong to one of the bodyguards who'd been stupid to leave it in the car. He pulled out and kept driving and, in the twenty minutes it took to get us to Jan Smuts, I couldn't stop my eyes from straying constantly towards that small, slim door.

After check-in there was time for us to snatch a few minutes together. We sat in the airport's dingy buffet, our cups of stewed tea resting on shabby linoleum tables. Looking back I can hardly believe how far we'd moved from discussing the state of Joe's health: what we talked about, because I was the one who steered us that way, was his political future.

He played along with me, constructing fantasies of what he might want to be in the new government. Ombudsman, he said surprisingly, or something to do with justice. Another uncharacteristic moment: my reticent father actually talking about his future. I realised that I hadn't yet caught up with him, nor with his South Africa. In my mind, his destined end had been a violent death devised by implacable enemies. It felt almost inconceivable that he should, one day, supplant those same men and end up as a minister sitting in the high-backed chairs that they had once ordered for themselves.

Chapter Twenty-One

I sat, with Andy and Cassie, on the hard, wooden airport bench, listening to the sound of a woman wiping a rag over the surface of her serving hatch. Apart from her, and the occasional blue overalled workman who would mop desultorily at a section of the grey tile floor before vanishing through an unmarked door, we were alone.

It hadn't been like this when we'd first arrived. We'd come out of customs to find the faded interior of Cape Town's international arrivals hall ringing with affectionate greetings and the sound of luggage being passed from trolleys into car boots. But soon afterwards our fellow passengers were all siphoned off and we were left alone. We sat, our garish suitcases piled precariously beside us, staring out at the unrelenting grey and at a line of taxis that, without an address to give them, we could not take.

There was no Joe, this time, to meet us. He'd said he wouldn't be there, but with Joe, you never could tell. In the years after Ruth's death, his movements had been unfathomable even, it appeared, to him. One minute he was coming to London, the next, the trip had been indefinitely put off. And it worked the other way as well. On our visits down south, all three sisters had become accustomed, after we'd made our travel plans, to have Joe tell us that he might not be able to fetch us from the airport. On every one of these occasions he had turned up – his early warning disclaimer produced, perhaps, to save us from possible disappointment.

Things had changed dramatically. Joe had made his final transformation, reaching the end of a career which had begun in what they called 'terrorism' and ended with Nelson Mandela proclaiming him the new South Africa's minister of housing. He managed the change brilliantly, using that combination of careful planning and flamboyant inspiration with which he'd once blown up oil refineries to woo industry and bankers into the slow business of housing the poor. White South Africa lapped it up: they took him to their hearts, this genial communist. Once he'd been their arch-enemy, now he was, quite simply, theirs.

Shimmering moments of the days since I had last seen him, bitter-sweet in the variation of their texture, come back to me – a newsreader's description of Joe dancing on the night of the election victory, the sight of Joe on TV in an expensive charcoal-grey suit walking to his seat at Mandela's inauguration, his jolly voice retelling the Fidel Castro joke he had used to break the ice at his first meeting with his ministerial staff and . . . And the moment when he told me that what he had predicted had come true. A set of medical tests showed that his remission was over. Hearing that, my upset was tinged by a sense of relief that Andy and I had already decided on an extended stay in South Africa. At least this time I would not be observing Joe's deterioration long distance.

In August a mortally ill Joe, suffering badly from a new round of chemotherapy, had gone with Helena to Italy. He was due back the day after our arrival, 1,000 miles away in Johannesburg.

We were to camp out in his ministerial house in Cape Town while we looked for a place to rent. In the weeks that preceded our arrival, I'd been on drip fax to his office, working out how we could get access to the house inside the presidential compound, enclosed as it was by high fences and armed policemen. The driver will have to pass you through, Joe's secretary (the first in his long career) told me – which is why, that early morning, we sat waiting.

I looked at my watch. An hour and a half had passed since we had landed. It was eight, if I phoned the ministry now there might be someone in. I got up.

At that moment I saw a red three series BMW saloon pulling up outside. I watched as a lean man, his muscular body enclosed in a fawn suit, stepped out of the car and, as if he had all the time in the world, ambled over. He was on a collision course with me but when he was a foot away, he stopped. 'Are you Gillian?' I said yes.

In the thick, accented English of a man who was only comfortable in his native tongue of Afrikaans, he proffered his name – Deon – and his job description, a member of the VIP protection squad who'd been allocated to Joe. He didn't smile. He said something, instead, about bad traffic that sounded more like an amateur radio report than an apology. 'I will drive you to the minister's house,' he said, making it sound like the stiffest of endurance tests.

We rolled our trolley out and heaved our suitcases into the boot, while he used distance to indicate that help was beneath his station. We managed without him, heaving what wouldn't go in the boot on the back seat. Then we were off.

The year before, I'd learned something about that peculiar mix of enforced intimacy and necessary distance that springs up between the guarded and the guards. But Joe's former companions had all been ANC members, friendly and relaxed, who moved in the same circles. This Deon was of an entirely different genre: a man whose working life had been spent deep in the old apartheid state, his job to defend his rulers from the likes of Joe. I sat up front, trying not to stare at him.

Half-way into Cape Town, as the startling outline of Table Mountain was given definition, I asked him about his family. It was a blind stab at breaking the awkward silence but it worked. Perhaps anything would have: perhaps all he needed was to know that we were not some spoilt ministerial brats who were going to take advantage. His sister, he told me, was also in the police – a member of the once notorious Internal Stability Unit. Both children had stepped into their father's shoes: it was an old-fashioned white South African police family.

We had left the flimsy, tin walls of the African squatter camps that line Cape Town's airport road behind. As the motorway forked left and we started gliding through white suburbia, I asked Deon what he felt about his new bosses. 'They treat me well,' he said.

I wanted more than that. I asked what it was like to be guarding the life of a man who, a mere five years previously, he would have shot on sight. 'Ag,' he answered, shrugging manfully, 'it's not a problem. After all, I'm not the kind of man to carry a grudge.'

Startled, I glanced left. Deon's hands were relaxed as he spun the steering wheel: a man at ease in this powerful car. Looking at him, I knew his words had contained no irony. He had meant what he had said, he bore no grudges. Except I couldn't understand from what source his grudges could ever have sprung. He was a policeman, a representative of the old order. He was too young to have been involved in the killing of my mother, but his was the heritage of those who had sent the bomb to her. He might have met them, might have been trained by them, might even have looked up, in admiration, at their past deeds.

And yet I knew that I shouldn't have been surprised by what he'd said because I knew something of this topsy turvy world of South Africa. It was a place where legalised apartheid had held sway for almost half a century but where it was almost impossible to find anyone who'd admit to having supported it; where the losers of a democratic election acted as if they had somehow, magnanimously, made the miracle; and where the backbone of the old regime moved smoothly into the new. It was different, though, to hear it expressed so baldly: *I bear no grudges.*

If he didn't, I thought, what about me? Me with my murdered mother and my disrupted life?

We were moving slower now. As we passed a fenced enclosure, Deon turned into a small, private road at the end of which was a set of massive gates, a solid guardhouse and a knot of uniformed men. While Deon slowed down, I found myself wondering whether this was why I had come to South Africa – to face my grudges. The guards had recognised the car: they pushed the gate open. We moved through as another thought took the first one's place. Perhaps it wasn't good enough to face my grudges, I thought, perhaps what I had come to do was to try and give them up.

★

In 1963, when I was eleven, a new member of staff had set our tiny Johannesburg school abuzz. While our teachers had previously been of one mould – greying matrons, secure in their years of past experience – the new arrival was completely different. She wore short skirts, had a beehive and long crimson nails and, most astonishing of all, she drove a red, two-seater convertible. We rich white girls, thirteen to a class, were entranced. We buzzed around her, breathing in the unfamiliar aroma of sex.

Although I can't remember her name I will never forget the way she made up for the unconventionality of her wardrobe by the orthodoxy of her teaching methods. We soon discovered that she took apartheid education to its narrow extreme: to her, history was a game of facts all marshalled together to build a picture of the way whites had 'civilised' South Africa.

We spent her lesson time copying down a set of questions which we were to answer – preferably in one word or one line – at home. They were the kind of questions that brooked no ambiguity, like the year in which Jan van Riebeeck rounded the Cape (1652), the name of the first Governor of Cape Province (Simon van der Stel) or the outcome of the 'kaffir' wars ('we' won). In case we didn't know them, the answers could be found in the only text book we were allowed. I remember that dry tome so clearly, the meticulous ordering of the facts of history and the illustrations which were, in the main, a set of gabled, Cape-Dutch houses so beloved of the first white settlers.

Joe's ministerial house was one of these come to life, but on a scale that made the pictures seem tawdry. Deon's BMW passed through the guarded barrier and crunched round the elegant oval driveway, purring to a stop in front of the huge oak door. The entrance hall was spacious enough to accommodate a formal dinner party; the sitting room had walls too vast to fit any but the most ambitious art; and through the door of glass, beyond the patio, was the rolling green of an immaculately tended lawn. It stretched on one side to a rose garden that would not have embarrassed Regent's Park and on the other to a huge border in which rows of pansies were laid out in the military fashion so beloved of the government's gardeners. I dropped my suitcase and stood staring. This was the most tangible manifestation yet of the long, long way my father had travelled.

I walked over to the French doors and opened them. As I watched Cassie, her arms spread wide, running joyfully down the long grass slope, I realised that I had finally bridged the 6,000 miles between my two worlds.

Chapter Twenty-Two

If it hadn't been for the rock face of Table Mountain backing on to the playing fields, the grounds of Cassie's new school would have looked just like a film set for an opulent Enid Blyton. And yet there was something utterly South African, and also so familiar, about the sight that confronted me. The place was a much grander, large-scale version of my Jo'burg primary, but the sight of happy little uniformed schoolgirls skipping their way to the tennis courts took me back. I stared at the spacious grounds, and I was assailed by memories of lawns like that, and of long trestle tables groaning with hand-made, wonky paper baskets full of Easter eggs that were our reward for taking part in a parade of home-made Easter hats. I was shown into the hall, and I saw myself, a child on another school stage, a necklace jiggling over my white bolero as I danced gaily in defiance of my mother's absence. I walked into the bright, light-filled classrooms with their separate desks, and I remembered how we had sat like that in rows, learning fractions against the fidgeting of the heat.

But at the same time as this world was so familiar, it was also foreign. I kept noticing little details: like the fact that when I had been at school the pinnacle of teacher achievement was an accent which hailed from England and now it was I who had the diction they aspired to. I was shown into the cool, calm school chapel and for a moment I was seized by the feeling that I was a Jewish interloper from the ghetto. And yet, I wasn't. I was a Slovo – and so was my daughter – a member of the new, ruling classes.

When I was at school the best my teachers could offer was a half-tolerant silence: now Cape Town's schools competed for the honour of educating Joe's grandchild. I watched nine-year-old Cassie moving round, carefree in the other pupils' admiration of her background and I thought how different it was from the half-truths and the silences that I had once had to swallow.

At home, we rattled around Joe's house, waiting for the day when our rental would kick in. The house had been built in another era and for a different lifestyle and the building, with its wide walls of mountain rock and its thatched roof, was structured around the past, with bell pushes to summon scores of servants, larders spacious enough to house a township family and two huge industrial cookers to cater for the parties of the old regime. Was it discomfort brought on by the past that made us feel as if we were gatecrashing? Or was it something else – the ghosts of old, treading softly beside us as we moved to chase squealing guinea fowls back into the garden, or smiled as one of the estate's many workers came to deliver that day's huge bunch of fresh-cut roses? I'm not sure, even now, which it was. All I remember is the uneasy feeling of being out of place, combined as it was with the fact that I had travelled all this way, but hadn't seen my father.

As the motorway veered left, away from Jo'burg's high-rise skyline, the taxi driver, a small, wiry loquacious man, wearing shabby trousers and an open-neck shirt topped by a greasy jacket, located me in his rear-side mirror. Having caught my eye, he threw me a question. 'Your father is a great man,' he said. 'But we never hear about your mom. Is she still alive?'

I told him no.

He shrugged and drove down Harrow Road, chatting of other, inconsequential things while I thought about his question and about the way that time had changed perceptions. While Ruth was alive, she had dominated our family. She was the star around which we moved. She was the bread-winner, the intellect, the ground breaker – she, not her husband. In many ways, I had stayed faithful to the image of Joe she had transmitted: a dreamer, a good-tempered if somewhat annoying romantic, who was not quite properly rooted in the realities of life. It was she, not he, who, in the decades after our flight from South Africa, had made a mark. If time had been frozen when she was killed, she would have been the one everybody remembered.

But time had not been frozen. It had moved on, propelling Joe ahead of it. The dreamer had been replaced by the pragmatic politician, the years of skirting failure by unprecedented success. Meanwhile death's decay was busy mutating memory: turning Ruth into a 'mom' – a woman who had once, sometime in her life, bolstered up the great man.

'Come on.'

Startled I looked up to find that the taxi had stopped in front of Joe's house and that Cassie and Andy were already outside. Pushing my thoughts into the present, I opened my door and followed them.

It was one of those clear, bright, warm Johannesburg days. I was conscious of the unseen presence of Joe's bodyguard watching through the video camera stuck up high on the garage door, as I rang the bell. The iron gate clicked open and we walked through and into the house.

Such a contrast to the grandeur of the Cape Town ministerial mansion: this was, by white South African standards, small and very cosy. This was Joe's home with Helena but my thoughts were full of Ruth. I couldn't help noticing how different this house was from any that she had ever occupied. She had gone for open-plan, bright lighting, elegant furnishings, all arranged in wide spaces. This home, in contrast, was an assortment of enclosed areas. Instead of one common space there was a dining room, a separate sitting room and, Joe's favourite, the small conservatory where he liked to sit and smoke his noxious cigarillos. As I looked around, I thought how well the house mirrored not only Joe's personality but also his Eastern European origins, much more than any he had previously shared with Ruth.

Helena was waiting for us by the door. The strains of Joe's recent health crisis showed on her delicate face and yet, smiling, she talked about how wonderful Italy had been, and how much stronger Joe was now. He was sitting on the stone patio, looking over a dying flush of riotous sweet peas as Jo'burg's spring gave

way to summer. I had expected him to be deathly thin: I was
pleasantly surprised. He was thin but he was also vigorous. I felt
his arms around me, full of vitality. Perhaps his boundless
optimism, which had reasserted itself, would prove correct:
perhaps this crisis, like the one before, was over.

And I thought, as well, that perhaps what Joe teasingly
continued to say about me – that I was far too oversensitive – was
right. When I'd phoned to tell him that we were coming to stay
in South Africa I heard him hesitate and I had thought: he
doesn't want me there. Yet now, experiencing the warmth of his
greeting, his hug for me and Cassie, his smile as he shook Andy's
hand, I felt myself relax.

He seemed so different, this man whose working life had
always been shrouded in secrecy, but who now talked openly
about his ministry. He was full of enthusiasm, almost boyishly
boasting about the things he would achieve, and yet it wasn't
boasting, it was real. Joe had got where he had wanted to be, and
his years of getting there had readied him for the enormity of the
task which lay ahead.

I sat beside him in the sun, and I felt his confidence embrace
me. The fear of what was to come, and the fear that had dogged
my past, seemed to leak away. Maybe I belonged somewhere in
Joe's world, maybe I could find a place in South Africa. I wanted
to stay there, to enjoy this unaccustomed relaxation. I couldn't.
I had an article to write, an appointment to keep. I had to go.

I was buzzed in through the glass security doors of the
headquarters of the miner's union. At the reception desk, I gave
my name to the two African men on duty. While one of them
picked up the phone to tell acting president, Kgalema Motlanthe, that I had arrived, the other looked at me and said,
'When are you bringing the old lady home?'

What followed was a moment of mutual incomprehension
that was endlessly familiar. While my surname gave me
membership to the wider family of the ANC, my life
experience meant we spoke a different language. *Old lady?*

Which old lady? Could he mean my grandmother?

He saw how I was struggling and expanded, 'Our comrades must not lie forever under foreign soil,' he said. 'Your mother must be brought back: they must all come home.'

Oh – that old lady: Ruth. I nearly laughed out loud.

Except it wasn't funny. Twice in one day, within a space of six hours, two men, one black, one white had asked about her – one because she'd dropped from vision, the other because he was telling me he had not forgotten her. Those two South African worlds, the black and the white, each struggling on parallel lines with the self-same issues. I was the irregular one, out of step, constantly wandering off track. 'Old lady', the man had said. I didn't think of her that way. But of course if she had lived, she would be old.

Death had made her seem forever young. She wasn't. And neither was Joe.

I had no time to think of that. Kgalema Motlanthe emerged and led me to his one VW Polo. As we drove out of Johannesburg, through sprawling industrial suburbs and past the huge mine dumps that are Jo'burg's most distinctive landmarks, we talked about the difficulties facing the new South Africa, about the vacuum that had been created as many experienced trade unionists left to take up positions in government. Forty minutes later, we had reached the bleak desolation that is the beginning of the Kinross gold mine complex. It was Kinross Day – the yearly commemoration of an underground explosion which had killed 177.

The first gate we came to was closed and guarded by a policeman who waved us in the direction of a second entrance. As we made the mile-long detour down an empty tar road, I felt a tourist in a country I didn't know. I looked around. The only visual break in the flat stretches of earth, contrasting colours of green and black, were distant power lines, the ugly outline of generating stations, and a low-build, high-security, brick grocery shop.

Another gate, another road block. There a policeman told us that with a demonstration about to begin, it wasn't safe for us to enter. Kgalema explained who he was: the policeman called his boss. And so I found myself in the car, marvelling at the new South African spectacle of a group of Africans briefing each other, while a senior white officer stood a respectful distance away, waiting for them to tell him what he should do.

It was desolate inside. We were in an eerie landscape, a self-contained city whose buildings were the low-flung, red-bricked prison-like structures of wretched mine hostels. We drove along a winding path to a dusty playing field. The lopsided goal posts looked like washing lines, decorated as they were with multi-coloured t-shirts for sale. By the field was another set of fences, the last bastions of an onion-layered blockade which guarded the entrance to the mine proper.

I could hear singing. I looked down the compound's inner road and saw the dust trails of a procession of young men, all of them dressed in that poor man's casual uniform of t-shirt, ragged jeans and worn trainers. They weaved their way round the field, toyi-toying over to the tiered spectator benches. A less menacing bunch of demonstrators I have scarcely ever seen. There was a kind of festive jocularity about them, a celebration of this precious few hours off.

When everybody was seated, the speechifying began. In that scrupulous attention to manners that is a mark of black South Africa, the speakers were each introduced. And me as well: pointing my way, the chairperson gave my name. I'd witnessed enough meetings to know how I should respond. I stepped forward, raised my fist and gave a weak '*Amandla!*' (Power). It was a first for me. As the reply *Ngawethu* (To the People) was delivered back, Joe's pre-election voice, questioning my place in South Africa, echoed from the past. Was Joe right? Was I a total fraud?

The speeches were in Zulu. Unable to understand anything but the slogans, I spent time looking around. I caught the moment when a man, one of a group dressed in a kind of makeshift military uniform who were standing guard, buckled and, elegantly, his body folded down into a faint. As men went to help him, I registered sounds of protest. Looking back I found the audience restive. Whereas they had arrived together, as if in one mind, now disagreement was destroying their cohesion: some kept their places, while others were already on their feet moving from the benches.

I asked what was going on. The mine owners, someone explained, had refused to let the crowd file through the security gates to lay a wreath on the stone commemorating the dead. Their reason was that the gate was too narrow, that somebody might get hurt in the crush. Their counter-proposal was for a small delegation of officials to be given access while the rest of us watched through the gaps in the metal fence. The crowd would have none of that. They were going in together. Even before negotiations with the mine's security force were over, they started moving.

I found myself in the centre of the crush to push the gates aside. I panicked, thinking I was going to be suffocated. I looked wildly around me – all I could see was men, pushing forward. I took myself in hand, forcing myself to relax and consciously breathe out and when I did I noticed Kgalema's eyes on me and I saw other union officials placing themselves strategically by my side, ready to pluck me out should things turn nasty.

The gates were opened wide, everyone pushed in. Anger gave way to dignity as a group of women, relatives of the dead, laid worn plastic flowers on a ring of stones. All around me, men stood in silence. I stood, taking in the intensity of that small ceremony, knowing that my reaction to the crowd had been completely off-key. No one would have hurt me: all they had wanted was to pay respect to their long-dead colleagues. Again it came to me, that sense of a world to which I was privileged to belong but which my white skin and my long years of absence had made only partly comprehensible.

That afternoon, when I got back to Johannesburg, I was full of the things I'd witnessed. I wanted to talk about them with Joe and I wanted to hear more of his stories. But I was too late: he had used up all his energy and was lying down. I sat in the garden he so loved, and wondered whether it would be always like this – whether we would always miss each other.

Chapter Twenty-Three

'I'm not going to tell you anything,' Joe snapped.

Shocked at the venom in his voice, I looked across the olive green wrought-iron table. He was sitting opposite me on a matching green chair on his broad brick patio in his ministerial home in Cape Town. Because the sun was hot, he had changed from his working suit into an open-necked shirt and I could see wisps of white hair and the concave area around his ribs where once there had been plump flesh. I couldn't help noticing as well how the relentless progress of his cancer had drawn his emaciated head down into his neck.

Perhaps he knew what I was seeing. If he did, it reinforced his fury. 'You have no right,' he said.

'But Joe . . .'

He overrode whatever it was that I was about to say. 'It's my life,' spitting out bitterly at the last word and repeating it as well, 'my life. Not yours.'

I guess he couldn't have put it any clearer than that. His life, not mine; his secrets, not mine; his property, not mine. His – all of it – and I was trespassing.

I'd been expecting something like this. Knowing I needed to talk to him, I'd simultaneously avoided each opportunity that arose. There had been plenty of excuses I could use to hide my cowardice. Although the end of the parliamentary recess had brought Joe and Helena back to Cape Town and under the same roof as us, I hadn't seen that much of Joe. When I was getting up, he was in the bath; by the time I returned from taking Cassie to school, he would have left for the ministry; and when he came back, his skin chalky white with fatigue, he would disappear into the other wing of the house to rest.

We ate together, all of us, but our meals had become

something of an ordeal. A glut of capsules lined the perimeter of Joe's plate, bitter chemicals which sapped his energy, vitamins to try and succour him, and a strange array of homoeopathic rememdies all of which had to be taken in a strictly preordained sequence. Joe found this pharmacopoeia almost as difficult to down as the tofu and the soup and the soft vegetables that Andy endlessly produced in an effort to tempt Joe's appetite. The rest of us sat eating, pretending that we were not painfully conscious of his thin stretched lips, forced swallows and his slow hand, scraping against his chin as if he could wipe the horror of swallowing away.

Pretence – life seemed to revolve around it. All those years of keeping secrets came into their own. Joe was public property: everybody wanted to know how he was. But when they asked about his health, we lied. 'He's fine,' I kept on saying over and over again. 'He's fine.'

It was a fabrication borne out of political necessity. And yet I wondered: did I also use those words to convince myself? He was working so very hard, I kept on thinking, he was achieving so much, could he really be that ill?

So much we left unsaid. So many half-truths. When he was well enough, he would wander through the Cape Town mansion, talking of how wonderful it was, and I would answer his smile with one of my own, although I really felt ill at ease in its alien grandeur, and I thought he did too. And then there was his repeated insistence that it was great to have us staying there: I wanted to believe it and yet I knew it was difficult for him and Helena as well, conscious as they must be of the shortness of the time that remained.

Most of the time, I kept my silence. I let Joe lead the way. I accepted the restraints with which he ringed all talk about his health. Using the lessons I'd learned long ago in childhood, I collected knowledge indirectly. From mutual friends I learned how, before their holiday in Italy, Joe had been too weak, even, to get out of bed. I learned to keep my observations to myself. The one time I made the mistake of referring to his fragility, he said curtly that he was better now. I wanted so much to believe him, for my own sake as much as his. And yet, when I walked into the television room and caught him on a low sofa, a mask over his nose and mouth as he breathed in the oxygen that was supposed to help his circulation, it was like a preview of a different, older, sicker sick man – the man I knew my father would soon become.

I told myself that if I let him lead the way, I would regret it. I had to talk to him, before it was too late. It felt so difficult. I took myself in hand, telling myself that I was being silly, feeding myself examples of how, in the past when I had raised a sensitive subject, Joe's initial combative response would soon be converted into calm. And then one early evening, lecturing myself this way, I came across Joe sitting on the patio. There was colour in his cheeks and he was smiling. He asked me to come sit with him. I did. And I raised the subject of my book.

Everything I had feared came true. Within minutes he had moved from pleasure at my company, through initial indifference into outspoken belligerence. When I asked him about Ruth and about their shared past, his reply was almost shouted.

'What gives you the right?'

I knew I had a right, that it was my past as well as his but when I tried to say as much, I found I was stuttering. There was a clamouring voice inside me which agreed with Joe, a voice conjured out of a past when necessity had made me protect my parents' secret world not only from hostile strangers but from myself as well. As a child, while Ruth and Joe had worked in the political underground, I had done my own kind of mining, burying my curiosity deep. I had internalised their proscriptions: to be 'good', I never pushed to know. And now, although I was rebelling against this enforced rectitude, still there was part of me that thought I was doing wrong.

Sitting at the table, I fought to suppress that part. There were things, I told myself, that I wanted to know. Joe was dying, I had little time left. For my own sake, not his, I needed to know.

I thought about the incidents that Joe had chosen to describe.

There were moments I found hard to take in, like the time in the sixties when he had almost left Ruth; or the time later, in London, when she had been so jealous of the good review he'd received for a piece he'd written on the armed struggle that she had used the offending journal to hit him over the head; or his saying that although she complained endlessly about his absences, she never acknowledged the way he had kept house for us while she had been constantly travelling. He had told me all these things because he wanted to: yet when I asked for what I wanted, he turned on me in rage.

He was glaring at me still. Shaking myself into the present, I tried a combination of argument and reassurance. I said that Ruth was my mother and it was her past I was exploring, not his. I told him I knew he meant to finish his autobiography and that I understood that his life was his territory. But, I added, there was a crossover between the two. And I lived those times as well, I added.

Violently, he shook his head.

I tried again. I mentioned a man whom Ruth had known during the Emergency.

'What do you know about that?' he said. 'Who told you?'

My answer, that it was he who had told me, was met by an irate, 'What business is it of yours?'

I tried to explain why it was my business, but arguing as I was against both myself and Joe, I sounded feeble. It didn't help that I was trapped in another of childhood's unhelpful hangovers – he was my father, I wanted him to understand. I wanted him to cross the barrier that separated us, to climb over the illness that sapped most of his energy, and the work that consumed the little that remained, and make contact. Couldn't he see that I wasn't only asking for the book?

Perhaps, right at the end of our exchange, he did see. He softened his voice from its former angry high. 'You can write what you want, but I won't tell you,' he said, more softly now.

He was determined: unlike all the other times, he was not going to change his stance. But then neither was I. I could have backed down and made it better but I didn't.

It was clear that our skirmish was over. I got up and walked back into the house. I was conscious of Joe behind me, of how frail he looked as he sat there, staring out at a neatly clipped and rolled government lawn.

He had held out his hand to me before I left — a peace offering, a truce. I had taken it and I had squeezed it, returning his soft pressure. But I think we both knew that what had been started between us was far from complete.

As I walked away I couldn't silence that part of me that sided with him. He was ill and he was busy. Being a daughter gave me no special right to chip away at his limited reserves of energy by selfish enquiry.

But soon afterwards I found that it rankled, what he had said. I thought about the way he'd galvanised his energy when a film crew came to interview him, and then I thought about the contempt that flickered across his face at the simplest of enquiries. It wasn't that he didn't want to talk, I thought. It was that he didn't want to talk to me.

Back and forth between these polarities I went, until I had a kind of conference call ricocheting round my head. His view, my view: I held them both inside of me. 'My life,' his voice kept echoing.

Joe's life. Joe's struggle. Joe's South Africa. But it was a big country with a long history. Was there not room for more than one of us?

Chapter Twenty-Four

I was heading deep into Johannesburg's northern suburbs and I was lost. As I executed another perfect u-turn, Joe's angry voice sounded in my head, 'Who told you?' At the time I'd answered that it was he who had told me. Now I was on my way to see the man whom he had told me about.

I checked the Jo'burg A to Z and drove down a set of soulless two-lane roads hedged by vast suburban houses sealed in by high-security walls. Eventually, following phone instructions which had mentioned garages and plant shops, both of which were plentiful in Jo'burg, I found his quiet residential street. I parked opposite his house and crossed the road. The property was set back, elegantly, from the pavement, where a patch of carefully tended shrubs masked a beautifully crafted fence.

I stood at the gate listening to ferocious barking, wondering what the hell I was doing there. The barking got louder. I could hear a man's voice, shouting at the dogs to be quiet. A man whose name was Donald Turgel, a stranger whom I had never met. Standing at his gate, fighting the urge to run, I was pulled back into the past, thinking about that time after my mother's funeral when we had sorted through her belongings. Joe took some jewellery – the rest, he had said, was ours. Faced with Ruth's possessions, I chose only one, a small brass tortoise that she had kept on her desk and I now keep on mine. I couldn't take anything else. They felt too close, these things, they still felt too much like hers.

Such a delicacy of feeling and yet, here I was, delving into a part of her life that she had kept secret from me. Maybe Joe was right: maybe it was their life, not mine. Maybe I should go.

Donald's voice was coming closer. I didn't hear what he was saying. I was too busy remembering those tributes at my mother's funeral, the words of heroism they had used to label her. I had stood there, listening, and I had thought that none of them came close to describing the Ruth that I had known.

Was that what I was doing, standing here? Was I searching for the woman I had known, whose image had been freeze-dried by her martyred death? And was I doing it now because my father was dying?

Donald Turgel was at his gate, it was too late to run. He turned a key and opened up. Conscious, mainly, of his dogs' snapping teeth, I managed only to take in a vague impression of his broad chest, his grey-brown beard and his strong, squat body as he led me round a corner of his lush garden. Past a messy artist's studio we went, and into a paved courtyard. A long, outdoor wooden table stood under a trellised creeper. Pointing me to a director's chair, he sat down at the table's head.

I had to twist round to face him full on. I saw how his face had been marked by a fire: one hand, as well, was distorted by ancient burns, its fingers badly bloated. I wondered whether he had been like that when Ruth had known him. I watched him pouring tea into cups that looked vaguely familiar. There were three pipes waiting by an ashtray. He drew on one.

I opened my mouth to ask a question but he forestalled me: 'How much do you know about my relationship with Ruth?' he asked as his pipe went down.

There was only one possible answer, 'I know that you had an affair with her.'

He looked almost relieved. 'If you hadn't known,' he said, 'I wouldn't have talked about it.' As his hand fetched the pipe to his mouth, he echoed Joe's question. 'Who told you?'

I said Joe had mentioned that Ruth had slept with some stranger during the Emergency but I didn't say that Joe had followed this revelation by confessing that when he had discovered what Ruth had been up to, the knowledge had almost ended their marriage.

'Joe didn't tell me your name,' I said. 'I got that from a friend of Ruth's.'

'I'm glad Joe knows,' he said, prodding at his swollen lip with his now unlit pipe. 'Or talking about it might be offensive to his ministry, his ministerial ...' As his voice tailed off, he put the first pipe down, picked up another and began loading it with slithers of tobacco.

While I'd been busy getting lost in Jo'burg, I'd been pondering which of my questions would unlock this man's story. I shouldn't have bothered: he needed no prompting. As soon as he'd lit his pipe, he launched right in.

'One night,' he said. 'I came home and in the kitchen was a strange dark-haired woman chatting with my wife. She was introduced to me as Ruth Gordon. I didn't know anything about who she was. [I was told] she is going to stay with us for a while ... I can't remember why.'

'I thought that she was from Cape Town,' he continued. 'And that's why she had no friends in Johannesburg. Although sometimes a car would come and pick her up.' His 'reputed wife' of that time, he said, was a strange person, who thrived on secrets.

I looked at him and nodded, wondering where this was leading.

'And then,' he said, 'a couple of days later, maybe two to three days, I came home one evening and there in the kitchen I found two roast chickens.'

Chickens – I did a double take. Was he reliving how it had happened? Is that why he kept switching to the present tense?

'My experience teaches me,' he said, 'that when I find two roast chickens in the kitchen it meant that [... my wife] had gone overseas – secretly, never saying where she was going.'

I didn't ask what kind of intrigue could have sent his wife overseas: I knew that whatever it was, it would have sprung from very different sources than the intrigue involving my parents.

'Two chickens means she'd gone overseas,' he repeated, 'which indeed she had, and left me alone in the house with Ruth Gordon ... I don't know how long Ruth stayed here ... I didn't know who she was. It only came out later – when

I don't remember – very considerably later ... Nobody came to see her. She didn't appear to go out. It was strange. One never knew ... a car would arrive ... Only later, when we became more open and frank with each other, did I know who she was.'

'Open and frank' – by which he meant they had started an affair. I concentrated on writing down his words despite the fact that what I really wanted to do was sit and stare. I wanted to roll back time and see him as he was in 1960 to see what it was that had attracted Ruth to him.

'Once or twice Joe came,' he said, referring to the time when Joe had been released from prison and Ruth was still in hiding. 'They went up to the roof terrace. I suppose they had private discussions up there ... I never went to Roosevelt Park,' he continued. 'I knew she had a house in Mendelssohn Road.' Abruptly he veered off on to another subject. 'She spoke quite freely about what she was trying to do,' he said. 'I used to sneer at Joe's incompetence at blowing up electric pylons.'

I was frowning while I wrote this sentence down. There was something not quite right about it but I couldn't work out what.

He didn't seem to notice. 'She told me quite a bit about her experiences in detention,' he said. 'She spoke a lot about the psychological effects ... apparently it's quite normal after long periods of interrogation to switch to suddenly being friendly with your interrogators.'

Detention? Now I was positive there was something wrong. In 1960, when the Emergency was declared, Joe was the one in detention. 'Ruth wasn't in gaol in 1960,' I said.

For the first time since we'd sat down, my companion looked less than certain. Was this because he had realised that I didn't know as much as he had assumed I knew? Or was it because he was genuinely confused? 'I thought it was 1960,' he said.

The phrase he had used – *blowing up pylons* – came back to me and I knew what was wrong with it. The armed struggle, and therefore Joe's involvement in any kind of blowing up, had started some time after the Emergency. Which meant, I thought, that Ruth's fling with Donald had not been confined to a few months in 1960.

His rounded tones confirmed it. 'It could have been later,' he said, 'because I saw her for years after she had been here. I continued to see her virtually until she left South Africa.'

Until she left South Africa which meant four years. The worst four years of my life.

'We discussed at great length whether she should or shouldn't go,' he said. 'She discussed with me whether she should stay and be caught. She felt people would think she was abandoning them.'

His words washed over me as I sat there, thinking how abandoned I had felt during those four years.

'We had an association, on and off, continuously until she went away,' I heard him saying.

I wrote it down and the dates as well: 1960 to 1964. The time when I'd gone from eight to twelve, the years that marked the end of my childhood's happy memories and the beginning of the nightmare. My mother had been driven then by tension, excitement, danger, anxiety in those years – almost to her death.

I hadn't blamed her for her distraction: I had protected her from my longings. I had kept repeating to myself that what she did, she did for an ideal, for the millions of the oppressed who needed her more than me. And yet now I had learned she had also been doing it with Donald Turgel. No matter how rushed she'd been, she'd found the time to meet him sometimes twice weekly in a friend's flat, not far from Marshall Square where she'd been imprisoned, in the Chinese area. For four years. Hardly a one-night stand.

He was looking at me. I didn't want him to know how his words had confounded me. I asked a question about Ruth's imprisonment.

'Ruth said at certain stages there was almost the wish to become friendly with her interrogator,' he said, 'even to become intimate with him. She was quite cold about that – that was the communist taking over. Ruth the communist was the one who was being interrogated. This was a different section of her being ... I found her to be very bright except with this field. It was as if she'd had a kind of frontal lobotomy.'

I asked him, coldly, if he thought there were two Ruths.

'The name Ruth,' he said, 'wasn't that the name of a woman who was schizophrenic or multiple personality? I suspected that there is a kind of blockage – two Ruths. One is the communist. The other one, that was Ruth, the one I liked ...'

Six months later when I met with Eric Pugen, Ruth's dress designer of old, he also said that there were two Ruths – the one who ordered clothes from him and the other who was involved in the 'game' of politics. He hadn't liked the communist, he said, and when he said it, I was gripped by the same sense of anger as now, anger that these men thought they could split my mother into two, excising her politics so they wouldn't have to deal with them. She wasn't like that, I thought: she was whole – the stylish woman and the communist were one.

Except, what was she doing hanging out with these men who had so much contempt for the thing that drove her on?

Did Donald Turgel notice how much his words disturbed me? He had moved on to talking about the lead-up to Ruth's mother's arrest, and about how aware she was that she would be targeted. 'She always carried a handbag,' he said. 'She was very distinctly noticeable.' Ruth, he continued, had an urge to be arrested, to show that she belonged. 'She needed to be one of the boys,' he said, 'and to be one of the boys she needed to be arrested.'

In 1963, Ruth had needed to be arrested. In 1995, I needed a break. I got up and followed his directions to the toilet.

The bathroom, like the house I had just moved through, was well-proportioned, elegant in white and unglazed terracotta tiles. I sat on the edge of the bath and thought about the things I'd just been told. The irony of it. I had decided that Joe's proscription was his way of protecting himself: now I thought that maybe it was me who needed the protecting. Big, brave me who had launched myself, despite warnings, into this investigation and who now felt betrayed because my long-dead mother had slept with a man I didn't really like.

It wasn't tragic: it was funny. I laughed out loud, shook myself and looked around. Which is when I realised that like the tea set that had come before, the bathroom seemed amazingly familiar. I was sure I'd never been here. I looked more closely at the detail. Which is when I understood why it was that the place looked so familiar: it was because of the tiles that lined its walls. I'd seen them before, not them but that same grainy finish, that same distinctive terracotta look. I even had one at home in London which sits on my marble table, waiting to receive hot pans. It has a seven on it: it used to be outside our home at Number 7, Mendelssohn Road.

Those tiles which my mother had loved.

I got up and left the bathroom. As I walked outside, I took in the greens and blues that draped the living furniture. All of them reminded me of Ruth. I thought of the pottery collection that was her passion: of huge modern, round, moss-green platters, scoop-bottomed soup tureens decorated by mysterious glazes, oversized salad bowls in dreamlike blues, many of which had since been stolen from a Maputo warehouse . . .

Outside, the third pipe was burning fiercely. I sat and I asked about the tiles. Donald said his son owned a pottery and that his ex-wife had designed and made the tiles when his son was young.

Looking round now, all I could take in was Ruth's distinctive stylishness. Except it wasn't hers alone: she had shared it with this Donald who ridiculed her hopes, who was sitting by me, telling me that he had in his possession, a chair that he designed and that my grandfather Julius had made up in his factory – a thank you present for sheltering Ruth during the Emergency.

We got up to go and find the chair. No luck, the main house was locked. I was relieved: while I was on my feet I might as well keep going. He walked me to the door, warding off his snarling dogs. He told me to come back, any time. I thanked him and I left.

Chapter Twenty-Five

A s Sea Point's fog-horn hooted dolefully in the background, I sat at my desk, leafing through a set of letters my parents had exchanged during the Emergency of 1960 when Joe had been in gaol.

I had been through this correspondence once before. I had read my mother's loving tributes to Joe, and his replies which were packed with boyish enthusiasm for the prison camaraderie he was experiencing. All this I'd registered and yet now, after my trip to Jo'burg, it seemed very different.

I was finding it hard to concentrate on the two sets of eccentric handwriting I knew so well: his looping with a backward slope; hers full of twirls and dashes that merged one word into the next. The fog that had descended on Cape Town was in me too.

My father had tried to stop me delving in the past and I had defied him. I sat wondering whether I'd made the right decision. Already my search had delivered more than I'd expected. When I'd started out, I told myself I was looking for the truth. Now I was no longer so sure that this was possible. It happened all the time: a cousin would tell me one thing, an aunt would contradict him entirely, and neither of them would be lying. Their memories were not the clean-cut, crystal versions of the past I'd once assumed they'd be. Each version had a subtle twist to it, each person reinterpreting what had happened through their experience of what came next.

In the distance, the fog-horn sounded. I shook myself and started rifling through the letters, concentrating not on the words Ruth and Joe had exchanged but on the details. I noticed that on each of his, Joe had put his prisoner's number where an address and date should have been. I turned to Ruth's. She, in contrast, had dated each of hers, methodically numbered them and, always the good student, had also inscribed her address on the top right-hand corner.

Her address: our home address, 7 Mendelssohn Road. It was a lie. From the moment of Joe's arrest, we had left home. Ruth had driven us, through one whole day of sizzling heat, across the border into Swaziland. I remembered how, on our arrival I had rushed into the shower in a desperate attempt to cool down. All that I remembered, and all that was real.

I have no memory at all of the journey back, made, presumably, by us three sisters in our grandparent's company. I have retained other things: walking through the Swazi hills, for example, or visiting Joe in Pretoria's central prison, or doing the rounds of two schools in one short term. All of that, but not the fact that, while we children came home, Ruth hid out in a suburban Johannesburg stranger's house. And shared his bed at night.

In Cape Town, more than thirty years later, the phone was ringing. I picked it up.

I heard Joe's voice. 'How are you?'

I knew why he was asking. It was because of what had happened that previous evening. 'A little bruised,' I said. A moment's silence, while we both relived it.

With my younger sister, Robyn in Cape Town, I had invited Joe and Helena to supper. Robyn and Helena turned up at the allotted time but Joe phoned to say he was in a cabinet meeting and would be a little late.

He'd been very late, not only because the meeting overran but because his police driver got badly lost. By the time they found their way to our door, Joe was exhausted and extremely aggravated. He was also unsteady on his feet as he climbed downstairs. The cancer was eating not only at his frame, but also, relentlessly, at his self. My father, who had always been the centre of laughter and of conversation sat at the table, eating slowly and without relish, speaking not at all. Within half an hour, he was finished and he and Helena got up to go.

When he'd come in, he'd put his briefcase and a sheaf of papers down on the sofa. Now, as he got ready to leave, I fetched them for him. In the act of hand-over, I glanced at the title page.

Which is when he'd gone ballistic.

'Don't you dare,' he shouted, so fiercely that the order forced an exclamation from Robyn. He wheeled round on her, directing a furious, 'What's it got to do with you?' her way before turning back on me, 'Don't you ever dare read other people's private papers.'

I felt it like a slap, which is exactly what had been intended. I opened my mouth to tell him that I hadn't read the page, but I knew already that this was hardly the point. Here it was again, his fury that I was prying into his life.

I closed my mouth, handed the papers over and watched in silence as he took them out of there.

Now, the morning afterwards, his voice was friendly. 'I knew you'd say that,' he said in response to my being bruised. 'You're too sensitive.' This a repetition of a criticism he always used on me. I held my tongue and heard his voice softening as he said he couldn't really understand why he'd snapped. The papers were neither interesting nor confidential, he said, just an agenda of a routine cabinet meeting. And then he asked me out to lunch.

Before I left, I shoved the letters Joe and Ruth had exchanged back into their cardboard box. I could no longer hear the fog-horn. Looking out, I saw that spring's sun had burnt off the morning mist. I stood pulled back for a moment into my meeting with Donald Turgel and I thought I should not have been shocked. My mother was unique – a radical who refused to fit the South African left's puritanical mould. If I was proud of her for that how could I then condemn her choice of lovers? Except, a small voice interrupted, during those four terrible years, when she should have been thinking of us, her children, part of her was no doubt involved with her architect friend.

Standing in the foyer of Cape Town's Plein Street ministerial buildings which fronted the parliamentary complex, I queued behind a line of vice-chancellors on their way to a meeting with the minister of education. When my turn came I gave my name, address, telephone number and profession to the uniformed Afrikaner policeman whose grasp of English made the process tortuous. When I had signed the registration book, he handed me an i.d. tag. And then, having funnelled my bag through the X-ray machine, I was in. On the walls of the lift, where once had hung stiff pictures of official buildings, now were photos of black nurses tending patients, and black teachers shaking President Mandela's hand. I got out on the second floor.

In my lifetime, I have visited only two of Joe's offices. The first had been his lawyer's chambers in Johannesburg, pre-1964. All I remember of that was a carpeted corridor and a bunch of big, smiling men who patted my head before talking over it. The second visit is fixed far more securely in memory. It took place at the back of London's Goodge Street, in an area crammed with Greek restaurants, wholesale stationers, travel agents and cramped rooms at the top of steep stairs. Joe had worked in one of them, sitting with his comrades behind wonky desks, talking in a code I never could crack about men and dlbs and their plans of military incursions. In a repetition of the earlier memory, their chat had gone completely over my head.

This Cape Town venue was as different from Joe's London base as anything could be. I walked down a hushed corridor, through an inner office where bodyguards and secretaries loitered, and into a room big enough to dwarf any normal mortal. It did more than that to my father, dressed as he was in a blue suit made voluminous by his shrunken frame. He was sitting behind his enormous desk, turning papers as he sipped at a bone-white cup of tea. Hearing me, he closed his file, and leaning heavily on his knuckles, hauled himself upright.

We left via the underground car park, and were driven to Cape Town's Atlantic Ocean sea front of Camps Bay. Joe had chosen to eat at Blues where a wall of glass overlooked the white sand beach. We sat on cushioned chairs, gazing out at bronzed, bikini-clad women who lay spreadeagled on bright coloured towels as blue overalled Africans shovelled the last ugly remnants of an oil spill from the sand.

While we stared out at them, our fellow lunchers sneaked curious glances at Joe. He didn't seem to notice: or at least he pretended that he didn't. He sat and concentrated on choosing something from the menu that he might be able to swallow. Opposite him, I registered his frailty.

While we waited for our food, we lapsed into silence. At a nearby table a group of four well-coiffed and manicured women tore a mutual friend's reputation to shreds. I listened as Joe sat, staring into nothingness. But when our waitress had brought our meal and gone, he launched into speech.

He had prepared what he wanted to say and he got on with it. First he spoke about his two marriages. He started by telling me how happy he was with Helena, how much he loved her.

I told him that I knew that. And it was true, I did know. I had seen them together, had registered the loving glances that passed between them, I had heard the gentle teasing that each could tolerate as well as the distant sound of their animated voices issuing from the baths that they liked to share.

So I told him that I knew he loved Helena.

I could see in his eyes that he didn't believe me, but he moved on anyway, to Ruth.

It was different and much more bitter than anything he'd ever said before. 'When I first got together with Ruth,' he told me, 'she'd sit at dinner laughing at what other people said . . .'

He was talking almost as if, in saying the unsayable, he had to be aggressive. His lips were stretched tight, a sadistic smile or a sad one?

'And then, afterwards,' he said, 'when we were alone Ruth would ask me to translate the joke.'

As I listened to my witty father's contempt for my mother's humourlessness, I thought about my recent visit to a Johannesburg garden, and about a man who had talked about Ruth's tremendous sense of fun. I kept my thoughts to myself. I hadn't told Joe about my meeting with Turgel and I wasn't going to.

Joe went on without me: he was determined to have his say. From tales of Ruth's humourlessness, he shifted to her competitiveness. Once again it came, that story of her blow delivered by magazine. And again, her Emergency affair. He told me how much it had hurt.

The words she had written to him while he was in gaol, those tender, loving words came back to me. I thought of her letter number 4: 'I've come to the conclusion,' she had written, 'that with all my show of independence, I'm a most clinging, reliant, dependent creature lost without you and in a new environment.'

Was that why she had done it? Because she had, quite literally, been lost without him?

And yet, what about the love she had felt for Joe? She wrote of that as well. Like, for example, in her letter number 11, dated 21 May: 'How could I be so generous to share you with a horde of your friends,' she wrote, 'Lucky dogs! But we have had wonderful years together and who can take those away from us? Or so much else to come? Soon. And better than ever . . .'

And again in number 14, written on 4 June: 'That's what the Emergency has done for us, old thing; it's turned me quite addled on you.'

When I had first read this, I'd been surprised that my mother's usually undemonstrative typing fingers could ever have allowed such sentiments to surface. I thought about the people who had read her letters, Joe and the prison censor and perhaps his fellow prisoners. I wondered how easy it had been to write for such an audience. But reading on, I'd got used to the way that, running through her twice-weekly missives was that same distinctive, unchanging narrative – her dependence on, her love and her admiration for Joe. No wonder he had kept her letters safe.

Except now they made no sense.

I saw Joe looking. 'I've been reading those letters,' I said. 'Hers were so full of love.'

'Those letters. Exactly!' stressing it, proving his point.

I stared at him, at the signs of acrid victory in his eyes, and I thought about what he had written back to her. Perhaps she'd been disappointed by his replies penned from the inside of a communal gaol cell; they were certainly less expressive, more heroic than hers. While she praised him, he answered in grand gestures.

'When you have no regrets in your personal life,' he wrote, 'when you have no regrets in your conduct and bearing as a social being then an upset in routine, an inconvenience, does not really worry you.'

And, a little later, '. . . those who don't like us are puny, savage, lost. Nothing can stand up against the warmth of 90% of humanity.'

She wrote of how much she missed and needed him, he, with almost boyish enthusiasm, of the brotherhood that had grown up between the incarcerated, of games of deck tennis and sessions of communal singing, and of the euphoria of a successful hunger strike.

But that's not all the truth. He did stop in full flight to acknowledge his feeling for Ruth. In one of his later undated letters, he wrote, 'I don't think I've ever been more in love with you than I am at the moment.'

On the face of it, the correspondence of two people who were deeply committed to each other. And yet she had got involved with someone else.

Perhaps the loving impatience which ran through his letters had something to do with this. In response to her frequent references to her own inadequacies, he had berated her. 'You made me cross,' he wrote on 22 May, 'at your underestimation of yourself . . . let me tell you a couple of home truths. Your ability extends mine. You are better looking than I am and you have a passion which if it disappeared would destroy you and a lot of me. What more do you want? Don't you change now!'

I heard Joe's voice in my head, saying these words, and I thought, whatever had driven Ruth into the arms of another man, this could not be it.

And then I thought of Joe, sitting in prison not knowing

when he'd be released, and of another thread that had run through what he wrote. 'If you don't keep your quota (of letters)' he wrote, 'I will misconstrue it . . .' and, later, 'you know me – how jealous I am by nature – but that's because I love you so very much. I'm selfish.' And later again, this same theme repeating itself, 'I understand,' Joe wrote, '[that] a red bearded man from Mars descended upon your community. Give him my regards but *that's all* see. Am I being foolish again? I suppose I am. I'm not really being serious.'

But of course he was being serious and now, it appeared, he had good reason.

I watched him putting down again the same mouthful of food that he had held up to his lips and I felt his anger at Ruth. No, not his anger. I felt mine as well. She had betrayed him. She had betrayed all of us. How could she?

He didn't need my anger. He kept on talking. There was no stopping him: he wanted to get it, all of it, off his chest. He wanted to tell me how hurt he had been by Ruth's affairs – how the affairs he'd indulged in had merely been his way of trying to pay her back. He wanted to tell me how unhappy the marriage had often made him. He wanted to, and he did, until finally he was sated.

While I sat and absorbed it all, this version of my parents' marriage.

When I could, I asked him questions. I asked him why he and Ruth had seemed so much happier in that period leading up to her death.

He said that was because they had decided to go their own separate ways.

I asked him why after she had died, he'd told me how much he'd loved her.

'A father trying to make his daughter feel better.'

When he said that, my anger turned from her to him. He was making himself the innocent party and yet I thought about the times in England, when Ruth had tried to get Joe to go on holiday with her. She had one destination in mind – Italy – she wanted them to travel there, to sit in trattorias consuming pasta and young wine, or to stay with friends in Tuscany and lie at night, gazing up at the stars.

He'd never found the time to go.

And yet, he had the time with Helena, and he had gone to Italy.

I looked across at my father, sitting there, consumed by his illness and by what he had to say. I knew that he believed it, but I also knew it was not all the truth. In the moment of his pain and his physical deterioration, this was how he thought of Ruth. It was part of the Joe I knew and the part which made him such an effective politician, this ability of his always to keep on moving forward. Perhaps he had made another 'switch', a purely personal one this time. He had looked back on a relationship that had been abruptly cut off more than a decade before, and he had interpreted it through his dying eyes.

But I knew as well that between my parents had been a connection and a passion that he was now busily writing out. He was acting her victim – I didn't like him for it.

I caught myself, swinging back in judgement and I wondered how I had ended up arbitrating between them in my mind, hating first one and then the other. Was this my punishment for daring to tread in a past that did not belong to me?

I looked at Joe. I thought that he was no longer the man I had known all my life, he was different, caught up in the prospect of his ending and I knew it was not a question of the truth. He was telling me how he felt. Now. At the moment. There was no arguing with that. My anger dissolved.

When it was over, we hugged each other.

He dropped me at home and I stood watching as his state BMW drove off. As it turned the corner a flash of how he'd looked in the restaurant, his half-closed eyes belligerent. At moments in the conversation, I'd wondered whether he was speaking to me, his daughter, or to his dead wife – Ruth. Was he angry with her for leaving him to die without her? Or was he angry with me, for forcing him to think of her when he had other, more important things on his mind?

Chapter Twenty-Six

The next time I saw Joe was at Robyn's seaside house where we met for lunch. I was already there when he arrived. Listening to him slowly climbing up the wooden stairs, I heard him slip. He came into the room, using those familiar words, 'The bad news is I fell: the good news, that I didn't break anything.'

He was white with fatigue and almost speechless and yet, when Robyn gave him her unsuccessful salad dressing to taste, he roused himself and doctored it into a Joe special, as it had been in those days of Ruth, when making a good salad dressing was his chosen domestic duty.

I saw him after that, again in Robyn's company. We were in Jo'burg and Robyn and I were visiting him at home. He seemed better, his voice had timbre and his movements were far more energetic than they'd been for some time. Maybe it was because of this that when he accused Robyn of something she thought she hadn't done, she responded with a shout.

What ensued was a familiar burlesque: the kind of drama we'd recently stopped enacting but which used to be a central part of family tradition. There was verbal attack and counter-attack, money thrown down on kitchen surfaces and finally, one of the daughters – in this case Robyn – running out. I was flung into the past and my old role. *Look after Robyn*: that's what my mother had once said. Ever obedient, I followed Robyn. So did Joe. Which is why we ended up on the pavement outside his house, shouting about the things that hurt, the things that, these days, we never mentioned.

At one point Joe turned to me, demanding to know why, when Andy and Cassie and I came to Jo'burg, we didn't stay with him. I repeated what I said before: that we didn't want to add to the heavy pressure he and Helena were obviously enduring.

'We like to have you here,' he said. 'We want you here.'

I knew it was true, and I also knew it wasn't. We were too much for them and, no matter how hard we all pretended, it was easier when we stayed elsewhere. I tried, as I had done before, to say so. He nodded as if he understood, just as he had always done before. Perhaps he did, or perhaps this was just one more misunderstanding that would run between us: his version and mine which could never, ever meet.

The conversation veered from me to Robyn and other ancient hurts. It was the strangest of encounters. We were no longer shouting at each other but with Joe's dinner guests and his new family waiting inside, we continued to stand on the pavement. I couldn't stop myself registering the video camera which was stuck high on the wall. I knew that inside the garage, Joe's bodyguards must be watching on their monitors.

I pushed the thought away. It didn't really matter. What would they have made of it, anyway, when they saw their boss looking at his daughters, tears in his eyes, his voice cracking as he said, 'You girls don't know how much I love you.'

Was that all I had ever wanted from him – to know that he loved me? When he said it and I believed it, I thought perhaps it was.

In South Africa's long summer break that kicked off in early December, Joe, Helena and Helena's two children went on holiday to the Eastern Cape. Cassie was to join them there. The day before she left, I phoned to check that they would meet her off the plane. Which is how I discovered that Joe, walking from the beach to his holiday house, had tripped on a pathway constructed out of rubber tyres. This time there was no good news. It had finally happened, that moment he'd been dreading: falling on hard sand, he had broken his shoulder.

Cassie came back from her stay, bubbling about long hours

spent with Helena's youngest daughter, Kyla, on long, white beaches, of the joys of solo flying and being picked up from the airport by Joe's two bodyguards, and of the evening when she had spilled coke all over the table, ruining three people's meals, and Helena had bumped the car. Of Joe she said little. When I pressed her, all I got was, 'Kyla says he's in such a bad mood because he's in pain.'

I saw him soon afterwards, briefly as he passed through Cape Town. He was on his way to the ANC national conference which was to be held in Bloemfontein. Meeting him by accident, I was shocked into a realisation that the process of his dying was reaching its final stages: it wasn't the sling around his arm that was so ominous, but rather his scarecrow neck, his skull-like head, the intensity of his teeth's grip on his jaw, as if he was in too much pain to let any words pass.

I watched him on television at the conference, standing on the platform besides a towering Nelson Mandela who'd just presented Joe with the ANC's highest award, the Isithwalandwe Seaparankoe.[1] When Mandela announced what he was going to do, the crowd (many of them the same people who had carried Joe on their shoulders up to the platform in Zambia in 1985, when he was elected the first white member of the ANC's national executive) roared. But watching on TV, I didn't feel like celebrating. As Joe held his thin arm and his clenched fist up into the air, I could see the effort it cost him. I remembered the sight of him on television, only a few months before, when he had stood in triumph at the successful conclusion of his housing summit. The speed of his health's deterioration was almost unbelievable.

In his short speech of thanks, Joe used the words which underpinned his whole life's work, 'I don't regret anything.'

---

1. Meaning 'he who wears the leopard skin'. Joe was the thirteenth person to be awarded the Isithwalandwe.

There was another thunder of appreciation from the conference floor.

By now, it was obvious that he was dying. And yet, still he fought it. 'I have cancer,' he told a journalist who pressed him on the subject of his health, 'but I also have feelings.'

But even if he wouldn't speak of it, he was ready to assume others did. To Jeremy Cronin who came to warn him of the Isithwalandwe, Joe asked whether the national executive now expected him to resign his post. To Thenjiwe Mtinsto who told Joe, '. . . you should know that all the time we felt you were there for us, and I want to thank you for your life', Joe's touchy response was, 'What you're saying is I'm dying.'[2] I wonder now how he dealt with Thenjiwe's reply of, 'No, I'm saying, thank you, I love you.'[3]

In the months since August, we his family had endlessly repeated that it was his work which was keeping him alive. Only once did I question this. Once when, speaking to Helena, I wondered out loud whether it wouldn't be better for him to give up work and spend the time remaining with his family and his memoirs.

Now, I witnessed the fallacy of what I had suggested. Ever since his diagnosis, Joe had lived in fear of broken bones. When it finally happened, it was as if all the fight went out of him. If his body was too fragile, he couldn't work: if he couldn't work, he wouldn't live.

Christmas was a strange time. On the day itself Andy, Cassie and I *braaied* crayfish, drank red Pinotage and went to Clifton beach. I was thrown back to childhood, remembering all those Cape Town holidays, the pink-striped candy strips draped festively around the fringes of our beach umbrellas, the dots of wooden

---

2. Thenjiwe Mtintso, 'Comrades who have made me', extracted from Joe Slovo, op cit.

3. Ibid.

houses in the distance, the green-fringed hill that led up to the mountain and the long, hot trudge up the concrete steps back to our car. Except this time a new experience was added since I was now old enough to appreciate the instant sobering effect of Clifton's freezing seas. I sat, reheating myself on the white sands, and thought that finally, when the circle of my childhood was rejoined, my father was dying.

By Boxing Day as Joe's ministry announced he was working at home, we knew that he didn't have much longer. My sisters flew out from London and we met in Johannesburg. Tied to each other by our traumatic past and by a sense that, with our parents away, we were all the family we had, we three sisters had kept in constant contact. But the days when we hung out, all together, which had reached a peak immediately after Ruth's death, were gone. In the more recent past we had chosen to conduct our relationships one to one in a constant changing constellation of twosomes.

Now we were all together, and with Helena, we made four. Four difficult women in one small space: before this moment, I had wondered what it would be like and I know that Joe had wondered too. In the event, the way we managed surpassed all our most optimistic predictions. We, Joe's women, organised shifts to keep him company and to help each other. By New Year's Eve, we were all together in Johannesburg, standing in Joe's garden at midnight, setting off fire crackers, watched by Joe.

In his lifetime, Joe had rarely been at a loss for words. He had produced them endlessly in jokes, in arguments, in ever-changing political debate. Now it was as if he had nothing to say. He stopped talking – almost completely – my genial, loquacious father. I had thought that his death, when it came on, would clear away the detritus of his life, revealing the inner person. But Joe was silent, absorbed in a space I could not reach.

I thought about the Rilke poem:

She was already loosened like long hair,
poured out like fallen rain,
shared like a limitless supply.

She was already root.
And when, abruptly,
the god put out his hand to stop her, saying
with sorrow in his voice: He has turned round –
she could not understand, and softly answered
Who?

Was it the imminence of death that had stolen Joe's words? Or
was it something else? In his childhood, he had experienced
such terrible loss and yet the boy who was effectively parentless
by the age of twelve grew up to be an irrepressible optimist,
almost as if his adult life was lived out in negation of his earlier
pain. His life's energies had been directed outwards, into helping
transform the world.

But now that life was draining out of him, was he returning
to a quiet aloneness? Or was his silence simply the pureness of
a man who had always favoured external to internal processes?

We brought Cassie to see him. He half-lay, half-sat in his
dressing-gown on a sitting-room sofa watching her. She knew
she was being watched: three feet away from him, she smiled and
sweetly talked. Joe looked entranced: it was as if he were
watching life itself. But the pleasure he showed seemed like an
expression of joy at the continuation not only of life in general,
but of my life, and of his. And the sadness that was also there: was
that his sorrow at leaving which he could not bring himself to
express verbally?

Although he spoke little, he kept on moving, from one chair
to the next, to bed, and back again, restless roving in search of
a comfort he couldn't find. Wherever he went, we would follow,
trying to make sure he didn't fall. We followed with the
trappings of life: with the endless glasses of ice-cold ginger ale
which was the only nourishment he'd accept; the ice he slid
across his face in a vain attempt to stop the insatiable itching that

was consuming him; and the packets of small cheroots, these remnants of his life-long battle with addiction, which no longer interested him but which we kept providing anyway.

When I was away from him, I was as restless as he. When I was with him, I felt at peace. If his death did not bring him to the place I had expected, it had brought me somewhere. All my life I had battled to get something from my father, some spoken recognition that would place me near the centre of his existence. All my life I had wanted him to value me as much as he valued South Africa. In moments of past clarity, I would face the possibility that my father was just not capable of giving me what I desired. I had wanted so much from him, too much perhaps. And yet I had kept on trying to get it out of him, this inner sense that he was there for me.

This battle that I'd fought with him, this fight over which of our needs would be dominant, had continued in the run up to his end. We acted it out continuously – over where I should stay when I was in Jo'burg, over which one of us had the right to ask the questions, and on whether it was his past or mine. I wanted him to understand my quest, he wanted quiet. He wanted me to sit out on the sidelines, I wanted him to comprehend my need.

But now, all that was over. In his presence, knowing that it was too late, I finally accepted what he did have to give. At last I could be with him and not want something more.

The day before he died, I put my arms around his fragile back, and helped him lie back on his bed. He was bird thin, so small, my father, like a baby. As I gently laid him down I heard him whisper, 'Thank you'.

On his last day, he spoke in front of me again. Lying on his bed, he repeated two words over and over again. Two words, 'Come on, come on'. He wasn't calling me, he was calling death.

Helena was exhausted and it was decided that we should join the night shift. In Joe's old comrade, Mannie Brown's house, a convenient walk from Joe's, we, my sisters, Andy, Cassie,

Mannie and I, ate supper together. It was the strangest meal. We sat outside on a discarded mattress in front of a swimming pool, eating overcooked fish along with small baby squashes that, even after two hours of boiling, had not got soft.

I was to be the first on that night's rota. At eight o'clock I gave up trying to eat and went to rest. I was nervous. I lay down, on Mannie's double bed in a dilapidated house awaiting renovation, thinking I'd never lose consciousness. In case I did, I set the alarm for one hour's time.

I was wrenched from sleep. Confused, half-in, half-out of a dream I couldn't catch, I reached for the clock. Only half an hour had passed.

I heard a voice, 'Hello'.

I looked out the window and saw Mannie walking to the gate. I heard conversation, Mannie talking softly to an unseen presence. He didn't talk for long. When it was over, he turned and walked back towards the house. I watched him, hunched in the darkness of the night. As he came closer, a security light clicked on and I saw how pale he was. I got up and went to meet him in the hall. He said that they had called for us. He didn't know why. Numb from sleep, I joined my sisters in the car and, unspeaking, we drove the less than half a mile to Joe's.

There was a hush at the house, people walking to and fro, avoiding each other's eyes. No one said anything: for a moment I thought that Joe was dead. But going to his bedroom, I saw that he was only sleeping. It took a while for somebody to tell us that we'd been called because the doctor thought the end was near.

We took it in turns to watch over him as he lay oblivious to the soft strains of Beethoven in the background. Each time I left his room I passed the television. It was on, as if normal life was continuing, but almost without sound. Women with tiny, pinched-in waists pirouetted round big muscled men, all of them singing favourites from *Oklahoma*. As I sat and stared, unseeing, at the screen, I remembered watching the Oscars in that room. Joe's jolly voice, live from that moment, came back to me. I heard again his perfect timing when, as the adverts came on, he had quickly quipped, 'I'd like to thank my daughter in advance for fetching the pineapple.'

He died that night, his breathing growing heavy, slow and finally gone.

Earlier in the day, his friend, Nelson Mandela had come to visit him. Mandela had sat by Joe's bed, talking softly, while Joe lay silent. About to leave, Mandela had got up and resting his cheek against Joe's forehead had said, 'Goodbye Joe.' Which is when Joe spoke. 'Cheers,' was his reply.

We stood in the living room after Joe had died, drinking a toast. We held our glasses up and repeated that one word, Joe's last, 'Cheers'.

Chapter Twenty-Seven

It was four in the morning as Joe's director general at the ministry of housing, Billy Cobbett, worked his way down a list of phone numbers. The door-bell rang – the undertakers coming to fetch Joe's body, bringing with them that uneasy aura of respectful death. We left the door open as they wandered to and fro, taking measurements. Within minutes another man, a squat, bullish African sauntered in. As I watched him moving closer I felt a vague relief that not all undertakers were as cadaverous as myth dictates.

Except he made no attempt to join the others. He looked at me. 'I've come for the president,' he said.

The president? Had someone promoted Joe? 'What president?'

'Nelson Mandela,' he said and seeing my incomprehension added Mandela's clan name, the one his friends and comrades used, 'Madiba'.

Oh. That president. I told him Madiba wasn't there. He looked alarmed, said something about having misunderstood and rushed out. Within twenty minutes he was back, this time with Nelson Mandela in tow.

As the sky lightened over Joe's city, we sat together in the living room. We, Joe's family, had few words left. Never mind – Nelson Mandela was more than capable of making the conversational running. He started, as was often his way, with a description of his travel arrangements. He said that having heard that Joe was dead, he had wanted to come immediately but there'd been no driver at his house. He'd gone on a telephoning spree, looking for a lift. He'd tried Gauteng premier, Tokyo Sexwale; deputy president, Thabo Mbeki; and ANC general secretary, Cyril Ramaphosa – none of them had answered their phones. Finally he'd come up with the number of one of his ANC drivers, who'd been suspended on suspicion of wrong doing – getting hold of the man he'd hitched a lift from him.

We listened to this story, half-smiling, half-numb. When it was over, there was a moment's silence. And then the president looked across at us – Joe's daughters – sitting opposite and, in the quietness of the day's dawning, he told another story. He told us how one day when he had gone to hug his grown-up daughter she had flinched away from him, and burst out, 'You are the father to all our people, but you have never had the time to be a father to me.'

He let that last sentence hover before speaking again. This, he said, was his greatest, perhaps his only regret: the fact that his children, and the children of his comrades, had been the ones to pay the price of their parents' commitment.

There it was – the one against the other: their work, our needs, their commitment, our lives, there was no squaring the circle. They knew it, somewhere, all their generation: as the state had poured out its wrath, they had watched their children suffer. And yet, and yet – what else could they have done?

After Mandela had left, Andy and I walked along the deserted streets back to Mannie's place.

In another part of the country, Omar, one of Joe's body-guards, awoke, frightened by a dream. He'd dreamt that he and Joe had gone into the Plein Street basement, where Joe's car was parked. As Omar had held the door open for Joe, he'd asked his usual question, 'What's the programme Chief?'

'No programme,' Joe said. 'Just drive.'

The sleeping Omar didn't like that: the old man always had a programme. 'Where to?' he'd insisted and heard again Joe's answer, 'Just drive.'

Omar sat up so abruptly he woke his wife. After he'd described his dream to her, she persuaded him to go back to sleep. And so it was that it was morning before he woke again and switched on the radio and heard that Joe was dead.

★

In Johannesburg, it was daytime and Cassie got up. I told her what had happened. She didn't know how to react: how could she? She was nine years old and she'd seen her grandfather only three days previously. As we ate breakfast I kept seeing how she sneaked glances my way almost as if she were trying to work out an appropriate response by mirroring mine. I smiled and she seemed reassured and then, together, we walked over to Joe's house.

They'd put barriers up at both ends of the street. We parked a block away and walked the rest, straight into a volley of clicking cameras. I took Cassie's hand and dropping my head led us past a group of journalists who kept their distance. Seeing us, three strangers heading for the gate, a uniformed policeman moved in to intercept but, enclosed in their familiar garage, one of the bodyguards must have spotted us. The electronic door rolled open and we were in.

Thus began days of the most bizarre socialising I'd ever encountered. There were moments of meaning, like the one when Walter and Albertina Sisulu sat side by side with us, their hands gripping ours, tears welling in their eyes at the death of their friend, this younger man, whom they had known almost all his life. But even this fragment of calm and of meaning was cut short as from centre left a woman, intent on her relentless networking, used an insistent hand to sever our connection.

And there were other moments, as well, which made me laugh: like the fax full of flowery expressions of condolence which was addressed to 'the family of the nation', or when I found myself sitting opposite a dignified line-up of men in suits, silenced by the sudden realisation that I'd forgotten who they were and what they were doing there.

I was no longer a beginner – I'd learnt something of tradition. During the run-up to Ruth's funeral it had taken me a while to understand that the gang of women who took over the kitchen and the telephone were comrades who'd come to help. Now what surprised me was not the generosity itself, but the fact that this was no group of hefty African mamas but a set of modern, successful professionals taking valuable time off from their work to be with us.

It was Ruth's wake magnified a thousand times over – friends, strangers, politicians, delegations traipsing through. In the garage stood vast aluminium coffee urns, six-foot industrial-style refrigerators packed with cold drinks, and cakes crammed on to makeshift trestles, enough to feed a multitude. There was nothing left for us to do: nothing but to sit and listen.

There were some things that happened that week which I will never, ever forget. The young African in the garden, for example, talking about being in MK and about the way he trusted Joe above all others because Joe had never lied to him; or the old soldier describing his first military mission into the country; or the women from a nearby township, grouped together in a circle, singing of Joe and, when Cassie's first tears streamed down her cheeks, taking her by the hand and teaching her to dance out her pain; or the group of youths who, catching a glimpse of the funeral committee with its complex mix of old-style traffic cops and new ANC stars in session in the garden, put new vigour into their toyi-toying, stamping the ground in riotous celebration of their leaders, their voices rising up into the air to drown out an unending discussion of food, toilets and crowd control.

It wasn't possible to talk to everybody nor to read everything that had been written about Joe. But even scanning the outpouring took precedence over any private reflective time. It was a purely public occasion: there was no way of making it different.

Midweek, Robyn and I sneaked out to the hairdresser. There was to be a memorial meeting for Joe, one of many held throughout the country, at Johannesburg's town hall at midday. We thought we'd told the hairdresser who we were and why we were in a hurry, but we were operating on a different plane from other mortals and, not understanding what we'd said, he moved agonisingly slowly. As the minutes ticked by we missed the family cortège into central Jo'burg and had to make our own way into the city centre.

The route we'd planned turned out to be a disaster – every road we tried was barricaded off. In the end, hysterical, we abandoned our car in the middle of the road and got out to tell two policemen, busy directing traffic away from the town hall, that we were Joe's daughters and that we needed help. In the old days – old but not so long ago – we wouldn't have dreamt of approaching two strange, white policemen. Now they used their radios to tell their bosses that they were leaving their posts. They got into the back of our car and waved us through the barricades.

We arrived just in time. As the singing started up, I sat on the platform remembering Joe's descriptions of forties meetings held on the steps outside this building, when blackshirts would come to do violent battle with the commies. I remembered another story as well, one my granny had told me of how the seventeen-year-old Ruth had stood on those same steps to deliver her first public speech.

The choir had finished singing 'The Internationale' in Xhosa and the speeches began. Khoisan X, the sweet-faced demagogue of the PAC, got up to deliver his. The PAC had once been infamous for their anti-white slogan, 'One settler, One bullet', which a PAC wit had once changed to read, 'One Slovo, One bullet'. Now I listened to a PAC heavy describing how when one of his young son's friends had spotted a photo of Khoisan X and Joe shaking hands, he'd asked why Khoisan X was friends with a white man.

'That's no white man,' the son had replied. 'That's Joe Slovo.'

The audience, mainly young and black, loved it: they roared out their approval.

When Joe died it started raining. It felt as if it would never stop. But by the Sunday of the funeral it did, by which time Johannesburg's red soil was saturated with moisture. We were all exhausted. The night before we'd gone back to the town hall for a private gathering. 'Private' where private meant hundreds of Joe's friends and colleagues sitting round linen-covered table-cloths while the Johannesburg Philharmonic played his favourite tunes.

The next day, a marquee was erected in the garden Joe had loved. Outside on the pavement was a row of portable toilets for the visitors who were to descend after the funeral was over. We walked to a nearby school where the cars for the family cortège had gathered. It was a marvellous and motley collection of different vehicles that met our eyes, drawn as they were from a group of Sowetan undertakers which the funeral committee had selected in a move to encourage small businesses in the township.

We ended up in the only approximation of a de luxe car, an ageing black Mercedes. In front of us, Helena rode in a Toyota Corolla while directly behind came a 1960s winged black Chevrolet. With traffic cops giving us a motor-bike escort, we set off in procession through Johannesburg and on to the motorway that would lead us to Soweto's Orlando Stadium.

In the hours after Joe's death, we had discussed with Nelson Mandela where the pre-burial ceremony should be held. We had suggested the town hall: the president had nodded solemnly before gently speculating that it might not, perhaps, be big enough. I wasn't so sure: I, who an hour before take-off always worried that nobody would come to my parties, feared that the vast stadium they had chosen would be three-quarters empty. I wasn't the only one. In the week preceding the funeral, reports of pre-funeral memorials all over the country had people muttering that attendance on the day might well be down.

It was not down. Orlando Stadium with its 60,000 person capacity was packed by the time we filed past Joe's corpse. It was laid out in an open coffin under a flagged awning. Quickly I passed the waxwork dummy, with its polished apple-peel yellow skin and its thin, tight red lips, that looked nothing like my father.

When the ritual was over, and when Nelson Mandela had stopped in front of the coffin and bent down to touch Joe, the ceremony proper began. There were three stages: one for VIPs, one for speakers, and one for family and friends. As we sat opposite the coffin, I was fascinated by a jerky band of imitation MK soldiers who kept changing honour guard. They were a hilarious reminder of Joe's military beginnings in the ANC – their exaggerated stiff-leg stamp downs, each one slightly out of step from the one ahead giving an impression less of military formation and more a quaint, and passing, wave. The coffin lid was sealed – the signal for the onset of the speechifying.

There were small segments that galvanised – like when South Africa's Chief Rabbi Harris thundered at religious Jews who dared condemn Joe while they had done nothing against apartheid's inhumanity; or the moment when a union representative vowed that South Africa would not rest until Ruth's murderers were named and the crowd shouted its approval; or the time when the Communist Party's Jeremy Cronin read one of Joe's favourite poems, Brecht's, 'In praise of Communism'. But for the remainder, I found my mind wandering.

As we sat passively listening to the endless stream of words, 12 kilometres away in Soweto's Avalon cemetery, there was a burst of frantic activity. It had rained so hard that the area around Joe's grave was swamped and they'd fetched the fire brigade to pump it out. The grave itself had been prepared some time before and was covered with wooden planks – it was only when the fire engines had left that somebody thought to look inside. They found that it was three-quarters full of water. Without time to fetch the fire brigade back, a line of blue uniformed policemen stood, half-in and half-out of the hole, passing buckets from hand to hand, emptying Joe's grave.

As the last bucket was handed up by a mud-streaked white policeman to a line of his black colleagues, the speeches finished. Joe's pine coffin was carried out and put on to the unadorned back of a gun carriage. It was the most symbolic and the most moving of moments. Joe's old comrades in the ANC military –

now ministers and deputy ministers in the government, or generals in the army – lifting 'red' Joe into the waiting hands of uniformed South African soldiers. And, as the gun carriage moved off, members of the crowd climbed on to it, keeping their Joe company. We climbed into our cars and followed.

Travelling through the exit, I got my first vision of what was to come. On the high-tiered steps which banked up on either side, stood hundreds of people, black people, watching Joe's coffin passing through. They weren't the only ones there. On the ground, the exit was a moving, fist-clenching buzz of humanity, of people who had decided to accompany us on foot. We were enveloped by bursts of chanting which issued from all directions, by faces coloured every possible shade of brown pushed up close to the windows, by blue jeans and white t–shirts and flags and posters. And that was only the beginning.

It took us more than two hours to reach the grave. We couldn't go any faster: the whole of Soweto had come to say goodbye. The roadside was lined by people, their fists clenched at shoulder height, saluting Joe's passing. Others charged forward, running in a proud, rhythmic and unrelenting 'hoff-hoff'. On and on stretched the procession, five deep, a carnival, a celebration of Joe's life. Echoing the old days when tear gas was the police's inevitable response to a crowded funeral, buckets of water and hoses connected to taps lined the roadside but now they were used to quench the thirst of passing runners. All around was the sound of singing, of 'Hamba Kahle Umkhonto' songs of the old days, of the camps and of Joe.

His face was everywhere, his picture printed on every third t-shirt. Amongst them, an original in black and white on which was printed the words, 'Goodbye – Nelson Mandela' and below that the words, 'Cheers – Joe Slovo.'

Ahead of us Helena's car overheated and lurched to a halt. No problem – there was a crowd of mourners competing for the honour of physically pushing the family through the last leg of its journey. Behind, there were other casualties: buses ready to topple over; steam issuing from under black bonnets; twisted ankles being treated by the side. The vehicular strain was so intense that most of the mourners ended up walking the last half mile, their high heels sinking deep into red-brown Soweto mud.

At the grave side itself there was chaos. A decision had been taken not to use the police or army to patrol the crowd but in getting monitors who'd learnt their trade during the election, the organisers had underestimated the crowd's strength. There was almost mayhem as we pushed our way through the churning mud to get up to the stage. The crowd stretched out, unruly now, jostling to come closer, angry that it was refused access. For a moment it looked as though the funeral might end in violence.

A family member, traditionally a man, was to give the graveside thanks: we, Joe's women, had decided Helena should do it. She started, but the noise was so intense she couldn't go on. Battling for order Cyril Ramaphosa and Thabo Mbeki finally succeeded in winning a moment's quiet. Helena jumped into it, reading the speech we'd written together, describing the man we had known. When she got to the part that called Joe 'endearingly messy', a man who'd loved 'peanuts, whisky, cigars, red socks, wine, women and song' the crowd roared out its one last collective gesture of approval.

It was almost over. Time for the moment of Ruth's funeral that I remember most clearly, when the mourners took turns to cover her coffin with dirt. But at Joe's funeral there were just too many people. I didn't know it was happening and didn't hear the simultaneous sound of AK 47s firing in salute. Only later was I able to sit in front of a television screen and watch my father's coffin being lowered and see the roses that went afterwards, the candles, and the spadefuls of Soweto dirt.

It didn't really matter. Joe's people, not just his family, had come to bury him and bury him they did.

As for me, I was left with one enduring thought. What Joe had said to me was absolutely right: in a very real sense, this was *his* South Africa.

Chapter Twenty-Eight

We were sitting in Joe's study, reading through his will, surrounded by pictures of Joe. I was fascinated by one in particular – a photograph of him standing beside Helena in a London doorway on the day in 1987 when he married her. Smiling broadly, he lifts up his trouser hem to reveal his red sock.

He looks so happy in the picture and yet . . .

I looked away from it, remembering how, on the day before his wedding, Joe, having just flown in from Zambia, had run between each of his three daughters, trying to placate us. When my turn came, we'd ended up in a wine bar, pushing wilted lettuce leaves around white plates as he, as near to tears as I'd ever seen him, tried to explain.

So did I. I tried to get him to understand that it wasn't that he was getting married which bothered me, but the fact that, although he'd come to London especially to tie the knot, he hadn't told us. How could he, having shared the knowledge with other people, have imagined that we wouldn't learn of it? The news of the impending wedding had circulated around North London and reached us in a flash. And if, by some miracle, we had been kept in ignorance, what would he have said if one of us had innocently suggested we meet up at the same time as he was due at the registry office?

That day before his wedding, none of his stuttered justifications rang true. I was too angry with him: angry that he hadn't trusted me enough to know that I loved him and would have supported his marriage; angry that, even if he feared my disapproval, he, who had faced the prospect of sending men he loved to their possible deaths, did not have the strength to face me.

But now that was all in the past. I sat in his study, in the present, looking at the photo, drinking in the sight of him as he had been then – chubby, smiling, alive. I could hardly remember him like that. His cancer had consumed not just his bones, but my memories as well, wiping away the image of my healthy father and replacing it with an emaciated, frail, forbidding, dying figure. I knew I would have to work hard to reclaim what once had seemed so familiar.

The will was straightforward and it didn't take long for Helena to guide us through. It had been written, she said, almost at Joe's end. I guessed this was another mark of his obsession with his work, but I also wondered whether he'd put it off because he, who'd never cared much for material things, just couldn't decide what to leave each member of his complex family.

Or perhaps it was something different again: perhaps it was that, even at the end, he did not really want to acknowledge that he was dying. He'd been so brave about it, so defiant in the jaws of death: and yet had this man, whose optimism had sustained him through terrible times, truly accepted that he was mortal?

So many unanswered questions: as they passed through my mind, I realised that the peace I had reached at Joe's end was being chipped away. I sat by the window seat, looking out at the garden, worrying that it would one day be completely gone, sealed up only in distant memory.

'I've looked in the obvious places,' Helena was saying.

She was speaking to me. I shook myself and concentrated.

'I know they're somewhere,' she continued. 'I'll find them and send them on to you.'

She was talking about Joe's medals which he had left to me so that I could hand them on in turn to my daughter. His medals: the Isithwalandwe which he had accepted a few short weeks before his death, and the others as well; the one, sparkling with tiny rubies that had been presented to him at the Kremlin on his sixtieth birthday; and the Czech stamped vision of socialist workers that had been a tribute to a fellow revolutionary. They were a mark of who he was, his history stamped in bronze and gold and they felt like the best of inheritances.

To Cassie, directly, Joe had left money. She had been so grown up these last few weeks, and so well behaved – now her chin wobbled and she quavered that she didn't want a cheque, she wanted something of Joe. At which point Helena disappeared into the house and came back with a hard-edged leather shoulder bag.

'See if you can find what's inside,' she said.

Cassie undid the clasp and opened the bag, rooting through its two lined compartments. Without success. She handed it on to us and we each had a go. Her lip trembled, there was nothing there. She passed the bag back to Helena who deftly showed her how to unlock its secrets. There were two compartments we hadn't located. Each was concealed in the lining behind the thick leather which, once parted, could be instantly velcroed back. The first was empty.

'Try the other one,' Helena said.

When Cassie tried it, she found a passport: a British passport, something that stateless Joe could never have legally owned. The name on the cover, which was echoed on page one, was a stranger's name but page three bore a picture of a man we all knew: it was Joe who, wearing an unfamiliar pair of thick-framed spectacles, his hair an uneasy, wig-like thatch, blinked nervously into the camera's lens, the portrait of a sleazy salesman. Helena couldn't remember exactly why the passport had been made – she had accepted it as a souvenir of his days of subterfuge along with the false moustache, the strange glasses and the lurid green contact lenses that Joe had stored, casually, in his bedside table and which were still there. They and the passport, due to expire sometime in 1995, had outlived him.

It was time for Andy, Cassie and I to go. At Johannesburg's Park Street railway station, we got on the train to Cape Town.

Almost sixty years ago, a steam engine had brought the ten-year-old, Yiddish-speaking Joe on the last stretch of a 6,000 mile

journey to this city, his new home. Now we were to make the trip
in reverse. As the train pulled out on the first leg of its journey into
the high *veld* and flat plains of the Orange Free State, I thought that
Joe must have endured the journey on wooden benches in third
class: we had a sleeper carriage to ourselves.

By dusk, we were still crossing the great expanse of the Free
State. As we neared the Karoo, buff-coloured hills took on the
burnished red and orange flame of the setting sun, descending
finally into the magically star-filled semi-desert Karoo sky. Joe
came to me again, his voice telling me that this was the best sky,
the best landscape, the best country in the world.

He had loved South Africa so. Did he know how much it
loved him back?

He was lucky: I'm sure he did.

Thinking about how different were our lives, I wondered
whether it was inevitable that we could not find a middle
ground. His secret world of guns and high-level politics – mine
of friends and family and inner callings. It seemed they had to
be in opposition. Except I couldn't let myself off the hook so
easily. Excluded from his male realm, I had learned from my
mother to defend myself with scorn. Now I wondered whether,
if I had opened up a little more, if I had shown Joe how much
I valued what he had done, perhaps he would have let me in.

We went to the dining car for supper. Our steward was a fat
man with a Chaplinesque moustache and dressed in trousers
held up by braces which went straight from belt to neck,
bypassing his stomach entirely, a white shirt to cover his massive
belly and a bow tie which served only to emphasise his bulk. An
Afrikaner from a dirt-poor family, he told us how much he'd
admired Joe and then he moved on to talking of his dream of
living in another country, somewhere where he could earn more
money.

The food was frozen fish and putty chips. I picked at it while
I half-listened to the conversation issuing from a nearby table.

'I'm glad he's dead,' I heard a vivacious blonde telling her
companion.

I looked up.

'If Mandela had gone first,' her high-pitched exuberance could not have been more resonant, 'Mr Slovo would have become our president and then we would have had to put up with his communistic ideas and it would all be over for us.'

It made me smile to hear the use of the word mister – good old authoritarian South Africa asserting itself – but at the same time I was conscious that she was talking about my father. I didn't think, I reacted. I turned and told her I was one of Joe's daughters. Only in the moment that followed her puce blushing and her stuttered apologies did I pull myself together. I shouldn't have said anything: Joe never would have. I left my supper and went into hiding.

I couldn't sleep. When the train stopped, I heard voices. Going into the corridor I saw that we had reached a station in the mid Karoo – the twinkling lights of a strange town in the middle of nowhere lit up the sight of Africans climbing into the carriages, exchanging low greetings.

I heard another sound, this one issuing from behind. I turned to find a thin, white woman with sad eyes and blue dangling earrings matching her blue trouser suit, clutching her tiny adored chihuahua, standing in the corridor. Seeing me, she disappeared back into her cabin.

The train lurched forward. As its wheels overtook the night I stayed in the corridor, staring out at nothingness, thinking that only two things had ever silenced my ebullient, optimistic father. The first had been my mother's death: the second was his own.

Part Four

Chapter Twenty-Nine

Andy, Cassie and I had come to South Africa for six months. We should have known it would not be enough and that Joe's dying would take up so much of it. Now we prolonged our stay, promising schools and estate agents and publishers that we would be back by May. And then, with the cut-off date looming, I pulled myself out of the lethargy that had descended on me since Joe's death. I brushed the dust off old files, wrote new letters protesting about the silence with which various ministries had met my requests for information, read books on death squads and made appointments with journalists who might point me in the direction of Ruth's killers, scanned letters searching out clues to follow and people to interview, set up library visits and then I did one more thing.

I was in a café in a shopping mall. The muzak was loud and cloying, the waiters wore clumsy white aprons over smart black trousers and my coffee was all milk froth and chocolate powder. None of that worried me: I was concentrating on the near-stranger seated opposite.

His name was Michael. As I stared at him, I was visited by a strange, insignificant memory dating back decades to a time when Michael and I had both been living in London. He was very young then, under five years old and I remembered him clinging shyly to his mother's legs while I waited in the doorway for one of my parents to pick up a document from one of his.

'This must feel odd to you,' he said. He was all grown up now, in his early twenties, drawing on a cigarette, but looking just as shy.

I knew my unwavering gaze must be disturbing him: I couldn't tear my eyes away. I took in the sight of his chubby cheeks, the awkward slant of his red lips, his high cheekbones and his short cut wavy light brown hair and I thought: he looks nothing like Joe. Which put me, apparently, in a minority of one. Everybody else whose opinion I'd polled insisted that Michael Sachs was the spitting image of the young Joe Slovo.

The explanation for this was simple: Michael was, by all accounts, my brother. Or, to be more accurate, my half-brother, Joe's son, born out of an illicit affair which had been concluded when Ruth was still alive.

Here was a piece of the family jigsaw I'd never dreamt might come to light. No matter what changes we had all endured, no matter how many different countries we lived in we had always been the same: Ruth, Joe, three children – three sisters – and definitely no boy. Except, it now appeared, there had been one: Michael, Joe's son, my half-brother whose existence slashed through my enduring image of my family.

It took only a couple of weeks after Joe's death for my sisters and I to be let into the secret that we, Joe's children, numbered more than three. The first I heard of it, I was in our Cape Town home when some friends dropped by. With Cassie in bed, we adults sat drinking wine. We were chatting aimlessly when one of our visitors inserted a *non sequitur* into the conversation.

'The reason why I'm here . . .' he said.

The reason? I'd assumed it was a social visit. My sense of relaxation fled. Glancing across at Andy, I saw a mixture of perplexity and apprehension working at his face and I knew it wasn't only my imagination that whatever it was we were about to hear was bound to be unwelcome.

Our visitor ploughed on, '. . . there's a problem,' he said, 'no, not exactly a problem, but something I have to tell you.'

By the studied calm of his tone and by the way his partner was staring fixedly at the floor, I guessed the problem must have something to do with Joe. It flashed through my mind that he'd committed some unforgivable ministerial misdemeanour which was about to come to light. But of course he wouldn't have, not my honest, incorruptible, moral father.

And of course it wasn't that. What Joe had done was much more personal. He'd had a son. Twenty-three years previously.

In that instant of hearing the news, I was thrown off course. I had thought that I was doing so well, that because of the public nature of Ruth's funeral I had been prepared for Joe's. I'd sat through it assuming that after it was over we would be left to mourn in private. Now my short moment of peace was annihilated, my grief stanched as I tried to fit this new information into the things that I had always assumed were the constants of Joe's life.

I guess that if I had been less shocked I would have seen the humour in the situation. After all, I had gone out, against my father's wishes, to uncover the past. I'd found nothing of which he could have been ashamed, until this moment when this piece of information had come looking for me.

After our visitors left, I lay awake, recapturing flashes from childhood. I remembered the time when I woke up to find Joe gently tucking me in, or that time on the beach when he had got down on all fours and barked like a dog to make us laugh, or his holding his precious guitar and singing a Yiddish lullaby that his mother must once have sung to him, or the joke he told about the sailors and the dead horses that went on forever but never got boring . . . scores of memories of my affectionate, happy, caring father whose daughters were all precious to him, who'd never had a son. Except, it seemed, he had.

The next day, sitting with my sisters on the wooden deck of a friend's beach house on Glen Beach, we talked above the crashing of huge Atlantic breakers. Robyn was almost completely silent – she couldn't deal with the news, she said, not then – while Shawn kept saying it didn't matter, that whatever Joe had done in the past was now irrelevant. I seemed to be the only one to be gripped by anger. Was it because I had defied Joe and set out on my quest, only to be landed with a piece of information I didn't want and that I hadn't been looking for?

It was that, I guess, and something else as well – the way the exigencies of public demand took precedence over our private needs even in the face of death. I knew the reason why we'd been let into the secret and it was a public reason. We were told because people feared that the newspapers might soon approach us and ask about Joe's son.

I could picture the build-up to the revelation: how, amidst the arrangements, the pandemonium and the grief that had centred on Joe's house after his death, there had been unfolding this separate drama. Michael, ambushed by unexpected feelings of loss at the news of the death of the famous father he had never known, had joined the throngs and tried to talk to us. He was kept at bay but, even though we didn't know of it, his insistence was enough to start the gossip going until it threatened to break out of the inner circle and reach the public.

In Glen Beach with my sisters, I stared as surfers in their gleaming wet suits lounged on boards waiting for the next breaker to sweep them forward, and images of Joe engulfed me. I thought about the moment when he'd sat on the patio of his ministerial house, grimly repeating that he wouldn't tell me anything, or the time, after that, when the two of us had been down the road at Blues restaurant, and I sat passive as Joe snowed me with his own irrefutable version of his relationship with Ruth.

He had been so determined to get his view across and yet, it now appeared, he had told me only half the story. He had laid the ground rules which were to govern not only his behaviour but mine as well. I had sat and absorbed his righteous indignation about Ruth's affairs and the dishonesty of her letters, and, having just had my own encounter with Ruth's lover, I had found myself agreeing with him. Not totally perhaps – I was still the daughter of two rebels brought up to argue my case, and I had kicked against his rules. But I was conscious that he was dying and I never pressed him again about the things I wanted to know, the things he wouldn't tell me.

And now I discovered that one of the things that he'd kept secret was that he had a son.

Could this have been the thing he wanted to hide? Was this

why he had insisted it was his life, not mine, his business not mine?

Perhaps it was.

I had thought that meeting Michael might bring me clarity. Now I was no longer so sure. As a waiter swapped one overflowing glass ashtray for another, I listened to Michael talking about the way he'd been brought up thinking of another man as his father, and how, when he turned sixteen, his mother had told him the truth about his paternity. Her hand was forced, he said, by the fact that as Michael had integrated himself into the ANC community in Tanzania where he'd been sent to school, people started commenting on his startling resemblance to Joe.

When I said I didn't see it, Michael rode right through my sentence. He sat, smoking, sipping coffee and continuing doggedly with his story. *My* father might be freshly dead, but my status was mere bit player – a witness to this young man's pain which he couldn't quite acknowledge, that he had lost the last possibility of contact with *his* father.

I told myself I was being unfair. I put myself in his place and I wondered how it must have felt to sit in the midst of that enormous funeral crowd and listen to a succession of speakers reading praise poems to your unacknowledged father. And yet, I wondered, if Joe had been a teacher or a milkman or a lawyer, would not knowing him have mattered so much to Michael?

He wasn't interested in what was, after all, only speculation: he wanted to tell his story. He and Joe met as adults, he said, on only two occasions and both of them had taken place inside South Africa. The first meeting happened a couple of years before the 1994 election. Michael had been in the centre of a crowd of people marching through Johannesburg in protest at the violence that was breaking out all over the country, when Joe had crossed his path. Joe, Michael said, looked lost and he asked where the front of the march was. When Michael pointed it out, Joe wandered off in the direction of his finger, thus ending encounter number one.

Listening, I thought it was absurd. With everybody going in the same direction, it couldn't have been so very difficult to work out where the front of the march might be. I saw Michael looking at me. I smiled and made some comment about the symbolism of Joe's sudden appearance and disappearance. Michael barely returned my smile: he was too busy moving on to encounter number two which was equally stained with meaning.

It had also happened during those frenetic pre-election years, this time at the World Trade Centre where the negotiations on the future of South Africa were in full swing. Arriving at the end of a long corridor Michael had seen his non-biological father Albie engrossed in intense conversation with Joe. Michael had thought about turning and leaving but the corridor was one straight line and he'd decided that this would draw too much attention to himself. So he kept on moving, slowly towards the two men until eventually he came abreast of them, enraptured as they were by their discussion of ANC strategy.

Michael made as if to pass them but Albie held out a restraining hand and, looking at Joe, said, 'I don't know whether you've met my son?' At which Joe smiled, said no, shook Michael's hand, told him it was nice to meet him and then returned, as Michael walked away, to his conversation.

It was so bizarre: this time I laughed out loud.

In the flash of Michael's answering grin, did I see my father? I don't know whether I could allow myself to – although I couldn't deny the surge of affection I felt for this young man I didn't know.

But I had other things to preoccupy me. I sat and tried to imagine what could possibly have been going through Joe's mind. I thought of him as he had been then, working ferociously in the race against the cancer that was eating up his bones, caught up in the fulfilment of his life's dream at the very moment that he realised his life was almost over. Was that enough to explain his off-hand greeting? Was it that, or had he decided long ago that biology had nothing to do with a relationship? And, of course, there was a third possibility: that Joe had not known Michael was his son. Part of me found it had to believe that he could have been quite so blasé in Michael's presence if he had known: and yet, as Michael and a host of other people kept telling me, Joe had been told about it more than once. Perhaps he was told, I thought, and perhaps he just didn't believe it.

All these questions – only one person could have answered them and he was dead.

I heard myself telling Michael that it was a pity he hadn't tried to talk to Joe. I tried to tell him how Joe, whose preference was to run from emotional conflict, also had an ability to face it head on. As I explained this, badly, to Joe's son, I saw his eyes glazing over. I stopped in mid-sentence, realising that the person I was really trying to convince was myself.

I needed to be gone. As Joe had done before me, I shook Michael's hand and said it had been nice to meet him and then I got up and walked away.

The strains of insipid orchestral pap pursued me as I rode the escalator, through two floors and all the way up to the top of the roof-terrace garage. Getting into my car, I drove it down the ramp towards the exit. At ground level there was a queue of other cars ahead – I wondered absently whether one might belong to my half-brother. I didn't look too closely. I sat, letting my concentration slip, vaguely wondering when they had started piping muzak into the belly of the garage.

But then I realised it wasn't muzak, it was something else. It was coming from the booths that stood at the end of each line of cars. Looking more closely I saw two African women who, sealed up inside the small plywood and glass structures, were alleviating the boredom of punching tickets and handing out change, by singing together in harmony. The song they were singing was familiar. I'd heard it last at Joe's funeral. It was the lilting strains of an MK song, a tribute to the military heroes of the struggle. And then, as my car inched forward, I realised something else: that the women had inserted one name in pride of place. One name – my father's name.

Chapter Thirty

I could feel Cape Town's midsummer sun burning my shoulders as I crossed Green Market Square. I weaved my way through canvas-covered stalls where long-haired white boys and their beach-bunny sidekicks were busy selling the same cheap jewellery, the same raw cotton shirts and the same angular candlesticks as in any London street market. Reaching the market's opposite corner, I crossed the road, walked past an Italian restaurant doing brisk imitation *cappuccino* business, and into a narrow Cape Town house which had been converted into offices.

It was much cooler inside. I took the stairs two at a time, up to the first floor and the law office where I'd previously gone for advice on how to wrest my parents' files from police archives. The receptionist was sitting behind her desk, flamboyant in a pleated, crimson dress that set off her chocolate brown skin. As I pushed the glass door open, she got up and walked, surprisingly quickly for a woman of her bulk, round her desk.

I was in a hurry. I handed her the poster – one of many produced after Joe's death which shows him, glasses in hand, staring preoccupied, into the distance – that I'd brought for her. She stared at it, long and hard. I had expected thanks, not this puzzling hesitation that had me thinking I'd done something wrong.

She was frowning as eventually she put the poster down. 'Please don't take offence,' she said. 'I know I asked you for a picture of our hero, but I don't like this one. I want to remember JS as he was at the peak of his powers, not as this distracted old man.'

I didn't take offence. I knew exactly what she was saying: after all I, too, had wanted to remember a different Joe.

*

A thump as another batch of black bound volumes of old newspapers landed on my table. I looked up to find the librarian already wheeling her trolley along the ranks of other, silent readers. Her delivery had arrived just in time: I pushed the volume I'd finished to one side and, reaching for the next in sequence, began turning at its pages.

I was on a roll, in perfect rhythm scrolling through decades of recent South African history which was also my parents' history. It was all there in newsprint, their lives chronicled. Reports of my mother's arrest in 1963 accompanied by conflicting accounts of Joe's whereabouts at the time, and the same pictures that lined the pages of our family albums – glamorous, professional shots of Ruth and Joe captured on the steps of Jo'burg's courtrooms. I looked at them, so happy then, so confident that they would win soon.

And yet their time of enchantment was almost over. In 1963 everything ended in rout. Those prominent activists who were not in prison fled into exile while the rest of the country, cowed by the ferocity of the repression, fell silent. While Ruth struggled to rebuild her life first in London, then in Durham and finally in Mozambique, Joe and his comrades drifted from one African country to the next, inching their way closer to the South African borders. That was the second time in his life, I thought, when Joe had been forced to leave his home: I wondered whether it had brought up echoes of the first.

I had finished with 1963 – I skipped some years and reached for 1967. Practice had made me adept at guessing the length of the sport reports and the full page adverts that lined the newspapers' final pages, and I expertly passed them by. I kept on going, working my way through each successive volume, through the late sixties and those long bleak years when Joe and his comrades had sat in their office near Goodge Street, at the top of a steep flight of stairs, using steam and oven cleaner and caustic soda and sometimes blood to send and decipher secret messages, in an attempt to get things moving in South Africa. I read of their blind stabs into danger, like the time in 1967 when a group of ANC fighters had tried to pass through Rhodesia into South Africa and had been trapped by the combined might of the South African and Rhodesian armies and almost wiped out in the game reserve of Wankie.

Joe must have known most of the men who were killed, I thought. It must have been a terrible moment and yet at the time I, fifteen and preoccupied with my own life, hadn't even noticed that this drama was unfolding. Now, in hindsight, I knew how different were the worlds that we have inhabited: while I was busy trying to pretend that South Africa had nothing to do with me, my father was learning to live with danger and with death.

I was at school during the Wankie disaster, and I was at university when another of Joe's ambitious plans went wrong. It started in 1972, around the time, I guess, when Michael had been born.

I leafed through months of newspapers to find an account of the trial of the six men who were eventually convicted of bringing arms, ammunition and explosives into the country. Amongst a list of their co-conspirators was a familiar name – my father's name.

It came as no surprise. Joe had told me already about this military operation which, code named 'J', had been a plan, guided by Joe and then ANC president Oliver Tambo to send a boatload of MK soldiers to the Transkei coast, their job to kickstart armed action inside the country. It all went disastrously wrong when a member of the boat's foreign recruited crew sabotaged the engines and the people who had been sent into the country as a reception committee were arrested. The whole incident had stuck in my memory because once, when I'd been in mid book and searching for an event around which to hang part of a fictional plot, Joe had described it to me. At the time, I was startled by his frankness and flattered as well. It felt like a turning point that he should share this secret with me. But now, seeing how details of the expedition were spread all over the South African newspapers of the time, I realised that it was a secret which had already been blown.

To historian Luli Callinicos, Joe had described Operation J:

> I remember sitting in Moscow with admirals and generals
> from the Soviet armed forces who were helping ... [There
> were] people inside country, on beaches, to prepare DLBs[1] for
> the weaponry that was coming ... OR[2] wanted to go as part
> of landing party ... When we said no, he broke down and he
> wept. You know tears were just streaming, it was phenome-
> nal, you know it was absolutely so genuine ... He couldn't
> expect others to risk their lives because this was the real first
> big thing, and he is the leader and he feels he has to be there
> and he tried to talk us into accepting that because this was his
> area, it was Pondoland you see and he knew the place...

I could imagine them together, OR and Joe, impatient to be in
the country that they loved, but sitting instead in Moscow,
powerless as the plans they had so carefully laid went wrong.
And, as I thought about Joe's description of OR's tears, I
wondered how he had coped with the bad news. He was a
general and risking men was a general's job, and yet there are not
many such leaders who know their men as intimately as Joe
knew his.

I heard the squeaking of the trolley, the librarian returning.
She raised a questioning eyebrow and I nodded: I had done with
1972 and she could take this instalment of my father's cuttings
away. As she did so, I reached for the next and for a while after
that I was in constant motion, flicking fast through the mid-
seventies until I reached reports of the Soweto uprising of 1976.
I slowed down then, reading through descriptions of the
thousands of children who'd started by protesting against the use
of Afrikaans in school and ended up dying in a hail of police

---

1. Dead letter boxes – safe places.
2. Oliver Reginald Tambo was called by the affectionate shorthand of
OR.

bullets. As I went through them, I was revisited by that memory of Joe, of his square face, his plump physique, his hair its old familiar, wavy brown and his eyes shining as he'd talked about the way that revolutions were made by the young because they were fearless, whereas old people were cowed by the thought of death.

I thought of how Joe had been, not cowed, but silent in the face of an end he could not avoid.

Sitting in a library, I passed through 1976 and on to 1977. Turning the pages of the tabloid *The Citizen* I found a banner headline. JOE SLOVO IS TERROR MASTER, it screamed, its effect slightly undermined by the incongruous framing of an advert for a karate centre and the photo of six women with big hair grinning madly under the title, 'Knicky Knacky Knoo'.

I read through the article that spanned not only page one, but the whole of page two as well. I knew that it marked the beginnings of a campaign in the demonisation of Joe which, in the black and white madness of South Africa, would eventually turn him into one of the country's most popular heroes. But what surprised me was that amongst a list of also-rans in this hall of infamy was Ruth – her name and her photo as well. Ruth whom the newspaper called, 'Slovo's wife ... worshipped by South African exiles in Britain who refer to her as the "high priestess" of the South African Communist Party. . .'

I paused long enough to marvel at the way apartheid's propaganda machine had banded my parents together. Joe might have been a military chief but Ruth, whose weapons were her high profile and her sharp tongue, was also fingered. Was this where it started, I wondered: had her assassins laid the justification for their act so far back in time? I wondered whether I would ever find anyone qualified to answer that question, and if I did, whether I'd be strong enough to ask it.

I copied down the phrase, 'high priestess', and thought of the way Ruth used to argue incessantly against the people she called 'apparachniks'. Her insistence that she be allowed to think and say what she wanted had led her almost to the point of expulsion from the Communist Party and yet this hadn't stopped some lazy journalist turning her into a high priestess of orthodoxy. I wondered whether she had laughed when she had read of it.

I didn't wonder for long. I had work to do. I was drawn on by this official catalogue of my parents' public lives, on through the end of the seventies and into the beginning of 1980, a year which must have made Joe very happy. I read the intensifying reports of actions inside South Africa, of bucket bombs spraying leaflets over city centres, of firebombs flung at police stations, of arms infiltrated into the country. And then there came the moment that must have numbered amongst Joe's most triumphant.

Flaming Hell was the headline to a front-page article which went on to describe how:

> Residents shaken from sleep by the explosions streamed from their homes into the biting cold to watch billowing towers of flame and smoke rising high into the sky . . . Fire engines with sirens screaming raced to the blazing tanks. As dawn broke over the sprawling complex the funnels of dense black smoke became visible against the lightening sky. The rising sun tinged the smoke red . . .

The event that had provoked this lyricism was the blowing up of the Sasol Oil Refinery on 1 June 1980, which Joe – now in sole charge of an ANC military unit called Special Operations (Special Ops for short) – had planned. I had known at the time that Joe was the brains behind Special Ops and yet, true to custom, we never talked of it. Even after his death the bombing still seemed to be shrouded by secrecy. It took me more than a year to track down the handful of people who were the only survivors of the original group that had carried out the Sasol raid[3]. From them I heard about the preparations that had gone

---

3. Most of the members of the original Sasol group were later killed, either in combat in South Africa or in Matola.

into the explosion; the men hand-picked from Funda, the ANC's training camp in Angola; their forays into South Africa to do reconnaissance; the stories they told about their bank-robbing exploits to explain away their eagerness to pay big bucks for genuine Sasol tin hats; the blue overalls they scrubbed at so that they would not look new; and then the final moment when they drove from Mozambique into Swaziland and across the border into South Africa and carried out their plan. I thought of the details my father must have stored in his head and I wondered whether, during my first visit to Maputo, it was last-minute Sasol arrangements which had got Joe to stop his car and hold his whispered meetings on the street.

Those were dangerous times. The exiled ANC was both infiltrated by spies and full of people who talked too much. In the years before Sasol, MK combatants who entered South Africa had been picked off one by one. To forestall this, Joe got permission to carry out his acts of sabotage without consulting anyone save the ANC's then president, Oliver Tambo. Even the men who had helped plan the bombing were only told it was about to go down a few hours before they crossed the border. Everything Joe had done had taught him that effective subterfuge was the thing that separated success from failure, life from death: no wonder his conversations with me had been restricted to trivialities.

The attack on Sasol was meticulously planned and it turned out to be Joe's most successful military coup. There were no casualties but the fire that followed the detonation of the limpet mines burned for three days and three nights – a R6 million jolt to the economic heart of South Africa and its capacity to circumvent the threat of sanctions by storing oil. But it was more than that as well: it put the ANC military on the map, and it gave to people in South Africa the feeling that the guns that they had always been pleading for were on their way. It was a blow against the apartheid regime: a blow they set out to avenge.

I had stuck strips of paper to mark the pages I wanted for photocopying. I carried the volume over to the main desk. As

I waited for somebody to come and take my order, I wondered whether it was Sasol that had sent the South African police after Ruth. Shaking myself back into the present, I handed in my request form, and then I walked back to my table, thinking that perhaps Sasol had been the trigger. But I knew it wasn't Ruth that they had got, or at least not then.

Seven months after Sasol the South African state hit back. I sat down at the table, in the quiet of a Cape Town library, remembering the sound of Ruth's voice in 1981, distant on the telephone, as she told me that Joe's commander, Obadi, who'd been wounded during the attack on ANC houses in the Maputo suburb of Matola, had died. I heard her voice, issuing from the past. 'Joe's very upset,' she had said, almost tentatively as if she wasn't sure whether I was old enough to countenance this long-distance reference to my father's distress.

Many years later I went to Matola to look at the place where Obadi had got his fatal stomach wound. It's a solid double-storey house with a road on one side and a field where Mozambicans lived on the other, contained within its own grounds and surrounded by fruit orchards. It had been restored after the attack, but the heavy peppering of shrapnel on the balcony floor was left as a reminder of what had happened. The house had been a base for the Special Ops group on that night of Monday 29 January, when a number of military trucks went past the house and pulled up beyond the property. A few men, dressed in Mozambican army uniforms got out and called from the gate in Portuguese that they had come to raid for weapons. By the time the ANC men, dazed by sleep, emerged from the house and one of them noticed that the soldiers were in black face and they all heard gunfire coming from where two other ANC residences were being attacked, it was too late. Those who didn't get away were gunned down, Obadi amongst them. He crawled back into the house and lay clutching his wounded stomach. Near him were two dead SADF soldiers, one with a swastika on his helmet.

Joe went to see Obadi in hospital. He was lying behind

isolation glass and he waved jauntily at Joe. The doctors told them that if Obadi lasted three days, he would most likely be fine. He died in two and a half.

It was the only time that Joe talked to me of the death in battle of any of his men. And what he told me was that after Obadi's mother crossed illegally into Mozambique for his funeral, he had gone to see her.

'I told her how sorry I was,' he said. 'And what a great guy her son had been. She didn't cry. She looked at me and quietly said that she was proud of her son, that what he had done was right, that he had given his life for a great cause.' His eyes had misted up. 'She told me to carry on,' he said and added, almost crying, 'These people: they are so wonderful.'

Defiance in the face of loss, bravery in death – that was my parents' world. Listening to Joe describing the moment, I wasn't sure I could be that wonderful.

Now, in the present, I thought about the things I had learned about Obadi – a pseudonym that the young Aubrey (Monsto) Mokgabudi had adopted when he'd joined MK. I'd heard tales of stones thrown up at Sowetan windows in the dead of night as students made furious by the killings of 1976 prepared to leave the country and bring back guns. Obadi had been amongst them, a 'township sharpie' with flair, a 'clever' with charisma. Everyone who'd known him was at pains to describe his many attributes: his bravery in battle; his flair for leadership; his humour; his brilliance and his vitality. And everyone said one other thing – of the special bond between Joe and this wild young man from the township. From several sources I heard the story of the time that Obadi got so drunk that he slept through the departure of his plane from Maputo to Angola's capital city of Luanda. It was a serious lapse: he had been due to bring his Special Ops group back into Mozambique so that they could set out on the Sasol expedition but because he missed the plane, and because there was only one flight per week, the first planned raid on Sasol was drastically delayed.

Joe had been furious but Joe had also forgiven Obadi. Their

relationship, a friend of both the men said, was very special. 'Joe loved Obadi,' she'd said. 'He said that there was no limit to how far Obadi could have gone in the organisation.' And then, knowing that Michael was on my mind, she added, 'In a very real sense, if Joe could have chosen a son, if he had a son, it was Obadi.'

Joe had loved Obadi and he had died. He wasn't the only one. Twelve ANC men were killed at the three ANC houses. Twelve black men and one white Portuguese engineer as well who had been caught up in the road block and killed because he was mistaken for Joe.

Was that, I thought, why Joe had always refused bodyguards? Had he been trying to even up the score?

Twelve men, whose graves bore the same date and the same headstones and which lie side by side with Ruth's.

I thought about the sequence. Was it all tit for tat? Sasol and then the attack on Matola: Samora Machel's defiant riposte and then Ruth's death? Were they all connected?

I didn't think I'd ever know the certain answer to that question. All I could do was skirt the fringes of that world, and gather my insight from them. I thought about what Philip Mabena, one of the men who carried out the Sasol attack, had said when I asked him if he had been scared when he was cutting through the perimeter fence. 'The struggle was between life and death,' he said. 'If it was possible for us to die, we would have died for it . . .'

Heroism and death – they lived by it and many of them did die by it as well.

The dust from old newspapers had gone deep into my skin. Looking round I saw that while I'd been concentrating on the past, the library had been almost completely emptied of other readers. I'd also had enough. I turned the heavy folder over, shut it tight and left.

Chapter Thirty-One

120 Plein Street was just as it had been when Joe was still alive. I rode the lift, past the fifth floor where a new housing minister was ensconced and up to the eighteenth – the building's pinnacle. As the lift doors opened, I found myself facing a brace of uniformed policemen gossiping in Afrikaans by a bullet-proof cubicle. By the time I'd stepped out, they'd gone silent.

Instead of asking them for directions, I read the wall signs. There were two: one, pointing to the left and the offices of deputy president F.W. de Klerk; and the other to the right, and NIS, the national intelligence service. I went right, conscious of the sound of their voices starting up again.

I walked down a corridor until I could go no further. My way was blocked by a security gate. I slipped my hand through its metal bars and rang the bell. From an inner office which had two doors, one wooden and one made of steel more than ten inches thick, a woman emerged.

'Gillian,' she said, opening up, 'Mr Nhlanhla is expecting you.'

The thick-pile carpet blotted out the sound of our footsteps as she led me through the NIS inner sanctum. Her knuckles rapped against the door and then she pushed it open and I went in.

Joe Nhlanhla, once head of ANC security in Zambia and then head of MK and now boss of South Africa's new-broom intelligence agency, stepped out from behind his enormous desk. His office spanned an entire corner of the building and as he came closer I couldn't help thinking that if he had been lucky enough to have his own space in exile in Zambia, it would have been tiny and dusty, crammed with broken-down furniture. I looked out. Far below stood Cape Town's parliament and the pristine gardens that enclosed the parliamentary complex, all dwarfed by the bluish bulk of Table Mountain.

A lithe, thin figure in an over-large blue business suit, Joe took my hand in his small, soft one and directed me towards a sofa. We were joined by Mo Shaik, former ANC underground operative, now an NIS high flyer. They made a fascinating double act, these two. Mo was a handsome, bald-headed gym fanatic from Durban, one of a new breed of South Africans, smooth, sophisticated and full of easy charm. He sat down, leant forward and started tapping his foot, eager to get things moving. But his boss was in charge and Joe was altogether much more measured, with a fine mind hidden under a sometimes incomprehensibly roundabout way of expressing himself. Legend has it that it was Joe who had stubbornly sat out the old guard's determination to keep a grip on this, once the most powerful and most dangerous of apartheid's structures. Eventually, or so the story goes, the old guard rolled over, defeated by Joe's prodigious patience.

Tea arrived in the same white china as at my father's former ministry. Glancing out of the window, I saw a thick cushioning of off-white clouds drifting to the mountain's blunt edge and then wafting back again.

'The files,' I heard Mo saying.

The files, of course. I looked back, that's what I was doing here, trying to enlist their help in getting hold of my parents' police, security and military files.

I'd started my search six months ago by writing to the relevant ministries. All I had to show for my efforts was a growing pile of bureauspeak. The ministry of defence had been the first to answer, if only to tell me that no MoD files had ever been kept on Ruth because:

She was not a specific subject of interest to military intelligences as her activities fell within the ambit of responsibility of the then Security Branch of the SA Police as well as, possibly, the National Intelligence Service.

Not a specific subject of interest: Ruth had been in Mozambique during the time when the South African state had been desperate to destroy the exiled ANC. Their spies put poison in ANC food, their navy infiltrated submarines around the Port of Maputo and sent men out into the city on deadly, night-time forays and their air force once bombed a jam factory in reprisal against an ANC military incursion. It was ludicrous to suppose that Ruth would not have got a mention in the intelligence reports that must have backed each of these incursions: if only as someone the invading troops might easily encounter. I wrote back, asking them to check again.

At least the military had bothered to reply. It took many more weeks, and countless phone calls, before I had managed to wrest an answer from their counterparts in the police. When it came, the letter though more expansive, was equally unhelpful:

> The South African police can find no files on the family of Ms Slovo including the late Mr Slovo. It is indeed possible that the South African Police might have assembled information regarding these persons and have kept personal files on them. If this was the case the South African Police would have disposed of the information in one of the following ways . . .

What followed was a four paragraph description of how lack of space and growing computerisation had led to a gutting of files. In addition they wrote, '. . . after February 1990 [the month Nelson Mandela walked free from prison], the approach of the South African Police moved from an ideological one to an approach based on criminal activities' – a long-winded way of saying that they had stopped keeping files on political activists.

This same sentiment was echoed by the military in their next letter to me. They, however, chose a different cut-off date: 'Since 27 April 1994 [the day of South Africa's first democratic election],' they wrote, '. . . the necessity to monitor these [organisations of security interest] lapsed and all the pertinent information was consequently removed from the SANDF data bases.'

Removed from the files – it felt like a bad joke. I thought about the stories I'd heard of other countries, in other times, where, instead of destroying information at the first hint of their master's downfall, security policemen had made sure to keep it extra specially safe. How else were they to prove, if they were later charged with crimes, that they had only been following orders?

In South Africa as well, rumours abounded of the wholesale theft of files by those who had once been paid to compile them. There were conflicting reports. A former employee of the state-run steel corporation had come forward with a tale of how, in the run-up to the election, policemen had fed reams of information into the steel furnaces south of Johannesburg. His story was backed up by home-spun tales of police shredding machines working overtime in the first phase of destruction.[1] And yet, so other stories went, the photocopiers were simultaneously churning as security policemen made samizdat copies of the things their officers had ordered should be destroyed.

These were after all precious files, collected over decades by a state which had prioritised security. They might contain not only the details of what Ruth had for breakfast in March 1964, but also the names of the men who had ordered her death. And other information as well – the names, for example, of spies inside the ANC or, more mundanely but perhaps just as hurtful, the names of who, in the past, had been sleeping with whom. It was in all, a political blackmailer's charter in a country in which there was still an uneasy amalgamation of different power blocks. And yet, all the officials would say was that the files had been destroyed.

In the calm of Joe Nhlanhla's office I looked around, taking in the cushioning on the floor and the way his door was constructed in two parts to ensure absolute security. His desk top

---

1. Since shredded files in Iran were painstakingly reassembled, it had become practice not only to shred, but also to burn.

was just as discreet, devoid of paper. Apart from an envelope which Mo had brought in for Joe and which was sealed at all its edges and had a signature and date over each seal to ensure that it had not been tampered with, the whole office was a document-free zone. Secrets within secrets, I thought.

The two men had lapsed into silence. They were waiting for me. I told them I wasn't going to give up. They nodded. They said they took the matter as seriously as I: without access to what had been done in the past, they added, a line could never be properly drawn underneath it. But, they told me, when they had tried to dig into their own intelligence files, they had also drawn a blank. Times were difficult, they said, echoing what my father had often repeated – the ANC might be in government, but it was not yet in power. But even though the files had done a vanishing act, Joe Nhlanhla concluded, they might still turn up, adding the South African catch-all of, 'It will take time'.

Time in which the files that were stored, away from the prying eyes of the new head of intelligence, could easily be gutted.

We pushed around the possibilities of an approach to the minister of justice and the president as well, drifting almost aimlessly through the options. When I got up to go, I glanced casually at my watch and was shocked to see I'd been there longer than an hour.

Mo walked me down the corridor. At its end, he unlocked the grating. I went through and was about to walk off when I heard his voice, calling me back. 'There are rumours that Craig Williamson wants to talk,' he said.

The mention of that name jolted at my spine. I turned.

'Why don't you give him a ring?' Mo asked and then, without waiting for a reply he smiled, pulled the gate shut, locked it and headed down the corridor, back into what he always affection-ately referred to as his world of spooks.

The floor of my makeshift study was polished wood. The desk, the room's main piece of furniture, was two, three-foot pieces of painted chipboard resting on four black metal trestles. I sat behind it, thinking about the name Mo had effortlessly dropped.

Craig Williamson: his name was a byword for betrayal. A former student activist who'd left South Africa and ended up working for an aid organisation which was closely allied to the ANC, Williamson was eventually exposed as having been a long-term spy. Forewarned that the ANC was on to him, he'd disappeared from Switzerland where he'd been living, and resurfaced, to a hero's welcome, in Pretoria's Wagtheis – headquarters of the South African security police. Like many of his colleagues, he had subsequently left the police to run his own business.

All this I knew about Williamson, it was common knowledge. But now I also knew one other thing: that there were strong indications Craig Williamson was implicated in my mother's death.

The first time I'd heard this story was from the mouth of another ex-policeman, a man by the name of Dirk Coetzee. Once a member of an élite killing squad, Coetzee had fallen foul of his police bosses in the 1980s, skipped the country and gone running to the ANC with tales of state-funded assassinations. Since then he'd turned into something of a confessional junkie, spilling out his tale to any one who cared to listen.

I had gone to see Coetzee to ask if he knew the identity of my mother's murderer. I had ended up sitting opposite him, listening as, exuding bonhomie, he'd described how he and other policemen had gorged themselves on beer and *braaied* meat beside the bodies of activists they had just tortured and killed. At the moment when my revulsion almost propelled me from the room, he told me that, on the day he'd heard the news of my mother's death, he had bumped into a smiling Craig Williamson in a Wagtheis corridor.

'Have you seen?' was what Williamson said to Coetzee.

Apparently in that secret world of double talk and 'need to know' this was Williamson's way of telling Coetzee that he had been involved in Ruth's death.

Have you seen? One policeman to another. How could Coetzee have made a murderer of Williamson from that one, simple sentence? But when I pressed him, Coetzee had been adamant. He was, he told me, 'one hundred percent sure', that Williamson had been at the centre of the plot. And now Mo had told me that Craig Williamson was ready to talk.

Sitting in my Cape Town study, I stared at the details with which Coetzee had supplied me. They included Williamson's home number, his work number, his fax number, his car phone number, his wife's name, profession and work phone number and the registration of his Mercedes 500SE. Glancing down the digits I remembered the glee on Coetzee's face as he had glibly reeled them off.

I sat thinking of my parents' universe from which I had been long excluded in which the bonds of loyalty, secrecy and realpolitik had all been intermeshed. But South Africa was now free and the truth was no longer so dangerous. The news of Joe's son had landed on me through no choice of mine but now what I had always told myself I wanted had become a reality: I could step out from behind the shining aura of their powerful destinies, and take the risk of making my own move.

And I had an indirect invitation, as well, to enter a parallel universe. I'd told myself and anybody who cared to listen that I was going to do it. I would ring Craig Williamson, I said, I would go and see him. And yet, even though I'd had the numbers for some time, I hadn't rung.

I had produced a myriad of reasons to justify my inertia: reasons like it wasn't the right time, or that my father was too ill, or that he had just died, or that I was busy recovering from his death. All reasonable, all true, all of them, except they were also all lies. The truth was that I was frightened.

Those two worlds of secrecy: Coetzee and Williamson's; Mo and Joe Nhlanhla's. On opposite sides of a bloody battle they had skirted each other's rules of engagement. It had been hard enough for me to get access to the way my parents had operated: did I also have the strength to investigate what made the enemy tick?

My thoughts were drawn back to the time before I had made this trip. I was eating out in London, when the subject of revenge had come up. Merry from wine, I had blithely said that I felt no need for retribution, but as my easy words issued out, I'd caught one of my companions shaking his head in disagreement. I asked him why: he said he thought revenge was one of the earliest emotions to be 'civilised' out of us and that, perhaps, if I searched deeper within myself, I might locate a different, more basic, range of responses.

Was he right? Were rage and revenge the murderous impulses lurking beneath my easy rationalisations?

I thought about Joe again, about his hidden knowledge and his fury at my prying. The identity of Ruth's killer had, ostensibly at least, been the one piece of our shared past that he'd conceded was equally mine. But even so, the manner of Ruth's death remained part of our taboo. When I'd told him I might go and see Coetzee he had nodded, friendly enough, and yet he had also been completely noncommittal. I guessed he might have met Coetzee, might even have questioned him, and yet if he had, he'd never told me.

If I wanted to know how Joe talked about Ruth's murderers, I had to read the newspapers, like I did in December 1994: 'I would like to know who killed my wife,' he had told a journalist. 'Not to see to it that he was hanged, but just to achieve inner peace. I've always thought that this is the best revenge I can take for the murder of my wife – to make these people live in a free society.'

From another journalist, I learned that, when the ANC and the government had made their first, holding indemnity agreement,[2] Joe had been in a hotel bar, drinking whisky. Hearing news of the settlement, he had said it had been one of his most

---

2. Before the 1994 election, the ANC and the then South African government agreed the rules by which people who had committed acts of violence for political reasons would be indemnified by the state (i.e. would never have to stand trial for their actions).

difficult nights ever because it had come home to him that he was now party to an agreement which would let Ruth's killer off the hook.

And yet we never spoke of it.

And never could now: Joe was gone.

Which left me sitting on my own.

I thought how, despite what he had just told me, Mo Shaik had also once gently tried to warn me off. He'd been talking of a mutual friend who was searching out her parent's killer. 'She'll never be whole,' he'd said, 'until she stops looking.'

I knew that he was also talking about me, saying that I would never be whole either. Was he right? Was I pursuing a phantom that would only end up damaging me?

I thought about the way Mo had spoken to me of his past, of his nine months in solitary detention, and of the death of his mother during his incarceration. I conjured up the sound of his suave voice as he described the experience: I heard again his calm as he insisted that, no matter what abuse and suffering he'd endured, he had emerged the victor. It was the same kind of thing that my father had always said and it was true. But I sat wondering whether, mingled in with that obvious truth, there was not a deeper, more shadowy reality. Ruth's side, Joe's side, Mo's side had won – and yet, did that mean that the feelings from the traumas were now erased?

Behind me, the front door opened and shut again. I heard Cassie's clear child's voice as she came in from school. I called out to her, saying I'd join her soon. And then, before I could change my mind, I grabbed the telephone. As I started dialling, I thought that all my apprehension had been a waste of time. It was possible that Joe might be right, that it was not my business. It was also possible that Mo was right and that I might regret what I was about to do. But I knew, more strongly than any of their prohibitions, that I had gone so far along this road I had to reach its end.

Chapter Thirty-Two

In the weeks that followed I dialled the phone numbers I'd been given. Eventually, after conversations with Craig Williamson's receptionist, his domestic worker and his wife, I managed to get hold of the man himself. I don't know what I'd expected, certainly not that he should sound nervous. There was no doubt, however, that something was shaking around the edges of his oily voice as he agreed to meet me.

Having agreed, he then made it almost impossible for us to set a date. Up until the moment when I got on to the plane for Jo'burg, I didn't know if I was wasting my time. He might be there, he had said, on the other hand, he might not, or else he might . . .

It was hot as I drove through one of Johannesburg's industrial suburbs, down a succession of bleak roads whose discount shops sold car parts, commercial kitchen equipment, and outsize foam off-cuts. Craig Williamson's office, from which he runs his import-export business, was in a new-build three-storey building just off the main drag. I drove past it at ten minutes to ten, turned left at the corner into a narrow street which some workmen had half-excavated before abandoning, and parked.

Our meeting was fixed for ten o'clock. My car was as hot as hell. I knew it would be cooler outside. I continued to sit. At five to ten, I rooted through my bag checking my notebook was there. It was: I pulled it out. If this had been any other interview, I would have written a set of questions on page one. But this wasn't just any interview and this time my preparations had consisted solely of me staring at the notebook's spiral binding before flicking its pink cover shut.

Two minutes to ten: I knew I should get moving. I shoved the notebook back in my bag, wrestled a rigid metal bar into its place around the steering wheel, opened the door and stepped out. But then, standing by the car, I didn't like the way I'd parked. I got back in, undid the steering lock and reparked – in all probability positioning the car in the same tyre tracks I'd already made on the mounds of sand heaped up by the gutter.

Ten o'clock. I couldn't delay, not any longer. With the steering lock on the floor, I slammed the car door shut, walked across the road, round the corner, into the building, up a flight of stairs and into Craig Williamson's office.

I laid my tiny mini-cassette on the desk that separated me from Craig Williamson's bulk. I switched it on: he put his hands down next to it. My eyes were to be drawn continually to those hands, to the nails cut short and very, very clean, and to the way his fingers either worked busily at each other, or were almost deathly still. There was an elaborate golden wedding ring biting into the flesh of one pudgy digit.

'One has to be very careful,' he said, 'because like there were differing types of communists there were also differing types of anti-communists . . .'

He was sitting on a mauve upholstered chair, in a small space whose walls had also been papered mauve, in front of an aluminium window. He must have been all of twenty stone: his head looked tiny, perched as it was on top of all that fat. His beard and his moustache were both light brown, so was his hair. It was parted sternly from the left sweeping over to the right as if to hide a receding hairline. Behind his hefty back, a grimy air-conditioning unit was noisily recycling stale air.

I can sit now in my London study, listening to the tapes of our meeting. My voice is almost inaudible while his drones on unceasingly. Above them both, I hear the sound of the air conditioner churning. I hear it sometimes as melodic chimes, at others as if it were a huge, malevolent insect rasping in the background. Listening, I remember how a strip of material had fixed itself to one of the unit's vents. I remember staring at it, as silently it rose and fell.

In the two hours I spent with him, Craig Williamson kept talking. His voice, slow and measured, mesmerised me. Even now, many months later, when I listen to it on tape, I feel as I did then, inexorably weary. I am drawn back to that moment, to the memory of how I sat in front of my mother's killer, hearing his story, waiting out the pauses and the unfinished phrases which grew longer as he got closer to the point, feeling myself weighed down by listlessness.

Was it his exhaustion that I was picking up? His, or was it mine?

His subject, at least at first, was the anatomy of one type of anti-communist, himself. He talked about his family background, about his boarding school in Johannesburg, and about his first 'political problem'. It was March 1960, he said, he was eleven years old, and because of the Sharpeville massacre, there was no black help to make his bed or sweep his dormitory.

I looked up from my notebook, checking whether there was any irony in this adult's description of his childhood acknowledgement of a massacre through the act of tucking in his own blankets but apparently not – he had gone on to something else.

I listened and wrote it down. He went on, keeping up his voice's deadly pace, talking through the moment when a pink-aproned African maid brought in a tea tray and beyond that as well. He described why he had joined the police and how he had soon outperformed much more experienced men until finally he was one of only a handful to pass a particular promotion exam. As a result, he was recruited into the security branch.

He was delighted. He, fat boy Craig Williamson, an English speaker in a sea of Afrikaners whose father's money bought him the car his new-found colleagues could never afford, had landed a job they all coveted.

'You were taken out of the normal part,' he told me, 'and really taken off somewhere glamorous.'

The 'glamorous' security branch, the most vicious of all the police units. It was here that Craig Williamson got his political education. The threat, his teachers told him, was communism with the ANC and PAC[1] puppets in the hands of an evil Soviet Union. This was the undercurrent that informed the young Craig's every action, this talk of communism, and of white revolutionaries who used gullible blacks as their foot-soldiers.

I kept on writing, thinking at the same time how easily we create stories to justify our misdeeds. Williamson was born in 1949, he was only three years older than me, and yet he presented his past as if it were pre-history. I thought that what he was trying to do was to pull me into the fiction that he had spun around his life. In this well-worn fable, my mother was a character – a Machiavellian white revolutionary – and Craig a pawn in the execution of his master's faulty understanding. Given the same information, he implied, anybody else would have made the same choices.

Except, I thought, not everybody in South Africa became a spy. Or a killer.

He was like a sloth, devouring my air. Only my hands, moving across the notebook's page, kept my sluggish circulation going. My mind strayed. I was aware of the tinkling of a piece of stray dirt against the air conditioner and of Craig Williamson's voice spinning out its tale.

'. . . the war was becoming a straight confrontation,' I heard him saying, 'the military input was too much . . .'

Wait a minute. He had skipped on to 1985, the time when, disillusioned with what was going on, he had decided to leave the police. 1985: but Ruth had been killed three years earlier, in 1982. I glanced at my watch. When I'd first arrived I'd overheard his receptionist telling him that his next visitor was due at eleven. I saw it was almost that now. I wondered whether he was about to end our meeting.

I spoke, 'How much time have you got?'

---

1. Pan African Congress, a breakaway organisation formed by former ANC members in the early sixties.

He had answered every one of my previous questions willingly enough but this one he met with silence. Listening to the tape, I can hear the clinking of his cup – he was drinking cold tea.

I spoke again, 'I'm just worried we're not getting to the later years.'

'Yah,' he said, in apparent agreement, and then, 'I was ... saying that the game we were playing ...'

His voice droned on. I thought about the word he'd used, the *game*. Was he playing it on me as well?

The phone rang. He picked it up. 'Tell her to ...' I heard him saying and then ... 'Give her some tea.' Which meant his visitor had arrived. I looked at him, wondering whether he was going to send me away without having told me anything. 'Do you have to go soon?' I asked.

'Yah. There's a bit of time ...' He was off again, talking of the old days and the rules of the game. As soon as I could find the energy, I spoke again. I remember the effort it cost me. I can hear my voice, cutting across his, 'You're talking about '85 now. Can we go back to '82?'

At which point there was a high-pitched squeal, my cassette running out. I remember how I laughed, reached forward, and grabbed for the machine. While I changed the tape, I must have told him that I wanted to know about Ruth.

In the hour that had passed, he had been talking very slowly. In the minutes that followed, he added meaningless filler words, words like 'okay' and 'all right', and 'let's', that almost halted him entirely. I had thought this was habitual with him: later when I heard him on tape in normal speed conversation with someone else, I realised that the sluggishness had something to do with me. Or perhaps not just me: perhaps it was what he had to say to me.

I can hear his voice, speaking softly, on side three. 'What are you going to do with this information?'

I had already told him I was writing a book. Now I answered that, since I had no idea what he would tell me, I didn't know what I would do with the information.

'Ruth,' he said. He paused, an immovable monstrosity in front of an ugly office window. '. . . Obviously the state was responsible for Ruth's death.'

The state. Not him. The state.

He started up again, fluffing his lines. 'The actual chronology and people involved,' he said, 'is something that's going to be detailed at the truth commission[2] – you know I want to . . . I want to give you the information that you need and you obviously deserve – but I want to do it in a way that obviously. . .'

As his voice tailed off, the phone rang. He picked it up. 'Hello,' I hear him saying on the tape. 'Yeah. Yes. All right. Yeah. I'm just in a meeting . . . quick.'

A meeting: was that what I was?

He had put the phone down. I sat, waiting out his next long pause. 'I don't want to go into names . . .' he said, '. . . it's up to the other people involved.'

Another long silence and then, again, 'Ruth.' He was staring at the overblown mauveness of his walls.

'I don't know,' he said, '. . . whether the device was aimed specifically at her or Joe. . .'

Here it was, the first of a number of claims he was to make that he had thought the bomb was meant for Joe. I read that sentence over and over again, and I listen to the tape, and I know it could not possibly have been aimed at Joe. After all, the parcel, which had Ruth's name on it, was sent to the university where she worked.

I guess the anonymity of the victim made murder seem less bad, even if it was, ultimately, all self delusion, and he really knew the bomb was intended for Ruth. But then Craig

---

2. The Truth and Reconciliation Commission is a government-funded commission with the two-fold task of giving voice to apartheid's victims, and of giving indemnity for past political crimes.

Williamson spoiled the effect by following his assertion that he thought the bomb was meant for Joe by detailing how the police had come across an envelope addressed to Ruth. Sighing heavily as if his knowledge was a burden, he described how in 1982, 'the security structure in the sub continent' was such that, unbeknown to the ANC, all post from Botswana, Lesotho and Angola was sorted in Johannesburg. Later, when I met with him again, he fleshed out the details. He described a cavernous basement room in Jan Smuts airport where retired security branch policemen used specially modified kettles to search the post. They were looking for anything of relevance: which included, of course, anything to do with Ruth.

After I saw Craig Williamson, I went in search of that basement room. Things had changed: I never found it. Instead, I ended up in the din of the Jan Smuts mail room, as scores of people tossed letters from conveyor belts into pigeon holes. I asked a man, who was wearing one of the most lurid purple kipper ties I've ever seen, whether he remembered the room where the security police used to check the mail.

'Oh yes,' he said cheerfully. 'I never went there, none of us did, but we had a special name for it. We called it the bomb room.'

'It was a small package,' Craig Williamson told me, 'posted from Lesotho to Maputo and addressed to Ruth,' and, here it came again: 'or Joe.'

He was so methodical, was Craig. He described the package's journey from the Jan Smuts sorting office and into the hand of his section chief, the late Brigadier Piet Goosen.[3] The Brigadier

---

3. Piet Goosen was known to his colleagues by the nickname 'Biko' because he was the Security Branch Colonel in charge at the time that Steve Biko was murdered.

At a subsequent meeting, Williamson was to tell me that the envelope had been given to Brigadier Goosen by the then head of the ANC desk, Brigadier Heuer.

gave it to Williamson, telling him to put an explosive device in it. Williamson gave it to his 'technical guy' who, without the sophisticated equipment necessary, took it to the main technical section.

It was all too clinical for me, this tale of passing hands. I interrupted to ask whether they celebrated when they saw the package.

'It must sound terrible and strange . . .' Craig Williamson told me, '. . . it was almost casual . . . it wasn't as though somebody was responsible for this kind of thing . . . we had a particularly good technical guy . . . it was almost luck of the draw.'

Almost casual, luck of the draw: writing those two phrases down, I underlined them.

After the envelope was armed, Williamson said, it was sent on its way to Ruth. He wasn't sure how it had been delivered – he doubted that they would have risked blowing up a plane from Jo'burg – somebody must have taken it there.

And then he said, 'When they brought it back, I wouldn't even touch it.'

I looked up, startled to hear that they had brought the envelope back to him and shocked by something else as well, something in his voice.

It was the only moment in my visit when he seemed to have forgotten who I was. Unaware of my reaction, he mimicked comic horror to describe how he had felt when the package was returned. It felt like a story he'd told before and which had gone down well. I could almost picture him, sitting in a police bar after work, his hand gripping a goblet of red wine as he entertained his colleagues with hilarious descriptions of his fright as a bomb had landed on his desk.

The expression on my face must have given me away. His laugh was abruptly stanched.

I asked him, 'Why Ruth?'

His answer seemed to go on forever. He talked about the general strategy of 'terrorising the terrorist', *which meant she was the enemy*. About 'psychological warfare', *which meant, kill enough*

people and you demoralise the rest, and only finally about the fact
that they were convinced Ruth was a 'key player . . . one of the
top . . . ideological thinkers in the South African Communist
Party' and that they were 'worried about her involvement in
Mozambique'.

So we were back in a Scorsese movie: it wasn't personal, it was
business.

Or at least, it wasn't personal to Williamson. He told me how,
to him, Ruth '. . . was a historical figure . . . just like a famous
person . . .' This wasn't true for all those concerned, he said, 'To
the older people in the security branch who'd been involved in
the time when she'd been active in South Africa, it was a more
direct communication.'

I thought about those men who included, Williamson told
me, Ruth's former interrogator J.J. Viktor, sitting in the security
branch headquarters in Pretoria's Wagtheis, discussing their
'communication' with Ruth. I wondered how well each of
them had known her and how they felt when they heard that she
was dead.

Afterwards, continuing my search for Ruth's files, I was to
visit the Wagtheis. On my way to a meeting with Commissioner
Grove, whose office was on the sixth floor, I walked down a
sombre corridor. I started confidently enough but half-way
down, I was trembling. I felt as if the dark wood-panelled walls
were closing in on me, and I blinked each time I passed under
the pinpoint electric lights which, stuck on the low ceiling, did
nothing to alleviate the gloom. By the time I got to the end, I
was possessed by a single thought – that this was the place.

When I sat down opposite Commissioner Grove, the first
thing I asked was if the security branch's section heads had once
met there. He said they had, and he later led me back down the
corridor and into a large, windowless room in which a set of
polished wooden tables was arranged in the unmistakable shape
of a coffin. He told me that this was where they used to hold
their daily meetings. 'It hasn't changed at all since those days,'
he said.

I looked along the tables, at the microphone which fronted each of the seats, at the wall at one end, and at the huge picture of a springbok quivering in a brightly coloured landscape, and I felt sick.

But that was still to come. Before it did, I was in Craig Williamson's office, duplicating a question, 'Did you celebrate when you heard the news of Ruth's death?'

I wonder now why I asked him that again. I guess I was searching for some emotion, at least a hint either of vulnerable humanity, or of inhuman savagery which might have made it easier for me to understand what they had done.

In which case, I was searching in vain.

'No, we didn't,' he said, 'the same as when bombs went off [killing our people] . . . we didn't mourn . . . Dreadful I'm sure for you to hear but we didn't . . . no I think the reaction was more what are they [the ANC] going to do now.' What the police did, Williamson continued, was set in motion a 'strat com thing'[4] briefing journalists that it was Joe who had killed Ruth because of ideological differences. Later, sitting in a newspaper office, I was to locate the articles that resulted from this duplicity.

'. . . information compiled by United States and British sources,' the South African daily, *The Star*, reported, 'suggests Joe Slovo engineered his estranged wife's killing . . .' because of Ruth's 'ultra-left outlook'.

That was the one accusation, amongst so many which were printed in the South African papers, that had provoked Joe to fury. Without access to South African courts, he eventually and successfully sued *The Star* in London. And now I was sitting opposite Ruth's killer, listening as he told me that he had been the source of this malignancy as well.

My fingers were cramped from writing. It was time for me to go. But I had a final question. I asked him why he had agreed to meet me.

---

4. Strategic communication – a psychological warfare operation.

He dropped his head, low down on to his chest, and said, '... God help us ... we must just try and stop this thing so we can move upwards and not downwards.'

We – he was enlisting me in his altruistic bid to set South Africa on its feet. It was more than I could take. He wasn't finished.

'I was in the loop, that killed your mother,' he said.

Loop? What was he talking about? A baton race? A high tech circuit? Or a group of men sitting in Pretoria's Wagtheis working out ways to rid themselves of Ruth?

'... the loop was quite big,' he added and another sentence as well, 'I didn't have the ability to give the types of orders that were being given.'

I got up.

He looked at me, this bloated man in his mauve chair and then he did something to regain control. He told me he had a copy of one of my books which I had signed 'with love'. He smiled at my startled reaction and said it had been a present from a fellow spy who had infiltrated the London ANC and who, having attended one of my book signings bought one as a joke, for Craig. I told him that I had once written a book about a spy.

'I know,' he said, as calm and cold as he had been throughout. 'I read it.'

He stood up then, and walked me to the door.

Chapter Thirty-Three

Somewhere, way down below, a car horn blared. I heard it in my sleep and then again, loud enough this time to waken me. I opened my eyes to find that I was lying on a bed, fully clothed in a room which was bathed in an eerie light. I got up and, going over to the picture window, lifted the blind. I saw Jo'burg's blood-red sky darkening, night was closing in.

It was only six in the evening. Turning away from the window, I walked to the elegantly furnished living room that spanned one corner of the fifth-floor apartment in Yeoville where I was staying. The room had windows on three sides: depending on which way I turned, I could see either the city centre's New York-style skyline or the sprawl of its imitation Los Angeles suburbs.

Night comes quickly in Johannesburg. Far down below lights clicked on until my eyes were met by miles of radiating fluorescence. Inside, the flat got darker as I sat by the intricately cross-hatched rosewood dining table, and thought about Craig Williamson.

I thought about him as he had been, a huge mountain of a man, all oil, and lies and half-excuses. The years that had gone before and the choices he had made meant that he had spent a lifetime gutting the emotion from what he did. Our meeting had been an exercise in dissociation from which I'd emerged in a stupor that had sent me straight into a dreamless afternoon sleep.

There was a part of me that couldn't believe I'd gone to see him and that I had stayed, politely, listening to what he had to say. I thought of other people whose lives he'd damaged – of Marius Schoon, husband of Jeanette, father of six-year-old Katrine, both killed by a single bomb who, on hearing that I was to meet with Williamson, had said, 'I don't know how you can. I couldn't. If I were in the same space as that man, I wouldn't be able to stop myself from stabbing him.'

I noted the word: *stabbing*. Not doing as Williamson had done, passing a bomb along a distant chain of death, nor standing back and firing a gun, but stabbing – getting up close and twisting a knife into that gut and watching as Williamson's life blood spilled out.

I knew other people as well, people whom Williamson in his incarnation as a spy had first befriended and then betrayed. I remembered their tales of accidental street meetings and how they'd cut him dead, of slamming the door in his face, of removing their children from nurseries rather than letting them mix with his. Each of these separate, furious reactions seemed sane to me and yet, I had done differently. I had gone voluntarily to his office, sat on his chair, sipped his tea and nodded as he spoke. And then I had come out feeling nothing.

I turned the tape recorder on. The sounds I heard were cold metal and plastic, his air conditioner grinding through his justification of the unjustifiable. Listening, I conjured up an image of Ruth as she had been – her flashing eyes, the way her quick fingers worked the air underlining her staccato words, her hair frizzed softly around a face so frequently animated by a provocative smile.

'It was almost casual,' I heard.

For the first time, I was seized by anger. Perhaps stabbing would have been easier than sitting and listening to this bully's bloodless tale of murder.

His meeting me had been an exercise in control. He had made the decision to talk to me, he had told me he felt he owed it to me, and yet, all he'd really said was that he'd been in a loop, a big loop, which I guess, exonerated him from blame.

I knew what he'd really been saying. It was war, he was a soldier, Ruth was the enemy. He was too sophisticated to risk the cliché that he was only following orders, but that was the sentiment which underlined his tale. He was happy to boast about his effectiveness as a spy, or explain away how he had been taught to view people like my mother, but those other qualities that I'd been searching for – regret, repentance, or conscience – had been conspicuously absent.

I looked up and saw that night had come and that, high above the city, was a formidable sable sky with its twinkling pinpoints of starlight. As I stared out at its immensity, I wondered whether, in some childish way, I had wanted something deeper from my mother's killers, something that might have made them more worthy of the act. She was so much to me and South Africa was so much to her: how could I bear the fact that her life could be snuffed out by a group of men, safe in Pretoria, who had converted the awfulness of what they were doing into a game? What they had done had such an effect on all of us, I wanted to know that it had done something to them as well.

But when I was to later press the point, asking Craig Williamson whether Ruth's death weighed on him, he seemed irritated by my persistence.

'Yeah,' he said grudgingly, 'I said that you'll never get rid of. You can wish or regret or do as much as you like but you can't change it. What's done is done and if you try and analyse why it was done and how it was done and what the strategy and belief behind it was . . . it's difficult to believe that it could have been done, but it was.'

That was his whole approach – it was done, it was over. He had acted the good boy by following the rules of this new society, by coming forward and owning up: now, what he expected to do was to dump the past and move on.

I thought about how I'd heard Archbishop Desmond Tutu talking on television about the imminent opening of the truth commission and how the emphasis he'd laid was on forgiveness. My rational mind knew he was right, that if South Africa did not find in itself the capacity to forgive, it might still go up in flames. And yet, in the face of the displaced responsibility and the empty justifications that the likes of Craig Williamson produced, forgiveness felt like just another effort, in a long string of previous efforts, that the victims, and not the perpetrators, would have to make.

I don't know what I expected when I started my search for Ruth's killer – some kind of understanding, I guess, which might lead to resolution. Instead I'd found myself in another, very separate world, as cohesive as the one my parents had inhabited, but this one partitioned into black and white, 'us' and 'them', the system and its enemies. Craig Williamson had regarded the whole thing as a game of manoeuvre, a jostling for positions, a war where morality did not count. In this scenario, my mother was reduced to the status of a cipher, a 'top ideological thinker', a 'white brain' behind the ANC – in other words, not the woman I had known, nor the person that they might have hated, but just another workaday target.

I reached over and switched off the tape recorder and as his voice was abruptly checked, I thought that this was perhaps why Joe hadn't bothered tracking down Ruth's killers: because he had known what I was just discovering – that meeting with them would never provide catharsis.

In Yeoville's distance, I could hear the sounds of police sirens, of someone shouting and someone singing. I put the tape recorder into my briefcase, made sure that the iron gate separating my apartment from the landing was locked, and then I went back to bed.

I was due to fly back to Cape Town in the afternoon. In the morning I went to Soweto, to visit Joe's grave. I'd been there only once before, during his funeral, and I knew I'd never find my own way there. I phoned the offices of the Communist Party and asked if they could free someone to guide me there.

They turned up, a full-scale delegation, three men and a driver. Knowing how hard it must have been for them to make time from their busy schedule, I didn't have the heart to tell them that what I had really wanted was to go there on my own.

Reaching the cemetery, we passed through a narrow gateway down a dusty and deep path into the sprawling grounds of

Avalon. On my first trip Joe's grave had been in front of a huge construction, the stage on which we had sat, with a canopy over it.

Now the stage and the canopy were both gone and in the desolation of that flat place, Joe's grave stood a few feet away from the others on uneven red-brown earth, blades of scratchy grass trying to push their way through. It was so much smaller than I had imagined, this mound of earth with a black cast-iron fence around it, settling crooked into the ground so the whole thing had the look of a cock-eyed cradle.

To the west I could see the signs of Soweto's squatters: tin shacks, fences made of iron bed frames, roofs made of cardboard. To the east were the brick buildings of the once exclusively Indian location of Lenasia.

Most of my companions kept a discreet distance away from me, but the driver came close. He stood beside me, looking down. 'He is only one of two white people buried in Avalon,' he said. Joe's grave was under a set of electric power lines, the same ones that during the funeral some of the mourners had risked death to climb. 'He was seen by our people as a black man,' the driver continued. 'They put him under the electric wire because he was giving people houses with electricity.'

There were sounds of traffic in the distance, travelling the road to Kimberley, centre of South Africa's diamond wealth. I walked closer to the grave.

They had his name written on a placard as Joseph Slovo. It was not really his name. Born Yossel Mashel, he had always been known as Joe. By the head of the mound someone had placed the wreath which had been the centrepiece of his funeral – a glorious black and red hammer and sickle etched in crêpe inside its circle. There were ribbons too, red, and blue and yellow, tied to the iron railings.

It was a grave unlike any others. Joe's grave.

As I stood and looked down on it, voices came to me. I thought of all the articles that were written about him after his death, of the woman who was quoted as saying of us, Joe's family, 'They are not crying. They know what Joe's life was like and they are proud of him', or the comment on Ruth:

> Slovo's marriage to Ruth First was fraught with passionate competition and argument. But the chemistry that held their relationship together was visible when he wept in his hotel room over the loss of his mentor after being elected chairman of the South African Communist Party in Moscow in 1984.

All those voices trying to put words to match my parents' complex lives. All those voices and one more as well . . .

I looked around me at the arid wastes of Avalon, without a single tree to keep away the burning of the midsummer sun and I imagined the laughter in Craig Williamson's voice as he'd told a journalist after Joe's death, 'Do you know why it is so hot? Someone forgot to close the gate when they let Slovo in.'

It was time to go. I turned and my companions stopped their hushed conversation and we headed towards the car. In the moment before we closed its doors, a plague of small black flies flew in. We spent the journey into Johannesburg batting them away.

Chapter Thirty-Four

The University of Cape Town nestles under the spine of Table Mountain overlooking the main route out of central Cape Town into the ritzy southern suburbs. It has a campus which has been sculpted in imitation English style, right down to its elegant, ivy-covered walls. From where I was sitting, in Professor Apollum Davidson's study, it was this dark, luxuriant green, and not the scummy brown mist that hovers over the huge expanse of the Cape Flats, which caught my eye.

'This is too intimate, too delicate a matter,' Apollum Davidson said.

I glanced up, surprised. Apollum was standing beside one of his glass-covered book shelves, leafing through a book as if therein lay an answer he badly needed. Seeing me watching him, he put the book down and walked over to his desk.

'I would question whether this should come out in public,' he said, sitting down.

How many times had I heard either these words, or sentences that carried the same meaning? I took a deep breath. 'It happened a long time ago,' I said. 'Most of the participants have been dead for many years.'

He nodded and, as if persuaded, said, 'That's also true.' But I could see the residue of his historian's unaccustomed uncertainty hovering in his brown eyes.

Nevertheless he began to tell his story – the bare bones of which I already knew. It dated back to the thirties, a time when both my parents were children, and it was a convoluted tale, full of the twists and turns of history as they skimmed at my family's life.

At the centre of the tale was a stranger. His name was Lazer Bach. He had been a career communist who'd fallen foul of the official line in 1935, and ended up dying, in 1941, in a Siberian concentration camp.

'I had a friend,' Apollum Davidson told me, 'who spent some time in the camp with Lazer Bach. He said that Bach's knowledge of English literature was brilliant. Bach gave my friend information about the latest English novels including *Lady Chatterley's Lover . . .*'

This was a glimpse of a Lazer Bach more alluring than any I'd been given. Since I'd started collecting memories of the man, I'd heard many testimonies to his character, none of them particularly complimentary. I'd built up a picture of a man whose over-whelming ambition was to exercise power over his comrades. He had kept it up throughout his life and, when finally he disappeared almost without trace, he seems to have left few fans behind.

Latvian born and an early party member, he had come to South Africa in 1929 to join his father who owned a tannery in the Western Cape town of Paarl. Trained in law, the young Lazer Bach was a thin, big talking, heavy smoker with one consuming ambition – to foment and lead a revolution. The impression I'd been given was not the refined, well-read communist that Apollum's friend remembered, but rather a man who had used a brilliant mind to manipulate and to win. From Jack Flior, who as a newly arrived communist had been sent to Bach for lessons in Marxism, I heard that Bach was known by the uncomplimen-tary nickname of 'The Inquisitor'. Ray Alexander whose knowledge of Bach stretched back into their shared homeland of Latvia said, 'He was a very sorry character who spoke rhetoric to attract people.'

'He liked women very much,' Apollum told me, 'they were his second profession after the propagating of revolution. I don't think he was handsome – but then I'm not a woman – but he was very active, energetic brilliant . . .'

Lazer Bach had liked women. He had a wife back in Latvia and a string of girlfriends in South Africa – Tilly, Ruth's mother, my grandmother was amongst them. Although that's not entirely true. Tilly might have known him in South Africa but, as the story went, she only had sex with him in Yalta.

How she got to Yalta was part of the extraordinary nature of those times. It wasn't because of her status in the party, that I knew for sure. She was a woman who spoke little, and with barely suppressed irritation, about her past but one of the stories she did repeat was that she'd been refused membership of the South African Communist Party on the grounds that she was married to a factory owner, an employer, an exploiter of labour. It made no sense: my grandfather Julius, the capitalist, was also one of the South African Communist Party's founding members, its chairman in 1929, and later its treasurer but I guess that was the strange logic of the rules by which they lived.

She might not have been allowed into the party, but she was given free passage to Yalta. 'Your grandmother went to Moscow maybe in June 1935,' Apollum told me, 'or possibly it was late 1934. She was given a holiday there because her husband was so important in the South African Communist Party: he gave so much money.'

And there was another reason, Apollum continued, for Tilly's invitation: an African woman, named Josie Palmer, had a place in Moscow's University of the Eastern Toilers but because she was black, she would never had got the travel documents necessary for her to leave South Africa. Which is where Tilly came in. She got a passport, and she took Josie Palmer with her under the pretext that Josie was her servant. Together the two made the long boat trip – the reverse of the one Tilly's mother had made with baby Tilly, almost forty years before.

Once they reached Moscow, the women separated. Josie Palmer went to start her studies while Tilly was taken to one of the best of the Soviet sanitaria in Yalta in the Crimea. In this old palace of the now-deposed Russian tsar, Tilly spent her days making her way from a clifftop hotel down through a long tunnel, its monotony broken by fish-filled aquariums which lined the walls, to do group callisthenics on a Black Sea beach. There she met up with Lazer Bach, also on r and r, and there they had a brief affair.

After the holiday was over, they never saw each other again. In fact Tilly was the last South African to see Lazer Bach alive. Listening to Apollum I was drawn back into those distant days, that strange world of conspiracies and intrigue that my grandmother had accepted as normality. Apollum Davidson said:

> In August 1935, the policy of the comintern went through a 360 degree turn. It was a few years before the Second World War: there was a smell of a future war. Stalin was afraid Hitler would fight against the USSR. He proposed a new and opposite slogan to the previous one: to organise a united world front against fascism. After that slogan was produced, Stalin began to repress all people connected with the old slogan. They were blamed as Trotskyites.

I wrote it down, this description of a change of line that must have rocked Tilly's world. To me she had been such a forbidding figure and yet, when many years later I watched her on film by her daughter's grave side, all I saw was a wizened, old woman fighting for dignity. Her voice, speaking in the gloom of the London flat, came back to me. 'All my life,' was what she had told me before she left on her last trip to South Africa, 'I have lived for other people.'

Now I had discovered that this wasn't entirely true. She'd done something at least once for herself – she'd had an affair. And I found that I was pleased for her. I was grateful that my stern, unsmiling, resentful grandmother had thrown off her overweening sense of duty and done something, anything, for herself.

And then I remembered my almost puritanical outrage at my mother's lover, and my father's son, and I wondered why, if I was so ready to let my grandmother off the hook, I couldn't do the same for my parents.

As Apollum kept on with his tale, I was drawn back to that time and the way Tilly had kept what had happened a secret even from her closest friends. She was a woman schooled in secrecy – she had lived her whole life in constant movement away from the past. And it wasn't just her, everything it seemed had conspired to bury her. In South Africa I had tried so hard to track her movements. I had a researcher delving through old street and school records, birth and death registers – nothing came to light.

She had learned how to forget, this eagle of a woman. It had started early when she forgot how to speak her mother tongue and therefore could no longer speak to her own mother. But she was a dutiful daughter: she continued on the path that her parents' relocation had intended. While they settled in a poor Johannesburg area from which they could never afford to leave, eking out a living from a combination of boarders and kitchen gardening, Tilly crossed suburb and class. She got a new accent, and a new life and, perhaps most important of all, she was able to give her children the education that she had so craved.

But Tilly had been even more ambitious than that: she didn't only want a good lifestyle, she had wanted to change the world. She was never given the chance: she was a wife and mother, born in the wrong age. But she didn't give up. She poured her ambition into her daughter, my mother, who ended up doing everything that my grandmother wanted her to do.

'Bach and Josie Palmer – who was given the pseudonym of Henderson – were both delegates to that Congress,' Apollum said. 'The comintern asked Henderson to give a speech. She made a speech according to the old slogan.

'After the congress,' he continued, 'there was a commission, chaired by the famous French communist Andre Marti, which was set up to try and understand the situation of the South African Communist Party. When the commission looked through the documents they found Henderson's speech and saw it was made according to the old slogans. They called Josie Palmer and asked her why. She told them that she didn't write it, but only read it from a text prepared by Lazer Bach and a Russian comrade.'

Which meant that the woman whom Tilly had helped to get to Moscow had blown the whistle on Tilly's lover.

Tilly left, Lazer Bach stayed on. Who knows what he actually did to bring opprobrium on his head. There are rumours that he was kept back not because of his friendship with those who opposed Stalin, but because some of his communist comrades back home wanted him out of the way. Whatever the truth of it, he was eventually tried and found guilty on all charges of plotting with Trotskyists and sentenced to the gulags of Siberia.

Meanwhile Tilly, Apollum told me, had gone to London. She had been there, once before, as a newborn before the turn of the century, when her parents had stopped off, courtesy of a Jewish benevolent society. Her father had been trained as a tailor before his family continued on their journey down south. Tilly had a photo of them in London, taken before she was born. It shows her handsome father, smartly dressed and beaming proudly over his walrus moustache, her beautiful mother, serious in a high-waisted skirt and lace blouse that reached almost to her chin, and Tilly's brother, Israel, splendid in a mock-sailor's suit that his father had just made for him.

This trip was different. Tilly was grown up and what's more, 'when your grandmother returned to London *en route* to South Africa,' Apollum told me, 'she found out she was pregnant.'

She was a married woman with two growing children, she couldn't go home. She contacted Moscow and asked for help. 'They found a Communist Party doctor,' Apollum said, 'who gave her an illegal abortion.'

Apollum looked at me, and, having said that this was as much as he knew of Tilly's involvement with Lazer Bach, he talked again about the delicacy of letting these facts be known.

I drove away from the university, travelling back along Rhodes Drive and heading into Cape Town, thinking of what Apollum had said and how he was only one in a long line of people who had warned me about the dangers of uncovering the truth.

At the top of the queue stood my father – him and his injunctions to keep away from his past. Below him was a whole series of other voices: the voices of friends of my grandmother who questioned my reasons for delving into Ruth's relationship with Tilly; of the police and the military agencies who didn't want me to get hold of any of my parents' files; of men like my mother's old interrogator General J.J. Viktor, who had phoned me briefly to say that he didn't think it was right for him to meet with me. So many secrets they all carried: and how they hugged them to themselves.

I thought of the photos that Tilly cherished. There was the one of Ruth that had ended up on her closet floor and another portrait – this of her blue-eyed, beautiful, blond mother which had hung above her bed in London and which had been amongst the possessions she packed on her final return to South Africa. She had lost her mother long ago, her daughter relatively recently. And yet in the end, memory was kind to her: having outlasted Ruth, she was at last allowed to forget her too.

I had thought that I was different, that I was going to uncover the unvarnished truth. And yet look at the standards I applied: I was happy for my grandmother that she'd had an affair but I was furious that my parents had also had affairs.

I heard Joe's voice again, describing with bitterness the anger and the misery Ruth's affairs had caused him. In the background was a different chorus: someone else talking about how jealous Joe's amorous entanglements had made Ruth feel. All these many, contradictory voices which kept on swirling: there was no way I could resolve them.

I turned off Rhodes Drive, heading into Oranjesnicht and up the hill towards the mountain, thinking there was one thing I had learned. People always put themselves into the starring role when they talked about their pasts. That's why none of their stories fitted together: what they had seen, they'd seen through their own eyes.

A roadside sign pointed to the right, towards the cable car. I kept on climbing up, thinking that maybe Apollum Davidson was right: maybe because there was no way of really understanding them, there are secrets that are better left alone.

I had reached Wolfie Kodesh's apartment block. I stopped my car and got out.

Small, round, funny, a quintessentially Jewish uncle, Wolfie was the man who had given my father permission to date my mother, and who had worked with Ruth and gone with her and Joe Gqabi to investigate the fifties farm slavery scandal. His hair had turned white since then, but he seemed to have changed little in my lifetime of knowing him. I'd come to return a book he'd lent me: when he opened the door I went in for tea.

As we sat drinking, Wolfie told me about a recent encounter he'd had with a township gangster whom he had politicised fifty years before. He described in his own, inimitable, roundabout way how he had met up with the gangster's son and how long it had taken them to realise that they had connections.

I was caught up in my own trawl through the past. I changed the subject to my own obsessions. We talked again of Ruth and Joe and of the old days in South Africa. And then I asked Wolfie a question, 'Were you all in and out each other's beds?'

Wolfie grimaced. For a moment afterwards he sat completely quiet. 'There was quite a lot of that sort of thing,' he said. He shrugged. I thought he was shrugging my question away. He wasn't. His eyes almost distant, he simply said, 'You know when you reach my age, you realise that the question of who slept with who or why – these are not the really important things of life.'

He let that sentence settle on me and I sat there, thinking that of course what he had said was true.

Chapter Thirty-Five

The last of our many suitcases was hefted on to the conveyor belt, the last of the labels stuck on: our nine months' stay in South Africa was almost over. The man behind the check-in desk looked at us standing there, surrounded by impossible quantities of hand luggage.

'Give me that one as well,' he said, pointing at the soft leather bag that Cassie was holding.

Stubbornly, she shook her head and shifted backwards in case he tried to grab it from her. Seeing her tears welling, he quickly told her it was fine, she could keep it.

'Have a good journey,' he said, watching in amazement as we new-wave emigrants staggered off, weighed down by our possessions.

We went through passport control and seated ourselves beside the coffee kiosk, an area made perilous by workmen's tools. All around, bored strangers sat on uncomfortable steel chairs or browsed disinterestedly through shelves of animal t-shirts and KWV wine. I put a coke by Cassie's elbow and I watched as she picked up her precious bag, Joe's leather bag. She pried the two pieces of velcro apart and pulled Joe's false passport from its hidden compartment.

I never found out why Joe had owned the passport. I'd collected a number of possibilities: it was so he could travel incognito through Africa, someone said; it was all part of Operation Vula, said another; a third speculated that it had been given to Joe so he could come into the country for a secret party meeting. Which of these explanations was the right one was perhaps one of the mysteries that would always remain. One thing was clear, however: whatever the passport's purpose, Joe had never actually used it. Perhaps it was just part of the kit of his life, just there, because it was.

I sat in the airport, wondering whether I could tolerate that uncertainty because of everything I had learned. I thought about the changes that our stay had wrought in me. When I'd first arrived, I'd had a jigsaw in mind, the kind that Ruth had relished in the months before her death. I had thought that all I needed to do was to collect the fragments of the past and I would be able to slot them one into the other to build a picture of the whole.

It hadn't turned out like that and now I understood that it never would. At the same moment that I had managed to persuade people to talk to me about Joe's secret military past, I'd found out something I had not wanted to know, that Joe had a son. But after my shock wore off all the knowledge did was add to what I'd learnt elsewhere. I'd realised that memory, experience, interpretation could never be fixed or frozen into one, unchanging truth. They kept on moving, relentlessly metamorphosing into something other so that the jagged edges of each fragment would never, ever slot together.

I thought of the images of my parents that I had collected; each one different from the one before. The dead stayed still but the rest of us kept going. When finally we looked back, distance distorted what we saw.

And then I thought that Joe had been wrong to try and stop my digging at his past – nothing I had uncovered had made me feel any the less proud of him. It *was* his South Africa, and it was his life as well, but it belonged to other people too.

His life, my life: they had crossed and they had diverged. I wasn't positive that what I had done was right but I knew I no longer felt so curious to dig out those surprises that might still be waiting out there for me. I, a child of secrets, had done something that I had needed to do. I had laid to rest some of the ghosts that had stalked my life and in doing so, I'd found a kind of peace.

A disembodied airport voice called out our flight number. As our fellow passengers started to queue, we got involved in the complicated business of sorting out our considerable hand luggage. I put one bag into another and I thought about the time that I had been sitting in Mo Shaik's office, watching in astonishment as he had pulled a document out of his safe and instead of showing it to me, read me selected highlights. Later, when we met at supper, I had teased him about the smallness of his safe and he had replied in kind, 'Joe Nhlanhla told me you wanted information about spies,' he said. 'He told me to speak to you, but to tell you nothing.'

As the queue moved forward, I laughed out loud. In a sense what Joe Nhlanhla had told Mo to do was what everybody else did anyway. They spoke to me but even when they thought they were saying nothing, their nothing was pregnant with meaning.

I could see passengers meandering their way over the runway towards our plane. It was definitely time. We followed them, going towards the exit gate. Which was when I heard, coming from the souvenir shop, a song that even after thirty years was startlingly familiar:

Ag pleez daddy, won't you take us to the drive-in,

All six seven of us eight, nine, ten.

We wanna see a flick about Tarzan and the Apemen,

And when the show's over, you can bring us back again.